STUDIES IN SOCIAL POLICY AND WELFARE XII

The Movement for Family Allowances, 1918—45:

A Study in Social Policy Development

Studies in Social Policy and Welfare
Edited by R. A. Pinker

In the same series

The Movement for Family Allowances, 1918–45:

A Study in Social Policy Development

John Macnicol

Lecturer in Social Policy,
Bedford College,
University of London

HEINEMANN · LONDON

Heinemann Educational Books Ltd
22 Bedford Square, London WC1B 3HH

LONDON EDINBURGH MELBOURNE AUCKLAND
HONG KONG SINGAPORE KUALA LUMPUR NEW DELHI
IBADAN NAIROBI JOHANNESBURG
EXETER (NH) KINGSTON PORT OF SPAIN

Macnicol, John
    Family allowances, 1918-45. — (Studies in
    social policy and welfare).
    1. Family allowances — Great Britain — History
    2. Great Britain — Social policy
    I. Title   II. Series
    362.8'2   HD4925.5.G7

    ISBN 0-435-82555-0

Printed in Great Britain by
Biddles Ltd, Guildford, Surrey

Contents

Acknowledgements

This is a reduced version of a rather long PhD thesis for the University of Edinburgh. Inevitably, some information has had to be omitted: for example, the cross-national comparative developments and the full political background to the Second World War period (especially the reaction to the Beveridge Report). I am also acutely conscious that some wider issues (such as the role of women, or the political economy of low wages) are left unexplored, given the terms of reference I set myself in the Introduction. To have covered everything would have required a book twice this length.

Some material in this book, particularly from Chapter 5, has already appeared in 'Family Allowances and Less Eligibility', in Pat Thane (ed.), *The Origins of British Social Policy* (Croom Helm, 1978).

I am grateful to the following for allowing me access to unpublished material, and in some cases to quote extracts: the British Library of Political and Economic Science; the House of Lords Record Office; Mr A. J. P. Taylor, on behalf of the Beaverbook Foundation; the Bodleian Library, Oxford; the Department of Health and Social Security; the Wellcome Medical Library, London; the Librarian, University of Liverpool Library; the Fawcett Library, City of London Polytechnic; the Scottish Record Office; Mr Will Soper; Messrs. Allen & Unwin Ltd.; the Public Record Office, London (transcripts of Crown-copyright material appear by permission of the controller of Her Majesty's Stationary Office); the Trades Union Congress.

The following libraries were of enormous help to me in researching into published material, and I should like to express my gratitude: the University of Edinburgh Library; the Central Medical Library, Edinburgh; the National Library of Scotland; the British Library; the Wellcome Medical Library, London; the Eugenics Society Library; the University of Bristol Library. Most of all, I wish to thank the staff of the British Library of Political and Economic Science, particularly the assistants on the reserve counter in the old library premises, for meeting every request for obscure material with unfailing efficiency and good humour.

A number of individuals very kindly consented to being interviewed, and provided me with invaluable information. These included: Sir John Walley; Air-Commodore John Cecil-Wright; the late Baroness Stocks; the late Professor David Glass; and the late Miss Marjorie Green (Mrs Marjorie Soper). In addition I received many helpful suggestions regarding source material and other problems from numerous fellow academics, among whom I should especially like to thank Paul Addison, John Brown, Alan Deacon, Jose Harris, Hilary Land, Derek Oddy, Terry Rodgers and Pat Thane. Sylvia Mann went to considerable trouble to lend me a draft copy of her University of Warwick MA thesis. Professor Robert Pinker has been a constant source of help and encouragement at various stages of my work. I am greatly indebted to all these individuals, and needless to say I absolve them from any responsibility for errors of fact or interpretation in this book.

The first three years of full-time research were undertaken with the financial assistance of a postgraduate award from the Social Science Research Council, to whom I am very grateful. My final debt of gratitude is to John Spencer, late Professor of Social Administration at the University of Edinburgh, who supervised my research and died on 25 June 1978, a few months after it was completed. John Spencer was much loved by all who came into contact with him for his rare combination of academic excellence and personal warmth. This book is dedicated to his memory.

John Macnicol
Bedford College, 1980.

Introduction

The aim of this study is to examine the development of one particular social policy, from the birth of the idea to its passage into legislation. In the process, it is hoped that some general issues about the functions of welfare will be raised.

Social policy history is a relatively new discipline, and has developed rapidly in the last fifteen years. In the past it tended to lack a distinctive identity and remained relatively neglected, perhaps because it was considered an unimportant sub-branch of social history or of social administration. Its relationship with the latter discipline was often merely to provide social work students with a brief summary of the main legislative achievements leading up to the foundation of the welfare state in the 1940s. This restricted function all too often caused it to be presented in the form of general 'Poor Law to welfare state' accounts in which reformist social science technocrats fought heroic battles against the dark forces of conservatism and vested interest.

This approach has been savagely (and deservedly) criticised in recent years as representing a latter-day version of the 'Whig' view of history (long since discredited in other branches of history) in which societies are seen as inevitably progressing upwards on a path to perfection.[1] Now a growing number of social policy historians are analysing welfare development by reference to the many different functions which social policies were designed to perform – of which the 'ameliorative' (or meeting of need) may well be the least important – and in the context of wider social, economic, political and ideological changes occurring simultaneously. The social policy historian is thus faced with an extremely difficult task. In contrast to, say, the political historian, who can produce a biography of a politician in which the civil service scarcely seems to exist, the social policy historian must combine the approaches of a number of other branches of history – economic, political, social, administrative, intellectual – in order to unravel what J. R. Poynter has called the 'intricate relationship between interest, ideology and the pressures inherent in administrative procedures themselves'.[2]

Of course, to adopt such an all-encompassing approach may prove very difficult in practice, if only because many of the issues raised are so open-ended. For example, it is arguable that all the really interesting questions about the functions of welfare are ultimately reducible to conflicting definitions of 'the State' — a debate around which the science of political theory is built. Again, there is the problem that 'social policy' is notoriously difficult to define, since of course it merges imperceptibly into many other branches of public policy.

Theories of welfare development are many and varied, and space does not allow an adequate discussion of all their subtleties here.[3] Briefly, it is possible to discern a spectrum of approaches. At the one end, 'pluralist' or 'consensus' models see social policy as the product of a fundamental consensus in society: empirical evidence of need, produced by social investigators, reformers, pressure groups and so on, arouses public opinion and, through the democratic process, eventually results in appropriate social legislation.[4] Consensus explanations tend to view governments as neutral arbiters, judging between the competing interests that constitute a pluralist society, and responding rationally with legislation. This, for example, was the view of the Fabian William Robson in 1943 after reading the Beveridge Report; the fact that Beveridge had recommended much the same as the Fabian Society had suggested in its evidence showed, Robson thought, that 'if persons with qualified and trained minds will apply themselves in a disinterested manner to a great social problem . . . the proper principles will emerge so unmistakably that the right solution will cease to be a matter of mere opinion and become a question of scientific knowledge'.[5]

In general, consensus interpretations maintain that welfare is antithetical to free-market capitalism. Thus for H. L. Beales, social policy was 'a collective term for the public provisions through which we attack insecurity and correct the debilitating tendencies of our "capitalist" inheritance'.[6] Perhaps the most lucid exposition of this view has been presented by T. H. Marshall, who maintains that 'the central function of welfare . . . is to supersede the market by taking goods and services out of it, or in some way to control and modify its operations so as to produce a result which it would not have produced itself'.[7] Marshall has also argued that as democratic rights were extended in Britain by stages, so also were 'citizenship' rights extended to a growing proportion of the population; part of this extension of citizenship rights was achieved through welfare provision, the aim of which is 'to give equal care to similar cases'.[8]

On the other hand, a challenge to this view has emerged in recent years from various writers, Marxist and non-Marxist, who have tried to analyse welfare in relation to its more ambivalent 'control' functions. The failure of decades of reformist legislation significantly to alter the distribution of wealth and power in society, plus the growth of a critical sociology, has encouraged an approach which views social policy as one element in a number of social, economic, political and ideological controls whereby inequalities may be perpetuated or even enhanced. Thus while social policy undoubtedly raises living standards (though arguably rising real wages deserve much more credit) and improves life-chances, it also imposes on recipients subtle economic, social and political sanctions. Roy Hay, for example, has shown that in the early twentieth century many employers were extremely interested in welfare policies as a possible means of counteracting militant trade unionism and imposing new controls on their workforce; by contrast, the older consensus-oriented school of social policy history tended to assume that employers were generally hostile or indifferent to the idea of welfare.[9] Central to this view is the contention that social policies do *not* come about through governments responding rationally to empirical evidence of an objectively-perceived 'social problem'. Political and economic pressure from below may force a ruling class to make concessions through welfare legislation, but those concessions may be granted very reluctantly or in such a way as to involve minimal redistribution of wealth or political power.[10]

Clearly, this study could have examined the movement for family allowances from a number of different perspectives: in the context of the changing role of women and children, and the history of the feminist movement (relatively under-researched for the 1918—45 period), or in relation to developments taking place in other countries, to give but two examples. Faced with a number of possible approaches, this study has confined itself to the answering of a basic question: *on what grounds* were family allowances acceptable to policy makers? In particular, did policy-makers admit the validity of the arguments put forward by the campaigners, and respond with appropriate legislation? By asking this question, one is implicitly or explicitly challenging pluralist explanations of welfare development.

Family allowances[11] provide a particularly interesting case-study for this approach for several reasons. First, the movement for family allowances attracted support (and opposition) from a very wide spectrum of opinion, often for very contradictory reasons. As Mary Stocks, one of the main campaigners, wrote: the topic of family allowances

could be approached from so many directions with such an
infinite variety of emphasis and application. It could be handled
as a problem of vital statistics, housing administration, minimum
wage legislation, child nutrition, national insurance, teachers'
salary scales, coal mining economics, feminism, social philosophy
or pure finance.[12]

Thus in analysing why family allowances were introduced one must
bear in mind the important point that a movement for social reform
may consist of many different interest groups, each with its own
perspective,[13] and that, in contrast to functionalist analyses of welfare
development, one must not assume that there was fundamental agreement on the nature of the problem and the necessity for solving it.
Family allowances were a social policy ostensibly aimed at assisting
children, and it is possible that since children are one of the few groups
in society incapable of campaigning for themselves the motives of
those who supported or opposed family allowances were, as a result,
more complex and revealing than in more orthodox cases of
self-interest.

Second, family allowances had implications for many other areas of
social policy. The case for their introduction was based on social
conditions in the interwar years and touched on many of the social
problems of that period – mass unemployment, poverty and malnutrition in the depressed areas, low wages, income-maintenance policies,
the decline in the birth-rate, and so on. The movement for family
allowances fits neatly into the 1918–45 period: the 1945 Family
Allowances Act was seen by Beveridge as 'in all the legislation of
recent years the greatest break with the old tradition', since in every
other respect the recommendations made in his 1942 report were
'no more than a completion of what was begun in Britain in 1911'.[14]

A third point is that despite these many implications the case for
family allowances as presented by campaigners was essentially based
on two clear arguments: that a considerable amount of poverty existed
in large working class families thanks to a wage system which took no
account of varying family needs; and that the steadily declining birth-
rate would eventually cause serious social and economic problems.
Family allowances were seen as a remedy for both of these, and in
Eleanor Rathbone's Family Endowment Society one has an excellent
example of a well-organised pressure group marshalling evidence and
repeatedly presenting it to the government. The presentation of this
evidence, and the response by the government, is essentially what is
under investigation in this study.

Notes and References

1. For example, Karl de Schweinitz, *England's Road to Social Security* (1947 edn), which concluded (p. 246):

   The realisation in statute and administration of the ideals of the Beveridge Report may take time; but there is a quality of inevitability about the project and its auspices . . . The people of England in their long pilgrimage have come at last 'to the top of the hill called Clear', whence they can see opening before them the way to freedom with security.

2. J. R. Poynter, *Society and Pauperism* (1969), p. xxii.

3. Detailed discussions of theories of welfare development are to be found in Ramesh Mishra, *Society and Social Policy: Theoretical Perspectives on Welfare* (1977); and Victor George and Paul Wilding, *Ideology and Social Welfare* (1976).

4. For an interesting account of the origins of this empiricist tradition in social policy, see Robert Pinker, *Social Theory and Social Policy* (1971), ch. 2.

5. W. Robson (ed.), *Social Security* (1943), pp. 4–5.

6. H. L. Beales, *The Making of Social Policy* (1946), p. 7.

7. T. H. Marshall, 'Value problems of welfare-capitalism', *Journal of Social Policy*, 1 (January 1972), p. 19. For a similar view, see F. Lafitte, *Social Policy in a Free Society* (1962), pp. 8–9.

8. Marshall, op. cit., p. 29. Marshall expressed similar ideas in 'Citizenship and social class', in *Sociology at the Crossroads* (1963), p. 67–127.

9. Roy Hay, 'Employers and social policy in Britain: the evolution of welfare legislation, 1905–14', *Social History*, 4 (January 1977), pp. 435–55.

10. For general examples of this approach, see John Saville, 'The welfare state: an historical approach', *New Reasoner*, 3 (Winter 1957–8), pp. 5–25; Victor George and Paul Wilding, 'Social values, social class and social policy', *Social and Economic Administration*, 6 (September 1972), pp. 236–48; V. George, *Social Security and Society* (1973).

11. Family allowances must be distinguished from family endowment. The former usually refer to cash allowances for children; the latter to any policy which provides assistance in relation to family needs. Often the terms were confused, particularly in the 1920s.

12. Mary Stocks, *Eleanor Rathbone* (1949), p. 102.

13. John Goldthorpe, 'The development of social policy in England, 1800–1914', *Transactions of the Fifth World Congress of Sociology, 1962* (1964), p. 56.

14. Beveridge, in epilogue to E. Rathbone, *Family Allowances* (1949), p. 269.

1 Historical Background

Modern family allowance systems are essentially a feature of advanced industrial societies which have placed restrictions on the employment of children and have introduced some form of compulsory education — thus creating a situation in which large families become a major cause of poverty, and giving rise in turn to demands that the wage system should take account of family needs.[1] This stage was reached by Britain in the late nineteenth century and the demand for family allowances grew in strength thereafter, reaching a peak in the early 1940s.

Yet paradoxically the idea of paying bonuses to parents with large families is also a very old one, and instances can be found throughout history. Glass found evidence of several ancient systems, including three laws introduced by the Roman Emperor Augustus sometime between 18 BC and AD 9, and showed that various pro-natalist policies have existed in Europe ever since.[2] All modern family allowance systems have thus inherited an interesting history, and in order to have a complete understanding of the movement for family allowances in Britain between 1918 and 1945 one must bear this in mind.

In Britain the most important historical legacy was left by the pre-1834 Poor Law, and in particular by the so-called 'Speenhamland System' under which payments based on family size and the prevailing price of bread were granted to labourers either as wage-supplements or in the form of relief.[3] The origins of this system are conventionally seen as Gilbert's Act of 1782 (which allowed the able-bodied to receive relief without having to enter the workhouse) and the famous decision of 6 May 1795 at the Pelican Inn at Speenhamland in Berkshire where, in a period of rapidly rising wheat prices, bad harvests, severe winters and a French blockade of British shipping, the local magistrates decided to adopt a scale of allowances in aid of wages graded according to family size as a means of alleviating temporary distress.[4]

Thereafter, it was long believed, this practice of supplementing wages had a disastrous effect. Labourers became idle (since whether they worked or not, their income was guaranteed) and bred recklessly (since the normal economic penalties of a large family were now removed); farmers were encouraged to pay lower wages (since they knew these would be made up to the agreed minimum by relief payments); and prices increased.[5] Most of all, Poor Law expenditure rose alarmingly, from £1¼ million in 1760 (equivalent to 3s 6¾d per head of population) to over £6¼ million in 1834 (8s 9½d per head).[6] From the point of view of the 1834 Poor Law commissioners, this experiment in family endowment had provided 'a bounty on indolence and vice' by establishing a family wage system under which 'idleness, improvidence, or extravagance occasion no loss, and consequently diligence and economy can afford no gain'.[7]

Modern economic historians, however, have almost completely demolished this view. There is evidence that Poor Law family allowances existed long before the 1790s.[8] Research now suggests that, if anything, allowances were a response to an already rising birth-rate rather than a cause of reckless breeding.[9] Similarly, it is likely that far from causing wages to fall they were in fact a time-honoured device for relieving acute distress in a period of falling real wages – and, it is important to remember, allowances were a way of avoiding raising minimum wages.[10] Finally, historians have demonstrated that despite the commissioners' rhetoric against them, allowances continued to be paid after 1834 to certain categories of Poor Law applicants, such as widows with dependent children.[11]

That the conclusions of the 1834 commissioners were in fact a wilful distortion of the evidence to fit Benthamite prescriptions is now well known,[12] but for over a century their view of the Speenhamland System remained the standard one and was repeated by subsequent writers to such an extent that the 1909 Majority Report of the Royal Commission on the Poor Laws could assert that 'no economic doctrine has gained wider currency than that public relief is a grant in aid of wages and tends to reduce them'.[13] By the early twentieth century 'Speenhamland' symbolised everything that ruling class opinion feared most from over-generous relief – that it would create an ever-expanding army of indolent, work-shy paupers who would breed recklessly and whose attitudes would eventually infect the rest of the workforce. From this point of view, the first experiment in family allowances appeared to have been an unmitigated disaster.

This historical legacy dominated subsequent discussions of family allowances and deeply affected the attitudes of those involved. Eleanor

Rathbone on one occasion referred to 'the disastrous experiment in subsidizing wages known as the Speenhamland system' which 'put the idle or inefficient family on the same level with the industrious',[14] and always insisted that by paying them to the mother family allowances would be kept completely separate from wages. Perhaps the most influenced were trade unionists, the majority of whom remained deeply suspicious of family allowances in the interwar years on the grounds that they might depress wages. In 1928, for example, a Trades Union Congress and Labour Party committee warned that 'the notorious Speenhamland System, originating in 1795, was an early example of the family allowance principle grafted on to the Poor Law . . . the disastrous effects of this policy in reducing wages are too well known to require comment'.[15] This opposition from trade unionists was a factor very much taken into account by civil servants when family allowances were first seriously considered by the government in 1939–42. The Treasury even composed a special memorandum on Speenhamland and wages since 'the Trade Unions have always studied Economic History and this point is in their minds when they express doubts about family allowances'.[16] Thus when the government published a White Paper on family allowances in 1942 (the purpose of which was to set out arguments for and against) they included in it a warning that to use family allowances to bring wages up to a specified minimum level would 'make the amount of his wages a matter of indifference to the low wage earner with a family, and this would lead to consequences similar to those which resulted from the wage subsidy associated with the name of Speenhamland'.[17]

However, alongside this rather negative legacy was the important fact that by 1918 the principle of family endowment had been quite openly endorsed by government spokesmen on several occasions. The earliest example of this was Prime Minister William Pitt's interest in family allowances as an alternative to a statutory minimum wage.[18] Speaking against Samuel Whitbread's wage-regulation Bill in the House of Commons in 1796, Pitt pointed out that a minimum wage that took no account of varying family needs would be useless, since 'were the minimum fixed upon the standard of a large family it might operate as an encouragement to idleness in one part of the community, and if it were fixed on the standard of a small family, those would not enjoy the benefit of it for whose relief it was intended'.[19] In a remarkable passage which presaged twentieth-century thinking (and which was greatly abhorred by subsequent Malthusian pamphleteers) he suggested that the solution was to make relief in cases where there are a large number of children a matter of right and honour, instead of a ground for opprobrium and contempt. This will make the large family a blessing, and not a curse; and thus will draw a proper line of distinction between those who are able to provide for themselves by their labour, and those who, after having enriched their country with a large number of children, have a claim on its assistance for their support.[20]

Quite how serious were Pitt's intentions it is hard to know. Certainly, he later attempted to introduce a Bill to give effect to his family endowment plan, but withdrew it in the face of hostile criticism over some of its other proposals.[21] What is so interesting, however, is that the 'family allowance versus a minimum wage' arguments, of which Speenhamland and Pitt's Bill were practical manifestations, were exactly those that were to be repeated again and again in the campaign for family allowances that began over a hundred years later.

In the early twentieth century there were two important practical recognitions of family needs in public policy (apart from the Poor Law). The first of these occurred in 1909, when Lloyd George as Chancellor of the Exchequer introduced income tax child allowances in his budget, casually admitting the family endowment principle when he reasoned that 'the family man is, generally speaking, a much heavier contributor to that portion of the revenue which is derived from indirect taxation and inhabited house duty, so that in comparison with the bachelor he is taxed not so much in proportion to his income as in proportion to his outgoings'.[22] The implications of this went completely unchallenged in a House of Commons whose members would have been horrified had the principle been applied to working class wages; indeed, the only point of dispute was whether the allowances were large enough.[23] These new rebates provided a £10 abatement for each child under 16 years of age for parents with incomes below £500 and above £160 per annum (the exemption limit), and in 1910 were benefiting 3½ million taxpayers out of an estimated 18 million income-recipients.[24] The importance of this quietly-introduced precedent is often overlooked; one economist has even suggested that the 1945 Family Allowances Act was far less historic than the 1909 precedent, since 'whatever revolution there was in 1945 was chiefly in the manner and coverage of family differentiation'.[25]

The second major instance of state family endowment took place during the First World War, when service pay separation allowances were extended to cover Britain's first conscript fighting force. Along with the significant, if temporary, step forward made by women through their entry into previously all-male occupations there occurred what Eleanor Rathbone saw as 'the largest experiment in the state endowment of maternity that the world has ever seen'.[26]

These separation allowances were additions to the serviceman's pay in respect of his dependants (including illegitimate children); servicemen had to make an allotment from their pay, to which the government added an allowance. Separation allowances varied greatly according to a number of factors — rank, size of family, even the time of year — and were subject to many intricate regulations (such as what should happen if a soldier deserted, or was reported missing).[27] Thus no single cash figure can be quoted as a typical allowance, but for the sake of illustration a private in 1916 serving abroad would have had paid to a wife alone 12s 6d per week (the allotment from his pay plus the allowance) and to a wife and four children 25s 0d, while for a warrant officer the equivalent amounts would have been 23s 0d and 35s 6d respectively.[28]

The principle behind separation allowances was interesting. They were intended 'to represent the loss which the dependant has sustained by the man's enlistment' and therefore were supposed to be 'based on the value of the support given to the dependants by the soldier before his enlistment'.[29] In other words, they contained the implicit assumption that an enlisted man's normal civilian wages were sufficient to meet his family's needs. In a sense, therefore, separation allowances were not a true family endowment precedent, since of course the justification for family allowances is that normal wages do *not* adequately meet varying family needs. This was a point made later by opponents of family allowances, such as Professor Alexander Gray, who argued that separation allowances had been paid 'because the State could not enter into a contract to pay to all the wages they had previously received' and that the principles behind the system were thus 'very different to those applicable to free and voluntary labour'.[30]

Yet in their administrative structure separation allowances did establish an important precedent: many aspects of their administrative machinery, such as payment through post offices by means of draft books, anticipated the 1945 Act. They also provided the precedent for dependants' allowances in out-of-work donation after 1918, which in turn led to the introduction of dependants' allowances (and thus the obligation to meet family needs) into the main unemployment insurance scheme in 1921. Separation allowances also appeared to demonstrate that family-adjusted income improved child health and nutrition — a point later stressed by supporters of family allowances.[31]

Such were the practical precedents. At the same time there were occurring important changes in the economic structure of the working class family. The nineteenth century saw the transformation of children from the role of producers of wealth to passive consumers, thanks to restrictions on child labour and the introduction of compulsory state elementary education. By the end of the nineteenth century, social surveys were revealing that the larger the working class family, the more likely it was to be in poverty. Seebohm Rowntree, for example, found that in York in 1899, 22·16 per cent of primary poverty was caused by 'largeness of family' (that is, more than four children) and a further 51·96 per cent of primary poverty was caused by 'low wages' (that is, wages insufficient to maintain a family of not more than three children in a state of physical efficiency).[32] More striking still was Rowntree's point, demonstrated through his 'poverty cycle' chart, that a high proportion of working class individuals were likely to fall into primary poverty at three stages of their lives — childhood, parentage and old age — with children a major cause at each of the first two.[33]

Alongside this change in the economic role of children (which was taking place in all advanced industrial societies) there was emerging in Britain the movement for women's emancipation. The three major leaders of the Family Endowment Society — Eleanor Rathbone, Mary Stocks and Eva Hubback — had been involved with the women's suffrage movement and used the same campaigning methods in their fight for family allowances.[34] More importantly, each saw the family allowances movement as a natural outgrowth of the struggle for the vote: like many feminists, they believed that only when political equality had been won could women move on to the much more difficult and lengthy task of gaining economic and social equality.[35] Family allowances were thus only one out of several causes which Eleanor Rathbone supported with the aim of winning economic justice for women.[36] Similarly, Mary Stocks regarded her campaigning for family allowances and birth-control as part of a much wider effort on behalf of women; she 'always regarded the two subjects as the positive and negative of voluntary parenthood'.[37]

By the early twentieth century state motherhood endowment was also being advocated by many socialists, who argued that capitalism had destroyed family life. 'People rear children for the State and the future', wrote H. G. Wells; 'if they do that well, they do the whole world a service, and deserve payment just as much as if they built a bridge or raised a crop of wheat'.[38] Wells saw state motherhood endowment as part of a general transformation of family life under socialism, with legal and economic equality for women as an essential cornerstone.[39] From other socialists came demands for improved maternity services, maternity pensions, the provision of free milk and state-run nurseries.[40] The most extreme language came from Sidney Webb, who advocated motherhood endowment for the eugenically-sound 'best members of the middle and upper artisan classes' in order to alter the existing situation where between one-half and two-thirds of married couples were practising birth-control but at the same time children were being 'freely born to the Irish, Roman Catholics and the Polish, Russian and German Jews on the one hand, and to the thriftless and irresponsible — largely the casual labourers and other denizens of the one-roomed tenements of our great cities — on the other'.[41] The form of motherhood endowment envisaged by such socialists was thus extremely paternalistic and sprang in large part from fears over declining national fitness, but other sections of the Labour movement were showing a more practical interest in the problems of mothers and children generally; for example, pressure from Labour MPs was an important factor behind the Liberal government's introduction of the 1906 Education (Provision of Meals) Act which allowed local authorities to provide rate-financed school meals for needy children.[42]

Yet another impulse behind the movement for family allowances was the question, much debated by economists, of how wages should be calculated. From feminists came the demand of 'equal pay for equal work'; from socialists, the demand for a 'living wage' or 'national minimum'; and in addition there emerged in all advanced industrial societies in the late nineteenth and early twentieth centuries a debate over whether wages should be 'industrial' (that is, solely based on the individual's productivity) or 'social' (also related to family needs). Against a background of growing international economic rivalry and a resultant increasing concern over the industrial efficiency of the workforce, plus alarm over an increasingly socialist Labour movement, economists were forced into the realization that wages which provided for minimum needs would result in higher productivity *per capita* and might also stifle political discontent. Perhaps the best example of this strand of thought can be seen in Seebohm Rowntree, employer and social scientist. Rowntree's interest in minimum human needs arose from his concern that a seriously underfed workforce was also a chronically inefficient one. 'The relation of food to industrial efficiency', he wrote, 'is so obvious and so direct as to be a commonplace amongst students of political economy'; what an employer got out of a worker depended on what he first put into him, and for Rowntree the significance of this had now acquired an urgency that it is not easy to exaggerate in consequence of the stress and keenness of international competition . . . the highest commercial success will be impossible so long as large numbers even of the most sober and industrious of the labouring class receive but three-fourths of the necessary amount of food'.[43]

The living wage, argued the Polish economist Piotr Prengowski, was necessary in order to maintain good relations between employer and employee, and to keep workers immune from 'the revolutionary propaganda of the enemies of social order'.[44]

Gradually the industrial advantages of the living wage began to be more clearly perceived, and in the process it began to attract increasing attention from academic economists, political philosophers and religious leaders, who attempted to construct elaborate ideological justifications for it. An interesting example of this was the anti-socialist papal encyclical *De Rerum Novarum* (1891) which suggested that 'the wage paid to the working man must be sufficient for the support of himself and of his family . . . if in the present state of society this is not always feasible, social justice demands that reforms be introduced without delay which will guarantee every adult working man just such a wage', and went on to praise the small number of industrial family allowance schemes then existing in Europe.[45] Similar sentiments were expressed by the American economist John Ryan, who argued that 'the right to a family Living Wage belongs to every adult male labourer, whether he intends to marry or not; for rights are to be interpreted according to the average conditions of human life, and they suppose the labourer to become the head of a family'.[46]

It was just after the First World War and during the 1920s that the discussion of wages and family needs reached a peak in Britain. Essentially the points of dispute were: (a) whether wages should take account of family size, and (b) if so, what size of family should be assumed as average.

On the first point, there was still considerable opposition from economic theorists to any concept of need in wage-calculation. D. H. Macgregor argued that family allowances would increase the birth-rate and thus exacerbate the wages problem they were originally designed to solve.[47] J. H. Richardson (though interested in family allowances for the low paid) suggested that 'as a general rule, the adjustment of needs to income is preferable to the family allowance system of adjusting income to needs'.[48] The most virulent criticism came from Alexander Gray, Professor of Economics at the University of Aberdeen, who maintained that not only were needs impossible to assess ('the needs of the loafer, by virtue of his leisure, may indeed exceed the needs of the worker') but that if needs were to be the future basis of wage calculation, then soon the rights of private property would be challenged and a redistribution of wealth demanded ('once a society has embarked on this slippery slope, there is no logical stopping-place until the community is at the mercy of those who ask loudest and are most unrestrained in the satisfaction of their desires').[49]

However, this opposition was more than counteracted by a growing support for the idea of the family wage such that a foreign observer could note in 1924 that the discussion of family endowment in Britain had already manifested itself in as many as five different forms: apart from the newly-formed Family Endowment Society (examined at length in the following chapter) there were the State Bonus Plan, Beatrice Webb's equal wage and child endowment proposals, Seebohm Rowntree's interest in a minimum wage plus family allowances, and a continuing discussion of motherhood endowment within the TUC and the Labour Party.[50]

The State Bonus Plan originated in 1918 when Mabel and Dennis Milner published *Scheme for a State Bonus*, in which they suggested that every man, woman and child should automatically receive a weekly 'State Bonus', to be financed by a 20 per cent levy on all earned and unearned incomes.[51] Thus a family of five whose income was £2 10s 0d per week would pay 10s 0d a week into a fund and would receive £2 5s 0d back (at a bonus rate of 9s 0d per person), making their final income £4 5s 0d.[52] The scheme would redistribute income and would provide a basic stigma-free guaranteed minimum which would be quite separate from wages.[53] Dennis Milner was the son of a Quaker manufacturer and together with another Quaker, Bertram Pickard, the Milners founded the State Bonus League in 1918. The League soon developed twenty-four branches and Dennis Milner contested a seat at the 1918 general election, campaigning on the State Bonus issue. In 1919 the League even managed to persuade the Labour Party (of which Milner was a member) to investigate the idea, but in 1921 the Labour Party Executive eventually rejected it, and the State Bonus League had to disband.[54]

Beatrice Webb's brief interest in family endowment occurred when she was appointed to a War Cabinet Committee on Women in Industry in 1918 which investigated, among other things, the question of women's wages. The Majority Report of the Committee rejected the idea of family endowment in wages,[55] but Beatrice Webb published her own Minority Report in which, while admitting that wages could not be determined by family obligations, she nevertheless supported the idea of 'a children's allowance on the scale of the present separation allowance' financed out of taxation.[56]

Probably the most coherent advocacy of family endowment in the early 1920s (apart from the Family Endowment Society) came from Seebohm Rowntree. Rowntree suggested that a distinction should be made between minimum wages and wages above the minimum: 'the former should be determined primarily by human needs, the latter by the market value of the services rendered'. After calculating the cost of minimum human needs. Rowntree arrived at a figure of 35s 3d (at 1914 prices) as a minimum weekly income for a man, wife and three children. However, although 49·6 per cent of families investigated by Rowntree in York had three or more dependent children (thus justifying the three-child minimum wage), 62·0 per cent of the children belonged to families having four or more dependent children; such a minimum wage would thus leave nearly two-thirds of all children unprovided for. The only solution, Rowntree believed, was a three-child minimum wage plus family allowances of 3s 0d per week for the fourth and subsequent children.[57]

Finally, family endowment was still being discussed within the Labour movement. In 1920—1 Labour MPs, led by Tyson Wilson, made several unsuccessful attempts to persuade the government to introduce a mothers' pensions Bill providing child allowances for women who had been widowed, deserted or left to support an invalid husband.[58] Pressure from the 1921 National Conference of Labour Women and the Labour Party Conference forced the Executive of the Labour Party to appoint a committee, which published a report in 1922 favouring extensions of services in kind (for example, universal free education from nursery school to university, universal free health services, better maternity care) as having greater priority.[59] Nevertheless, interest in various forms of cash family endowment remained strong within the rank and file of the Labour Party, even if its leaders were by and large opposed.[60]

However, one difficult problem encountered by all who supported the principle of the family wage was the question of exactly what constituted the 'average family'. Generally, this was assumed to consist of man, wife and three children, but critics of the family wage principle were quick to point out that only 9 per cent of married workers had the supposedly 'average' family of three dependent children; 42 per cent had none, 23 per cent had one, 16 per cent had two and 10 per cent had more than three. Thus a three-child minimum wage would be on the one hand wasteful, since it would provide more than was needed by the 81 per cent of married workers who had fewer than three children (plus the single workers, who constituted 26·5 per cent of the workforce), and on the other hand would be insufficient for the needs of the 10 per cent with more than three.[61] This former point gave rise to moralistic warnings that single and small-family men would fritter away the surplus income on drink, gambling and cigarettes,[62] while the latter point Rowntree attempted to overcome by recommending that the three-child minimum wage be supplemented by family allowances starting with the fourth child.

But a more serious criticism made against the three-child minimum wage was its cost. The economist A. L. Bowley calculated that to raise all adult male wages before the First World War up to the Rowntree 'Human Needs' level of 35s 3d per week and women's wages up to 20s 0d per week would have cost about £250 million and could only have been achieved by the nationalization of all unearned income except that belonging to persons with less than £160 per annum all told, and by the reduction of all other sources of income from salaries, profits, earnings, down to £160 per head per annum.[63] Similarly, Sir Josiah Stamp calculated in 1921 that if all persons with incomes over £250 per annum pooled the excess over that amount and re-distributed it (after deductions for public expenditure) the resulting sum would provide less than 5s 0d per week per family.[64] Such figures seemed to provide reassuring proof to opponents of the family wage that the concept was pure economic moonshine.

Finally, no historical introduction would be complete without a brief reference to what was happening in other countries. While the family wage question still remained purely theoretical in Britain, in several countries family allowance systems were developing rapidly in the early 1920s. By 1925, equalization funds in France were paying family allowances to 1 210 000 employees: on average these gave additions to a married man's wages of 4 per cent for one child, 9 per cent for two, 16 per cent for three and nearly 25 per cent for four.[65] France, of course, had a long tradition of pro-natalist policies (often for militaristic reasons), and was subject to the same family wage controversy that Britain experienced at the turn of the century.[66] After the First World War, French employers took the initiative in introducing their own family allowance schemes, as a means of enforcing industrial discipline (allowances could be withheld in cases of strikes, lock-outs, absenteeism, or lateness) and as a cheaper alternative to across-the-board wage rises.[67] Similar developments, for similar reasons, took place in Belgium and, to a lesser extent, Germany, Austria, Czechoslovakia, the Netherlands, Switzerland, Poland, Sweden, Norway, Denmark, Finland, Yugoslavia, Italy, Spain and the Irish Republic.[68]

This, then, was the situation at the beginning of the movement for family allowances in Britain. The principle of family endowment was a very old one, and had manifested itself in public policy on a number of occasions — of which child tax rebates and service pay separation allowances were the most recent. Classical economic thinking tended to oppose any application of the principle to wages, holding up the apparently disastrous Speenhamland System in justification, but by the beginning of the twentieth century this was being counteracted by a growing interest among employers, politicians, social scientists and economists in the concept of the family wage for reasons of social justice, national efficiency and industrial discipline. Already by the early 1920s family endowment was being interpreted in many different ways, and seen as capable of achieving a wide variety of aims: on the one hand, it could be viewed as the essential corner-stone of an exclusively socialist approach to the family; on the other, as a means of weakening trade union solidarity by 'buying off' married workers. It was in this intellectual climate that Eleanor Rathbone formed the Family Endowment Society and began her campaign.

Notes and References

1. J. H. Richardson, *Economic and Financial Aspects of Social Security* (1960), p. 141.
2. D. V. Glass, *Population Policies and Movements in Europe* (1940), pp. 86–98.
3. For example, when a gallon loaf cost 1s 0d every man would receive 3s 0d per week for himself, and 1s 6d each in respect of wife and children, either in wages or relief. Sir George Nicholls, *A History of the English Poor Law* (1898 edn), p. 131.
4. Mark Neuman, 'Speenhamland in Berkshire', in E. W. Martin (ed.), *Comparative Development in Social Welfare* (1972), pp. 85–9.
5. *The Poor Law Report of 1834* (ed. S. and E. Checkland, 1974), pp. 140–79.
6. Nicholls, op. cit., p. 225.
7. *Poor Law Report*, op. cit., pp. 121, 156.
8. S. and B. Webb, *English Local Government: English Poor Law*

History: Part I, The Old Poor Law (1927), pp. 149–50; E. M. Hampson, *The Treatment of Poverty in Cambridgeshire, 1597–1834* (1934), p.37; Mark Blaug,'The Poor Law report re-examined', *Journal of Economic History,* 24 (June 1964), pp. 231–2.

9. For example, J. P. Huzel, 'Malthus, the Poor Law, and population in early nineteenth century England', *Economic History Review,* 22 (December 1969), pp. 445–51.
10. J. D. Marshall, *The Old Poor Law, 1795–1834* (1968), p. 13.
11. M. E. Rose, 'The allowance system under the new Poor Law', *Economic History Review,* 19 (December 1966), pp. 613, 616.
12. For an account of how this was done, see S. E. Finer, *The Life and Times of Sir Edwin Chadwick* (1952), pp. 39–49, 69–78.
13. Quoted in Rose, op. cit., p. 607.
14. E. Rathbone, *The Disinherited Family* (1924), p. 12.
15. Trades Union Congress General Council and Labour Party Executive: Joint Committee on the Living Wage, *Interim Report on Family Allowances and Child Welfare* (1928), p. 6.
16. Margin comment by Sir Horace Wilson in E. Hale to B. Gilbert (8 October 1941), PRO T 161/1073.
17. *Family Allowances: Memorandum by the Chancellor of the Exchequer,* Cmd 6354 (1942), p. 3.
18. This precedent has been noted by many writers. For example, V. George, *Social Security, Beveridge and After* (1968), p. 187.
19. Quoted in J. R. Poynter, *Society and Pauperism* (1969), pp. 58–9. Poynter mentions (pp. 59–60) that the question of the family wage was discussed in several popular pamphlets at this time.
20. ibid., p. 59.
21. Sir John Walley, *Social Security: Another British Failure?* (1972), pp. 17–20.
22. *Hansard* (5th series), vol. 4 (29 April 1909), col. 507. Child tax rebates had previously operated between 1796 and 1806.
23. ibid., vol. 11 (20 September 1909), cols. 182–6.
24. Allen M. Cartter, 'Income-tax allowances and the family in Great Britain', *Population Studies,* 6 (March 1953), p. 219.
25. ibid.
26. E. Rathbone, 'The remuneration of women's services', *Economic Journal,* 27 (March 1917), p. 55.
27. War Office pamphlet, *Regulations for the Issue of Army Separation Allowances, Allotments of Pay and Family Allowances During the Present War* (1916).
28. ibid., p. 30. For the administrative machinery, see E. Rathbone,

The Muddle of Separation Allowances (1915).

29. War Office pamphlet, *Recoverable Advances, Supplementary Separation Allowances and Temporary and Special Grants Authorised Under Part II of the Regulations* (1916), pp. 4, 12.

30. Alexander Gray, *Family Endowment, a Critical Analysis* (1927), pp. 23—4.

31. E. Rathbone, op. cit. (1924), pp. 59—61. Some observers maintained, however, that this had been caused more by high wartime wages. See T. E. Gregory, 'The endowment of motherhood', *The Common Cause* (18 October 1918), p. 311.

32. B. S. Rowntree, *Poverty, a Study of Town Life* (1902 edn), p. 120.

33. ibid., p. 137.

34. Involvement with the women's emancipation movement taught Eleanor Rathbone much about pressure-group tactics. Rathbone 'Changes in public life', in Ray Strachey (ed.), *Our Freedom and its Results* (1936), p. 21.

35. E. Rathbone, *Milestones: Presidential Addresses at the Annual Council Meetings of the National Union of Societies for Equal Citizenship* (1929), pp. 6—8; Vera Brittain, *Lady Into Woman* (1953), p. 7.

36. Mary Stocks, *Eleanor Rathbone* (1949), pp. 115—18.

37. Mary Stocks, *My Commonplace Book* (1970), p. 162.

38. H. G. Wells, *Socialism and the Family* (1906), pp. 57—8.

39. ibid., pp. 56—9. Wells also mentioned motherhood endowment in his satirical novel, *The New Machiavelli* (1911), pp. 410—15.

40. Henry Harben, *The Endowment of Motherhood* (1910), pp. 12—21; M. D. Eder, *The Endowment of Motherood* (1908), pp. 11—12, 46—52.

41. Sidney Webb, *The Decline in the Birth Rate* (1907), pp. 16—17, 19.

42. J. R. Hay, *The Origins of the Liberal Welfare Reforms, 1906—1914* (1975), pp. 43—4.

43. Rowntree, op. cit. (1902), pp. 260—1.

44. P. Prengowski, *Workers' Family Allowances* (1931), p. 53.

45. Quoted in the *Family Endowment Chronicle*, 1 (July 1931), p. 1.

46. John A. Ryan, *A Living Wage* (1912 edn), p. 120. The living wage was also discussed in S. and B. Webb, *Industrial Democracy* (1919), pp. 590—9.

47. D. H. Macgregor, 'Family allowances', *Economic Journal*, 36 (March 1926), pp. 4—5.

48. J. H. Richardson, *A Study on the Minimum Wage* (1927), p. 15. For a similar view, see D. H. Robertson, 'Family endowment',

in *Economic Fragments* (1931), p. 150.

49. Gray, op. cit., pp. 27, 32.
50. Paul Douglas, 'The British discussion of family endowment', *Journal of Social Forces*, 3 (November 1924), pp. 118—24.
51. E. Mabel Milner and Dennis Milner, *Scheme for a State Bonus* (1918), pp. 4—12.
52. E. Mabel Milner and Dennis Milner, *Labour and a Minimum Income for All* (1920), pp. 2—5.
53. Bertram Pickard, *A Reasonable Revolution* (1919), pp. 14, 52.
54. Douglas, op. cit., pp. 120—1; *Labour Party Annual Conference Report for 1920*, pp. 185—6, and *for 1921*, pp. 60—2.
55. *Report of the War Cabinet Committee on Women in Industry*, Cmd 135 (1919), pp. 177—9.
56. ibid., pp. 285—7, 305—7.
57. B. S. Rowntree, *The Human Needs of Labour* (1918), pp. 15, 30—48, 121—9, 141—2.
58. For example, *Hansard*, vol. 125 (13 February 1920), col. 388, and (20 February 1920), col. 1233.
59. Labour Party, *Report on Motherhood and Child Endowment* (1922), pp. 3, 5, 10—16.
60. Stocks, op. cit. (1949), p. 101.
61. Figures (from 1921 census) in Paul Douglas, *Wages and the Family* (1925), p. 32.
62. Some even made this point about the existing wage system. See Mrs H. A. L. Fisher, 'Family allowances', *Quarterly Review*, 480 (July 1924), pp. 76—7, 83—4.
63. A. L. Bowley, *The Division of the Product of Industry* (1919), pp. 95—7.
64. Sir Josiah Stamp, *Wealth and Taxable Capacity* (1921), pp. 95—7.
65. Hugh Vibart, *Family Allowances in Practice* (1926), p. 31; J. H. Richardson, 'The family allowance system', *Economic Journal*, 34 (September 1924), pp. 382—3.
66. Glass, op. cit., p. 100.
67. Vibart, op. cit., pp. 158—60, 167—71; Douglas, op. cit. (1925), pp. 62, 67, 89—90.
68. Vibart, op. cit., pp. 47—50; Douglas, op. cit. (1925), pp. 119—47; Mary Waggaman, '"Family wage" systems in Germany and certain other European countries', *United States Department of Labor: Monthly Labor Review*, 18 (January 1924), pp. 25—9.

2 Eleanor Rathbone and the Family Endowment Society

The Rathbones were a prominent Liverpool family who had built up a large importing and shipping business by the beginning of the nineteenth century, and wielded correspondingly great social and political power in Liverpool society. It was exactly the same background as had produced the pioneer social investigator Charles Booth, and, like Booth, the Rathbones' Nonconformism imposed on them a religious obligation to take an active interest in philanthropy – so much so that at times they even regarded business activity as merely a means to an end, as a way of financing their charitable work.[1] William Rathbone, Eleanor's father, displayed all those contradictory motives that characterized his fellow Nonconformist merchants: a frugal and abstemious man (and well-liked), he apparently pursued wealth solely for the power and social status enjoyed by rich men, yet was continually afraid that excessive wealth would cause 'too much enervation to a man's self and still more to his children'.[2] Always acutely conscious of the duties of the rich, throughout his life he gave away a proportion of his income to charity, this proportion rising as his income rose.[3] This insistence on self-imposed ethical standards often posed the Rathbones with serious moral dilemmas in their everyday affairs in the brutally competitive Liverpool shipping business – as in their quandary over whether to participate in the Chinese opium trade of the 1850s – but despite these uncertainties the family had amassed enough of a fortune by the late nineteenth century to let the business run down, leaving them free to pursue public activities.[4]

In William Rathbone's case this was philanthropy, and his work in Liverpool provides a fascinating microcosmic view of the growth of charity organization outside London. Indeed, along with Thomas Chalmers in Glasgow in the 1820s, William Rathbone was one of the great pioneers of charity organization and social casework.[5] Rapid commercial expansion in Liverpool in the first half of the nineteenth century had brought with it the attendant problems of overcrowding, disease and poverty — all exacerbated by the city's dependence on its docks, and hence on a large army of casual labourers, many of them rootless immigrants.[6] By the 1860s there were growing fears among the wealthy merchant community that pauperism was getting out of control and expanding too fast for existing charities to cope. In the opinion of the merchant class, the causes of this new urban danger lay partly in the failure of the Poor Law to stick to the principle of less eligibility and partly in the chaotic and indiscriminate way that existing charities handed out relief to all who applied. William Rathbone deplored the wastefulness and inefficiency of the latter. He visited the German town of Elberfeld in 1869 and was very impressed with its use of citizen committees to administer relief according to strict rules; the system appealed to his conviction (already voiced in books and pamphlets) that business methods could be used to solve social problems, and he persuaded the Committee of the Liverpool Central Relief Society to adopt a similar approach.[7] Thereafter his commitment to the aims and methods of the newly-founded Charity Organisation Society greatly increased, and it was in this social and intellectual atmosphere that Eleanor grew up.

The ideology of the Charity Organisation Society (COS) was complex, and a full analysis of all its subtleties is obviously well outside the scope of this study.[8] However, two contradictory strands of thought need to be mentioned briefly. On the one hand was the class-conscious, highly individualistic analysis of social problems, which saw poverty as a product of the individual's own moral failings and thus opposed state intervention. The intense fear of a pauperized army of indolents roaming the streets and threatening private property haunted COS thinking, and gave rise to a highly emotional and moralistic approach. Yet on the other hand, the COS claimed that it was offering a new, dispassionate and scientific analysis of social problems, and evolved rigorous casework methods to put this approach into practice.

These two contradictory approaches were evident in William Rathbone, and Eleanor inherited them. She more than anyone else carried the Rathbone tradition on into the twentieth century. Born in 1872, she grew up when the influence of the COS was at its zenith, and died in 1946, just as the Beveridge proposals were coming onto the statute book. Her life thus spanned the formative years of the welfare state, and the greatest period of women's emancipation. Significantly, the changes in her attitude towards social problems mirrored almost identically the general changes of attitude in the British political mainstream in the years 1872–1946.

At Oxford (1893—6) she developed a fondness for metaphysics, but this was gradually tempered by the influence of Edward Caird and D. G. Ritchie, two teachers who were disciples of the T. H. Green idealist school of philosophy that preached the individual's Christian duty to social reform and had such a powerful influence in the years 1880—1914 on Oxford undergraduates who later entered many branches of public life.[9] After graduation, the strong pull of her background brought her home to Liverpool to immerse herself in various aspects of charity organization and voluntary work. In addition to COS case-work as a visitor for the Liverpool Central Relief Society she also served on the board of Granby Street Council School and as honorary secretary of the Liverpool Women's Industrial Council.[10] Thus began the first phase of her public life, in which an involvement in local politics taught her many important lessons for the future.

During this period she appears to have accepted the rigid principles of the COS quite readily. In 1896, for example, she wrote to her father complaining that the Liverpool Central Relief Society was not keeping up to strict London COS standards: the proper business of charity caseworkers, she maintained, ought to be 'not so much to relieve as to prevent the poor from needing relief, and when relief is given to let it be in such a form as may, if possible, help them into a position of self-support'; thus no relief should be given for such regular events as 'the wife's annual confinement', for thus 'the fear of being driven into the workhouse, which is the only inducement likely to drive the average labourer to save, is removed from him'.[11]

However, her attitudes gradually changed. By the time she published *How the Casual Labourer Lives* (1909) and *Report on the Condition of Widows Under the Poor Law in Liverpool* (1913) the years of personal contact with the day-to-day realities of working class poverty plus her growing interest in feminism had left their mark. The upper-middle class moralizing remained, but it was increasingly tempered with genuine sympathy for the problems of working class women. Thus while on the one hand she could look on Poor Law widows who were inadequate mothers as 'the grossly negligent and slatternly, as well as the chronic drinkers and loose livers', suggesting that their out-relief be stopped and their children confiscated, yet on the other hand she could also see that 'it is hard for a woman to be an efficient housewife and parent while she is living under conditions of extreme poverty . . . The astonishing thing to us is not that so many women fail to grapple with the problem successfully but that any succeed', and recognize that since they suffered from 'a completely blameless misfortune' widows should be removed from a Poor Law based on the principle of deterrence.[12] Again, her inquiry into dock labour in Liverpool[13] was a pioneering example of the new empirical approach to the analysis of unemployment, and anticipated Beveridge's more famous study by several years.[14]

By the 1920s Eleanor Rathbone's social and political views had become so idiosyncratic as almost to defy analysis. There still remained a deeply conservative vein which surfaced from time to time — as, most notoriously, in her campaign on behalf of Indian women, where what one writer has aptly described as 'her characteristic bull-in-a-china-shop indignation'[15] revealed a complete inability to understand Indian nationalist aspirations.[16] In this context, it is interesting that some recent feminist historians have emphasized the underlying conservatism of the movement for family allowances spearheaded by Eleanor Rathbone: they argue that it was a watered-down version of far more radical demands for payment for motherhood, free nursery education, child welfare clinics and so on, being made by labour women, and in fact envisaged women being tied more closely to the home through their dependence on a family wage earned by the husband when what was really needed was a raising of women's wages and equal opportunities in the labour market.[17]

Mostly, however, this conservatism was hidden beneath a vague liberal reformism. She steadfastly refused to commit herself to any political party and throughout her parliamentary career (1929—46) remained an Independent Member of Parliament for the rather anachronistic Combined English Universities seat. The causes she espoused were many and varied: besides family allowances and feminism these included Spanish Civil War and Czechoslovakian refugees, the rights of coloured women in the British colonies, child poverty and malnutrition, stopping the persecution of the Jews, anti-Nazism and housing reform.[18] Indeed, these campaigns received far more of her attention during her parliamentary career than did family allowances.[19] All this brought her into contact with a wide range of political opinion: when first developing the idea of family endowment she worked with the socialist H. N. Brailsford, yet when campaigning to stamp out female circumcision in Kenya her companion was the arch-conservative Duchess of Atholl.[20]

Her personality, too, displayed many contradictions. Though generally formal and serious in her everyday manner, she attracted the support and admiration of easy-going, whimsical people like Robert Boothby. Meticulously careful in matters she regarded as important, such as checking an article for publication, she could be appallingly absent-minded at other times – on one occasion setting off for the House of Commons with one sock on and the other dangling from her hand. She could spend several weeks touring around South Wales mining areas (transported in the motorcycle-sidecar of the local Family Endowment Society organizer) and be warmly received by audiences of miners' wives; yet she could be equally at home addressing a meeting of the highly conservative, arch-elitist Eugenics Society.[21]

Why, then, did a wealthy upper-middle class woman steeped in COS philosophy, and with ambivalent political views, eventually lead a campaign for a cause which proposed a drastic reorganization of the wage-structure and was initially supported by many left-wing intellectuals?

The starting-point was undoubtedly her interest in feminism. The demand of 'equal pay for equal work', an important feminist cause, was usually met by the argument that men should be paid more than women because they had wives and children to support. But if this was so, surely men with large families should be paid more than men with no children? Eleanor Rathbone's mind was working on this question when she published a pamphlet in 1911 in which, she later said, the idea of family endowment was 'hinted shyly at'.[22] In fact, far from being shy, the language was strongly feminist and uncompromising: observing that in the existing wage-structure 'economic and social forces have worked out a solution satisfactory alike to masculine sentiment and to masculine love of power', she insisted that

> the community must provide somehow for the rearing of fresh generations. Hitherto it has provided for it indirectly and only half consciously by paying through the employer of the adult male worker (who is assumed to be normally a husband and father) enough to cover the prime cost of the maintenance of his own family.[23]

The seeds of her future arguments were all there – in particular the crucial point that the existing wage-structure treated all men as 'hypothetical fathers' – but they remained undeveloped.

Gradually, she began to examine the whole problem of the economics of motherhood. She discovered that the wives of both dock labourers and seamen suffered greatly from the irregular way that their husbands were paid, and that no amount of moral exhortation should change this.[24] She investigated the financial circumstances of Poor Law widows and their children in Liverpool, and was shocked at their plight: 'it may be said that thousands of non-pauper families of Liverpool live under no better conditions', she wrote, and hinting at her future ideas added, 'true, but the community has not assumed direct responsibility for the welfare of these families, as it has done for those of the widows'.[25]

By 1917 she had rejected the feminist slogan of 'equal pay for equal work' because the real problem was a wage-structure that took no account of varying family needs. The rearing of future generations was of vital importance to the state, yet the state did nothing to improve the lot of the average housewife, who would still be dependent for money on the whim of her husband since 'whether he expends the wages so received upon his family or upon his own "menus plaisirs" depends, of course, entirely upon his goodwill, since the State, though it recognizes in theory the rights of wife and children to maintenance, does practically nothing to enforce it'.[26]

Finally, the experience of helping to administer separation allowances during the First World War set the seal on her ideas. Just at the time when she was ruminating on payment for motherhood there was instituted this highly-organized state family allowance system. In her work for the Liverpool branch of the Soldiers' and Sailors' Families Association she met a far wider section of the working class than when with the Central Relief Society (thereby grasping the full extent of family poverty), saw that often these allowances were the only means of preventing such families from starvation, and witnessed their beneficial effect on child health. She also had to investigate cases where Liverpool servicemen had deserted their wives, and this led her to the inescapable conclusion that 'as for the actively unhappy marriages, it is probably safe to say that in the large majority the rift has begun in quarrels about money, in the husband's inability to earn, or refusal to give, enough for the support of the home'.[27]

By 1924 her thoughts on family endowment had crystallized, and in that year she published her *magnum opus, The Disinherited Family*. It is a remarkable book, in which ruthlessly logical argument, practical experience, sympathy for the problems of working class women and a sardonic feminist wit are combined into a devastating attack on male-dominated economic theory. She starts from the fact that although much had been written about family life nowhere is the importance of the family as an economic unit considered.[28] Although 'the whole business of begetting, bearing and rearing children is the most essential of all the nation's business', generations of male economists have refused to recognize this; indeed, 'if the population of Great Britain consisted entirely of adult self-propagating bachelors and spinsters, nearly the whole output of writers on economic theory during the past fifty years might remain as it was written'.[29] Their most recent creation, the living wage concept, is a fallacy, since to base such a minimum on the supposedly 'average' family of two adults and three children would be both wasteful (in that it would make provision for over 16 million non-existent children and 3 million non-existent wives, in families containing fewer than three children and in the case of bachelors), yet at the same time insufficient (because in families containing more than three children, over 1¼ million children would still remain unprovided for).[30] To talk of 'low wages' or 'large families' as causes of poverty (as Rowntree had done in his York survey) is to miss what for her is the crucial point that 'by far the greatest cause of poverty is the failure of the wage system to adapt itself to the needs of the variously sized households actually dependent on the wage-earner'.[31]

It is when she goes on to describe the effects of the existing wage-system on family and home life that she shows greatest sympathy for working class mothers. Even a married couple who were models of thrift and abstinence would be 'not a match for the laws of arithmetic' if their family size increased while their income did not. In addition to this wellnigh impossible task of running a household whose needs leapt ahead of income (likened to 'making bricks without straw') the wife must live in a state of legal and social disadvantage — yet at the same time accept hypocritical praise for her invaluable role in society ('popular sentiment places her little lower than the angels, the law a little higher than a serf').[32]

The second part of the book gives a comprehensive survey of foreign family allowance systems, and considers possible schemes for Britain. Rejecting fears over the possible adverse effect of family allowances on the birth-rate, parental responsibility, wage levels and industrial costs, she investigates the unconscious irrational opposition that such a family-oriented measure is likely to arouse, naming it the 'Turk complex'. This, she believes, is the real underlying force behind male opposition — stemming from the man's psychological need to dominate and possess, and his refusal to recognize his wife and children as separate personalities with rights equal to his own. Thus, she argues, opponents of family allowances may pretend to put forward reasoned arguments, but when examined none of these stand up, and ultimately the task of family allowance supporters must be the very difficult one of overcoming the irrational prejudices of this 'Turk complex' which permeates politics, the civil service, the professions, the trade unions – indeed, all walks of public life.[33]

The most striking feature of *The Disinherited Family* is thus its iconoclastic challenge to existing economic theory, and its attempt to re-direct economic thinking towards the needs of the family. Accordingly, no one particular scheme of family endowment is suggested: a state-financed system of cash family allowances would be best, but one run by private industries might be easier to achieve in the short term.[34] Essentially, the book is a plea that the *principle* of family endowment be applied wherever possible in social and economic policy.

This was to be Eleanor Rathbone's aim throughout the movement for family allowances, and was the policy of the pressure group formed by her. Having examined Eleanor Rathbone's background, motivation and growth of interest in family allowances, we must now examine the composition, aims and methods of the Family Endowment Society.

The Family Endowment Society[35] originated in a small committee assembled by Eleanor Rathbone in October 1917 to discuss possible schemes of family allowances. Clearly, she wanted to share with some sympathetic companions the vague ideas expressed in her article in the *Economic Journal* of March 1917, and shape them into a coherent plan. The composition of this 'Family Endowment Committee' had strong leanings towards feminism and socialism: apart from Eleanor Rathbone, three of the members (Kathleen Courtney, A. Maude Royden and Mary Stocks) were active in the National Union of Women's Suffrage Societies, one (H. N. Brailsford, the journalist) was a prominent member of the Independent Labour Party, and the remaining two (Emile and Elinor Burns) were similarly inclined.[36] The Committee began by examining the question of equal pay for women, at that time attracting much attention owing to the greatly expanded employment opportunities presented to women by a war economy. Rejecting the slogan of 'equal pay for equal work', they maintained that family allowances would achieve wage equality between the sexes anyway, since it would automatically rob men of the excuse that they needed higher wages because they had families to keep. By a majority they came out in favour of a national family allowance system providing 12s 6d per week for mothers, 5s 0d per week for the first child and 3s 6d per week for each subsequent child, to cover children at least up to the age of 5 and preferably up to 14. The language of the Committee's report reflected its political complexion: along with a visionary utopianism there was a strong element of state paternalism, with allowances being payable to the mother only on condition that she 'obtained at regular intervals from any registered infant welfare centre, nursery school, or qualified visiting officer a certificate that the general condition of her children was satisfactory'.[37]

The Committee thereafter gradually built up publicity for its cause. Collectively it gave evidence to the 1918 War Cabinet Committee on Women in Industry,[38] and individually its members tried to influence branches of the Labour and feminist movements. Brailsford began a long campaign to persuade the Labour Party to accept family allowances as official policy, while Eleanor Rathbone and Mary Stocks aroused the interest of the National Union of Societies for Equal Citizenship. By 1924 the Committee had expanded into the Family Endowment Society.

From the beginning, the Family Endowment Society's aims were kept deliberately vague — 'to collect and disseminate information, to promote discussion and to take action, with a view to bringing about as quickly as possible a more adequate method than at present of making provision for families' — so that all shades of political opinion could be accommodated.[39] Its object was to stimulate public discussion with a view to getting the *principle* of family endowment widely accepted.[40] Membership was never large — only 77 in 1925, rising to 123 in 1930, equally divided between the sexes and predominantly university-educated middle class professional people of some public standing.[41] At no time did the Society ever attempt to become a mass movement, powerful through weight of numbers: instead it concentrated on 'capturing' influential public figures who knew their way round the corridors of power in Westminster, Fleet Street and the civil service. These figures would be utilized at the appropriate moment to put the Society's case on a particular issue to those in positions of real power. Eleanor Rathbone soon realized that 'in a subject so new it is very valuable to have a strong list of names, representative of different sections of the community', since the idea would have little chance of catching on 'so long as those pressing for it are a small group of people, mostly women whose names naturally carry little weight with large employers, trade unionists, politicians, etc.'[42] These important names made up the Council (numbering about fifty in the 1920s); in addition there were the ordinary members and subscribers; and at the heart of the organization worked the small group on the Executive Committee, carrying on the day-to-day business.

For most of the 1920s the Society's joint presidents were Professor

Gilbert Murray, Sir Henry Slesser, KC, and Lord Balfour of Burleigh.[43] The Council included such names as Sir William Beveridge, the Bishop of Manchester, H. N. Brailsford, Lady Astor, the Archbishop of York, Professor R. A. Fisher (the statistician), Ramsay Muir (historian and a Liberal MP, 1923—4), Sir Arthur Newsholme (former Chief Medical Officer at the Local Government Board), Ernest Simon (prominent in Manchester local politics and a Liberal MP, 1923—4 and 1929—31), Sir Arthur Steel-Maitland (Minister of Labour in the 1924—9 Conservative government) and Barbara Wootton (the economist).[44]

With one or two exceptions, these prestigious Council members took no part in the Society's day-to-day business.[45] All of the administrative work was carried out by a small group consisting of Eleanor Rathbone, Mary Stocks, Elizabeth Macadam, Eva Hubback and the Society's official secretaries — Olga Vlasto (1924—30), Mrs E. M. L. Douglas (1928—30) and Marjorie Green (1930—9). Mary Stocks (1891—1975) had been born into a prosperous upper-middle class London family which had Charity Organisation Society connections; like Eleanor Rathbone, she had worked for a time with a COS committee and was active in the women's movement. After graduating from the London School of Economics in 1913 she became a part-time economics lecturer there. On moving to Manchester in 1924 (where her husband, John Stocks, had become Professor of Philosophy) she was less able to take part in the day-to-day running of the Society's affairs in London, but remained one of Eleanor Rathbone's closest friends and allies.[46] Elizabeth Macadam (1871—1948) had been a young social worker in Liverpool when she first met Eleanor Rathbone in the early 1900s; a strong friendship developed, with many common interests, such as feminism (in 1919 she became honorary secretary of the National Union of Societies for Equal Citizenship (NUSEC), and in 1923 joint editor of its organ, the *Woman's Leader*) and the two lived together; although Elizabeth Macadam tended to keep in the background in the campaign for family allowances she provided Eleanor Rathbone with considerable emotional and practical support.[47] Eva Hubback (1886—1949), like Mary Stocks, was from a prosperous upper-middle class family, and after graduating from Cambridge in 1908 also worked for COS-influenced bodies in London. An interest in feminism took her into work for NUSEC from 1918, where she met Eleanor Rathbone, and from the 1920s onwards she worked in a number of areas — in the various campaigns run by NUSEC (such as the one resulting in the 1925 Guardianship of Infants Act), in the work of the Family Endowment Society (which she joined in 1924), and as Principal of Morley College from 1927 until her death.[48] Eva Hubback was particularly adept at lobbying politicians and civil servants, in contrast to Eleanor Rathbone who was often shy and rather awkward in male company.[49]

Marjorie Green (1905—78) was of a younger generation. After graduating from the University of Edinburgh in 1928 she worked for the Liberal Party in Scotland for two years, and then in 1930 became the Society's full-time secretary; in addition, she was secretary of NUSEC (1934—7) and of the Children's Minimum Council (1934—9). Many of the Society's anonymous pamphlets published in the 1930s were written by her, and she edited the *Family Endowment Chronicle*, making it a well-presented, lively and readable record of the Society's activities in the 1930s. Possessing great organizational ability and tactical skill, Marjorie Green's role in the family allowances and child nutrition campaigns of the 1930s was of immense importance: like Eva Hubback, she was particularly adept at enlisting the support of prominent politicians, social scientists, nutritionists and other public figures where Eleanor Rathbone would have been less successful.

With the exception of Marjorie Green, all these women came from a class background that blessed them with complete financial security.[50] This enabled them to devote themselves full-time to the various causes they espoused, and also ensured that such causes were financially self-supporting. Thus the Family Endowment Society was largely financed by Eleanor Rathbone; the bulk of each year's donations and subscriptions (amounting in 1930, for example, to just over £507) came from her own pocket.[51] In addition, their social and educational backgrounds provided them with a myriad of connections in all areas of public life; even geographically they worked close to the centre of power.[52]

However, despite these inherited advantages the leaders of the Family Endowment Society clearly felt that because they were women their campaign began at a great disadvantage. Accordingly their aim was to get the idea of family endowment discussed as much as possible, so that other political parties and pressure groups would become interested and offer assistance in leading the campaign. Propaganda was all-important, and was directed through as many channels as possible. Lectures were given by the Society's members (particularly the leaders) to as many audiences as might care to listen; books and pamphlets were continually sent free of charge to numerous organizations (the Society published brief and inexpensive pamphlets presenting the case for family endowment in different ways); articles were written (in 1924—5, for example, at least nineteen journals and twenty-one newspapers ran articles on family allowances); meetings were held with political parties; Parliament was lobbied each time a Bill with family endowment implications appeared; and public figures were wooed whenever they displayed the slightest evidence of sympathy to the cause.[53]

Because the Society aimed at popularizing the principle of family endowment rather than any one particular system, it tried to present its case in language attractive to the listener. By the end of the 1920s many different organizations were showing interest in family endowment as an appendage to their own aims, and this resulted in a certain amount of confusion. There began to develop the situation (which was to be a feature of the family allowance movement) where the idea took on many different meanings. Mary Stocks, whose Labour Party sympathies led her to support a universal scheme financed out of taxation, was by 1927 clearly regretting the way that the original 1918 'Equal Pay and the Family' scheme had become 'embodied in a host of projects, many of them drawn from contemporary experience overseas, and supplying according to the vagaries of individual political taste' many different versions.[54] Yet Eleanor Rathbone firmly believed that a pressure group led largely by a few women would have no chance of success if it presented its case in a narrow, over-defined way such as might immediately alienate people who would otherwise be amenable to gentle persuasion, and thus the Society subtly altered its propaganda depending upon whom it was trying to convert.

To women's societies it stressed that political freedom was not enough: economic equality must now be achieved, and this could best come about by altering the wage-structure in favour of women and children, thereby achieving the old feminist aim of payment for motherhood.[55] In her role as president of the National Union of Societies for Equal Citizenship (1920–9) Eleanor Rathbone stressed this interpretation;[56] with Mary Stocks, Eva Hubback and Elizabeth Macadam she served on two special NUSEC committees investigating family endowment as one of several measures needed to improve the status of women,[57] and together they succeeded in persuading NUSEC to adopt family endowment as part of its official programme of aims.[58] Thus when pressing for aspects of family endowment that represented economic justice for women and children (such as higher allowances for widows and orphans under the new contributory pensions scheme) Eleanor Rathbone's language would be strongly feminist, angrily declaring that 'Parliament is still under the domain of the tradition that a woman is a kind of grown-up child, with no rights but only privileges which can be given or withheld at the discretion of her betters'.[59]

But in its overtures to the political parties the Society proceeded carefully. Labour supporters tended to favour a universal family allowance scheme financed solely from taxation, Liberals a contributory insurance one and Conservatives (the least interested) inclined if anything towards the 'equalization fund' type of system introduced in private industry in Europe. Thus Eleanor Rathbone was careful not to alienate any of these views: though she favoured the first alternative, she would still advocate the third as more practical in the short term, and tried to combine both by suggesting that the best course of action would be 'to make the State system a flat-rate one and secure the necessary gradation by supplementary allowances from an occupational pool for all the higher-grade occupations'.[60] On the one hand she tried to allay the fears of trade unionists who suspected that an industry-financed scheme would be used by employers to avoid paying across-the-board wage rises;[61] yet on the other hand she would emphasize to employers that family allowances 'would not involve a penny extra taxation nor any addition to the cost of production'.[62]

Family allowances were thus presented as a way of achieving a multitude of aims: they would lower the birth-rate among slum dwellers by enabling them to obtain roomier accommodation,[63] they could be used to preserve wage differentials between skilled and unskilled workers (which had been narrowing since the First World War),[64] or they could be a method of redistributing income.[65] Indeed, the only point upon which the Society stood firm was that allowances should be paid to the mother. Apart from the fact that this would tend to keep the allowance distinct from wages,[66] it would help rectify the situation in which motherhood was 'generally regarded not as a service necessary to the community but as a service to an individual man, a private luxury on which he may or may not choose to spend his surplus income', and would guarantee that the money would be wisely spent on the children.[67]

The Society supported almost any form of family endowment, and consequently directed its campaign towards securing short-term results as well as the long-term aim of a universal state scheme of child allowances in cash. Even a measure as insignificant as the introduction of separation allowances for married Indian Army officers was regarded as a step forward, another acknowledgement of the basic principle.[68] Literally anything with family endowment implications was made the object of a campaign. In particular, this involved watching out for any Bills in the House of Commons that might be relevant, and attempting to insert a family endowment clause. For example, in the 1924 parliamentary session considerable effort was expended in an attempt to secure amendments in two Bills. The Society persuaded a group of MPs led by Francis Acland to press for the insertion of a permissive clause in the Agricultural Wages Bill to enable County Wage Boards to require the payment of children's allowances in addition to the statutory wage, the cost to be met out of a fund to which employers would contribute according to the number of workers they employed.[69] Also, an attempt was made during the passage of the Wheatley Housing Bill to direct local authorities to differentiate rents according to family size in the case of houses receiving the higher rate of subsidy.[70] Both failed, but set the pattern for subsequent campaigning: the lobbying of MPs and the organizing of deputations would be accompanied by publication of specialized pamphlets on the particular topic, with articles and letters in the Press.[71] In all this Eleanor Rathbone followed two firm rules: first, to campaign only for what could realistically be achieved at any one time, and never to ask for too much;[72] second, to get in early and lobby politicians and civil servants, while proposals were still in the early stages of consideration when they would welcome evidence and suggestions rather than resent criticism.[73] The Family Endowment Society was thus a classic example of a middle class pressure group — elitist, gradualist, subtly working within the existing power structure, placing great faith in the willingness of governments to listen — and used the campaigning techniques that had been developed in the past by groups like the anti-slavery movement, the Anti-Corn Law League and the Suffragists.

The best specific example of how the Society conducted its campaigning can be seen in its relationship with Sir William Beveridge and, through him, its attempt to get family allowances introduced into the mining industry. Beveridge was Director of the London School of Economics (1919–37) and by the 1920s had established an enormous number of personal contacts with public figures through his experiences in journalism, the civil service and academic life; he was thus exactly the kind of person the Family Endowment Society were looking for, Eleanor Rathbone later referring to him as 'my prize convert'.[74]

Beveridge had heard of family endowment before 1924, though he probably had a fairly hazy notion of what it involved. In September 1923, for example, he had chaired a meeting of the British Association in Liverpool on the role of women in industry, where Eleanor Rathbone and the economist F. Y. Edgeworth had spoken in favour of family allowances, and had been rather lukewarm towards their proposal.[75] By April of the following year, however, he was an enthusiastic supporter: he had been given *The Disinherited Family* to review for a journal, the *Weekly Westminster*, and reading the book produced 'instant and total conversion' to Eleanor Rathbone's cause.[26]

Immediately, the Family Endowment Society leaders took notice. Three days after the review appeared Eva Hubback wrote to Beveridge, congratulating him on it and asking if the Society could use the London School of Economics for a conference. Beveridge's reply was encouraging, and Eleanor Rathbone wrote again: could the Society reprint his review as a pamphlet, and would he allow his prestigious name to be placed on the Council membership, and on the headed notepaper? Beveridge agreed, 'provided I do not have to do anything'. Inching her way forward, Eleanor Rathbone then asked him to become the Society's president, emphasizing that this would not commit him to any one particular scheme of family endowment, but would simply provide them with a much-needed important figurehead. Beveridge refused to go this far, but enough friendly contact had been established for the Society's leaders to realize that they had a most valuable ally.[77]

One of Beveridge's first practical responses was to introduce a family allowance system for teachers and senior administrators at the London School of Economics. Sir Arthur Steel-Maitland (a governor of the School and a member of the Family Endowment Society Council) actually seems to have thought of the idea around the same time,[78] but it was Beveridge who was instrumental in persuading the governors to introduce what was one of the first occupational family allowance schemes in Britain. By 1927, two years after their introduction, the allowances amounted to £30 per annum per child from birth to the age of 13, followed by £60 per annum to the age of 23 for children in full-time education, and added just under 4 per cent to the total salary bill.[79]

Almost as soon as he put down *The Disinherited Family*, Beveridge began working out for himself a plan for a national family allowance scheme, based on the insurance principle: it would cover only those within the scope of health insurance and in return for a total weekly contribution of 2s 9d (1s 0d each from employer and employee, 9d from the state, with half these rates for women), an allowance of 3s 0d per week for each child up to the age of 15 could be paid — payment being made to the mother. Beveridge was attracted to the insurance principle (despite the fact that having children could be said not to be an insurable risk), because of its administrative convenience, because it could be 'a simple first step' leading on to the eventual introduction of a universal state scheme, and because, of course, for social, economic and political reasons he was a convinced 'insurance man'.[80] It was an interesting scheme for a number of reasons, not the least of which was that it showed how far the original 1918 concept of family allowances as a method of redistributing income from rich to poor could be altered into something very different.[81]

Throughout the 1920s the Family Endowment Society leaders kept up close contact with Beveridge, calling upon him whenever they felt his name might be useful. In December 1924 they asked him to speak at a proposed conference on family allowances and teachers' salaries; the conference was cancelled, but Eleanor Rathbone asked him to put the case to Lord Burnham privately.[82] In October 1927 he organized a conference at the London School of Economics (which resulted in the book *Six Aspects of Family Allowances*), where six speakers looked at the subject from different points of view.[83] In January 1928 and May 1930 he helped the Society lobby the TUC and Labour Party over their report on family allowances.[84] In October 1929 the Society asked him to be one of their witnesses to the Royal Commission on the Civil Service.[85] Three years later there was another conference at the London School of Economics under his auspices,[86] and on many occasions during the 1920s the Society's leaders sought his advice.[87]

The most interesting episode — and the one most illustrative of the Society's aims and methods — occurred when Beveridge was appointed to the Royal Commission on the Coal Industry under the chairmanship of Sir Herbert Samuel. The mining industry was a particularly fruitful ground for a family allowances campaign. Nearly all European mining industries had family allowance systems and by the mid-1920s these were working quite successfully. More importantly, miners in Britain had a high fertility-rate relative to the rest of the population (an average of 1·3 children per man as compared with 0·9 for agricultural workers and 0·6 for teachers),[88] and the distribution of their children made them a group in particular need of some system of family support: 47 per cent of miners' children under 16 years of age belonged to households with more than three dependent children, and a much larger proportion were members of such households at some stage in their childhood. The Miners' Federation demand for a minimum wage was seen by Eleanor Rathbone as unrealistic, since to base this on a three-child family would still leave nearly half the miners' children insufficiently provided for at any one time, and would also be wasteful, since 48 per cent of miners had no children under 16 years of age; in fact, only 9 per cent of them had the supposedly 'average' family of three children.

Again, wage levels in the mining industry were such as to cause great concern over the condition of the children: using Rowntree's 'Human Needs' standard, Eleanor Rathbone calculated from the table of miners' wages in 1925 that 32·9 per cent of their households, covering 66·5 per cent of the children, were below the poverty line. If one took a midway point between this 'Human Needs' level and the much more austere poverty line calculated by Rowntree in his 1899 study, this would result in a figure (at 1925 prices) of 35s 0d for a man, or man and wife, plus 5s 7d for each child. A child allowance of 5s 7d per week could be introduced into the mining industry without any additional cost simply by imposing wage-cuts of 5s 10d per week on all male workers: the result would be that the lowest-paid childless miners would still receive 35s 3d per week and every miner's wife and child would be raised out of poverty. The health of the children would benefit, industrial relations would improve since the real cause of hardship was being immediately met, and maternal mortality would probably diminish.[89]

The Family Endowment Society campaigned in the period 1924—7 to get some sort of family allowance system introduced into the mining industry. *The Disinherited Family* included a brief outline of why the industry was a suitable case,[90] and in the month it was published (March 1924) the pamphlet *Family Allowances in the Mining Industry* was sent to all district secretaries of the Mining Association and Miners' Federation, 1500 collieries and the Press.[91] By 1925 speakers from the Society were touring mining districts, discussing family allowances with meetings of miners, who showed great interest and enthusiasm 'in striking contrast to the ostrich-like attitude of the official representatives of the Miners' Federation at the Coal Commission'.[92] In 1926 the Society decided at its annual general meeting to concentrate on the mining industry, and set up a special fund to finance the distribution of information: 29 000 copies of the pamphlet *Family Allowances in the Mining Industry* were sent out to branches of the Miners' Federation; 100 copies of *The Disinherited Family* were sent to miners' institutes and libraries in mining districts; reprints of the Society's Evidence to the Samuel Commission were also made available; and in addition between March and October 1926 seventeen circulars and memoranda were dispatched to mineowners, mining directors, Miners'

Federation branches, MPs, libraries and the Press.[93]

&0. The Society's most intensive campaigning was directed at the Samuel Commission, which was set up in September 1925 to investigate the whole range of economic problems that had beset the British coal industry since the relinquishment of government control in April 1921. Beveridge was appointed to the Commission, and throughout its work he carefully shepherded the Family Endowment Society's leaders through the protocol of submitting evidence. Of his own accord he wrote to Eleanor Rathbone on 19 October 1925, discreetly pointing out that as a commissioner he was not permitted to make the first move in inviting evidence from them, but he was expecting them to give evidence and they should do so.[94] The Society had in fact already written officially to offer evidence, and Eleanor Rathbone was clearly delighted that Beveridge had been appointed to the Commission since he would guarantee them a sympathetic hearing.[95] In December she and Lord Balfour of Burleigh gave evidence to the Commission, and thereafter Beveridge worked on his fellow-commissioners to persuade them to include a recommendation of family allowances in the final report.

Beveridge saw family allowances as a means of facilitating wage-cuts he believed were essential to make the British coal industry competitive on world markets once the government's subsidy ended in April 1926. As opposed to introducing longer hours while leaving wages untouched (the only other alternative envisaged by the Commission), wage-cuts would be easier to restore once prosperity returned and if accompanied by family allowances would not result in undue hardship.[96] Above all else, the cost of the wages bill had to be reduced, and Beveridge warned Eleanor Rathbone that unless she accepted this presupposition in her evidence she would not be listened to seriously; if, for example, she used Rowntree's 'Human Needs' standard as a desirable minimum 'and add 42% so as to allow the present rating for skill, you get above the present wages even before you have provided your family allowances, and thus become obviously a mere visionary'.[97] Together they agreed that it would be most practical to adopt a standard midway between Rowntree's 'Human Needs' level and the level he used in his 1899 York survey; this would result in minimum wage levels of 34·20 shillings for a man and wife, and 51·70 for a family of five, at 1925 prices (to which would be added increments for skill).[98] A weekly allowance of 6s 0d for each dependent child up to the age of 14 would cost £286 000 per week, and would result in an overall wages bill £105 000 less than at present − a saving of 4·5 per cent. Were this £105 000 distributed equally to all miners as a flat-rate wage increase not taking account of family size, then more than a quarter of the children would be left below this poverty line.[99]

Beveridge won his fellow-commissioners over, and their report, published in March 1926, included a recommendation of family allowances as a means of ensuring that wage-cuts did not result in undue hardship. Family allowances were seen by the Commission as

> one of the most valuable measures that can be adopted for adding to the well-being and contentment of the mining population. If the total sum available for workers' remuneration can be kept at the present level, the allocation of a small part of this to children's allowances will raise materially the general level of comfort; if the full remuneration cannot be maintained, the harmful effects of any reasonable reduction can be largely mitigated.

The allowances were to be paid for as long as the father remained on the books of any colliery or attached to the mining industry during unemployment, and the report also suggested that absenteeism among single men would be reduced because they would have to attend more regularly in order to make up the percentage removed from their pay to finance the family allowance scheme.[100]

Thus did family allowances receive their first government-sponsored recommendation, albeit for reasons that were anathema to most trade union leaders, confirming their suspicions that allowances would be used by employers as an alternative to wage-rises.

Some interest had already been shown by the mineowners. On 25 June 1925 the Central Committee of the Mining Association had discussed the question of minimum wages and had concluded that family allowances would be cheaper to introduce than an all-round subsistence wage.[101] The South Wales and Monmouthshire Coalowners' Association, for example, had tried to introduce a family allowance scheme in August 1925;[102] their proposal was not accepted by the miners, but in April 1926 the South Wales mineowners were still keen to introduce a family allowance scheme, which would add to a miner's rate per shift, 1s 0d for his wife and 4d for each child, as an alternative to a subsistence minimum wage.[103]

In the aftermath of the General Strike and the miners' lock-out, however, such ideas were forgotten. Indeed, only two months after the Samuel Report was published Eleanor Rathbone seems to have realized that its proposal for family allowances was now of academic interest only, and would not be implemented.[104] But the Society continued to campaign. In the summer of 1927 a Family Endowment Society local organizer went on a tour of two large mining districts to measure rank-and-file opinion. Generally, the ordinary miner was in favour of family allowances, though not without suspicions (in the aftermath of the lock-out) that they would be used by mineowners to weaken trade union solidarity.[105] Certainly, the Society's campaigning succeeded in one respect, in that from the late 1920s onwards the leaders of the Miners' Federation were the strongest supporters of family allowances within the trade union movement.[106]

The campaign aimed at the mining industry set the pattern for subsequent lobbying, and in the late 1920s and early 1930s the Society tried to get family allowances introduced in certain occupational groups. This was very much in line with Eleanor Rathbone's 'minimum possible advance' approach: better to achieve a series of minor victories and hope that occupational schemes would spread, than keep on campaigning for a universal state-financed scheme which could only come about in the very long term.

Thus in February 1930 the Society gave evidence to the Royal Commission on the Civil Service. Preceding this, there was the usual flurry of activity: meetings with civil service organizations, articles in journals, a conference, questionnaires dispatched to those European governments that ran family allowance schemes, and so on.[107] In its evidence, the Society stressed that considerable hardship was felt by low-grade civil servants with large families.[108] It also suggested that family allowances for the professions might have a eugenic effect by raising the birth-rate of the 'white collar' occupational groups, quoting Professor R. A. Fisher's warning that 'in about thirty years, more or less, with our present birth rate, whatever is worth keeping in the genetic potentialities of the upper and middle classes in England and Scotland will have been reduced to half its present quantity'.[109]

This was one of the first expressions in the Society's propaganda of the eugenic fears that were growing at the time (discussed fully in Chapter 4), and as it directed its campaigning at selected professions these pro-natalist reasons began to take an equal place alongside the anti-poverty ones. Thus when making the case for family allowances among the clergy the Society mentioned family hardship among those with low stipends, but also 'in the interests of the community' suggested that the children of clergymen born of parents whose mental and moral qualities are presumably above the average and reared and educated in Christian homes, are a particularly valuable addition to the population . . . unless something is done to lessen the financial burdens of parenthood, the dis-eugenic decline in the birth rate will continue.[110]

But in addition to the tactical reasons and the growing eugenic fears, there was a third factor behind the Society's decision to concentrate on specific occupational groups. This was that in the aftermath of the 1931 economic crisis in Britain any social reform as expensive as a universal state-financed family allowance system would stand little chance of being accepted by a National Government pledged to keep public expenditure as low as possible. The 1931 crisis had also resulted in salary-cuts in certain professions, and thus by campaigning to get family allowances introduced into one such profession — teaching — the Society believed that it was following the only policy likely to succeed.[111] Mary Stocks expressed this dilemma when she spoke at a conference organized by the Society at the London School of Economics on 29 and 30 April 1932. She was a supporter of a state-financed universal scheme as a long-term aim, but in a situation 'in which we have a Government in power which, for better or for worse, has declared war on the social services', the only hope was for the adoption of limited occupational family allowance schemes. She felt it was very unfortunate that the trade unions had missed the opportunity of pressing for family allowances on their own terms, and had thus let the initiative pass into the hands of the employers; but she supposed that an employers' scheme might be better than none at all.[112]

The 1930s were years of disappointment for the Family Endowment Society, in which the promise of the previous decade was not fulfilled. The Society's annual report for 1933, for example, stated rather woefully: 'the most, perhaps, we can hope is that efforts, which now seem fruitless, may yield results upon which we shall be able to congratulate ourselves in some future Annual Report'.[113] At the Society's annual general meeting that year Eleanor Rathbone reviewed the progress made since she organized the 1917 discussion group: there had been many developments abroad, but in Britain 'there had been more thinking on the theory of family allowances than practical experiment'. Some advances had been made — dependants' allowances in unemployment benefit, rent rebates proportional to family size in some local authorities since 1930, the London School of Economics scheme, the interest shown by the Labour movement in the late 1920s — but for the moment the campaign for family allowances was 'in the trough of a wave'. She thought that the falling birth-rate would add strength to their case in the future, and expected that employer-financed industrial systems would probably be the form in which family allowances would spread, though she 'looked forward to a State system, probably partly contributory, as the end to aim at'.[114]

Faced with this bleak economic situation, the leaders of the Family Endowment Society tended to divert their attention to other causes they regarded as of more immediate importance — for example, the Children's Minimum Council, which was closely linked to the Family Endowment Society. In addition, Eleanor Rathbone (now a Member of Parliament) was devoting a lot of time to many other activities, such as the condition of Indian women. Nevertheless, the Society continued to campaign, and by the late 1930s the cause of family allowances was again experiencing a revival. Having examined the composition, aims and methods of the Family Endowment Society, subsequent chapters will show how the arguments for family allowances influenced those within government.

Notes and References

1. Sheila Marriner, *Rathbones of Liverpool, 1845—73* (1961), p. 3.
2. Eleanor Rathbone, *William Rathbone, a Memoir* (1905), pp. 113—14.
3. Marriner, op. cit., p. 4.
4. ibid., p. 131.
5. A. F. Young and E. T. Ashton, *British Social Work in the Nineteenth Century* (1956), pp. 67—80, 95.
6. Margaret Simey, *Charitable Effort in Liverpool in the Nineteenth Century* (1951), pp. 8—12.
7. Young and Ashton, op. cit., p. 79; Rathbone, op. cit., ch. 10.
8. Two important studies are C. L. Mowat, *The Charity Organisation Society, 1869—1913* (1961), and David Owen, *English Philanthropy* (1965), pp. 215—46.
9. T. S. Simey, *Social Purpose and Social Science* (Eleanor Rathbone Memorial Lecture, 1964), pp. 8—9.
10. Mary Stocks, *Eleanor Rathbone* (1949), p. 50.
11. ibid., p. 51.
12. Rathbone, op. cit. (1913), pp. 24, 29—30.
13. E. Rathbone, *Report of an Inquiry into the Conditions of Dock*

Labour at the Liverpool Docks (1904).

14. Beveridge acknowledged his debt to it. W. H. Beveridge, *Unemployment, a Problem of Industry* (1910 edn), pp. 95—6, 108.
15. Vera Brittain, *Lady Into Woman* (1953), p. 5.
16. Much material on this is contained in the Eleanor Rathbone Papers (Fawcett Collection) and the Eleanor Rathbone Papers (University of Liverpool Library), XIV. 1. 6—13. See also E. Rathbone, *Child Marriage, the Indian Minotaur* (1934).
17. Sylvia Mann, 'Trade Unionism, the Labour Party and the Issue of Family Allowances, 1925—30' (University of Warwick MA thesis, 1978), ch. 2.
18. For example, on the Jewish question, see E. Rathbone, *Rescue the Perishing* (1943) and *Falsehoods and Facts About the Jews* (1945).
19. Evidence for this can be found in a digest of speeches and questions by her in the House of Commons. Eleanor Rathbone Papers, XIV. 3. 5.
20. Stocks, op. cit., pp. 200—2.
21. Personal reminiscences of Baroness Stocks, Marjorie Green and John Cecil-Wright in interviews with the author. Comments on her personality are also to be found in several Eleanor Rathbone Memorial Lectures.
22. Speech for Family Allowances Reception (13 November 1945), Eleanor Rathbone Papers, XIV. 3. 82.
23. E. Rathbone, *Disagreeable Truths About the Conciliation Bill* (1911), p. 10.
24. E. Rathbone, op. cit. (1904); E. Rathbone and E. Mahler, *Payment of Seamen* (1911).
25. E. Rathbone, op. cit. (1913), p. 17.
26. E. Rathbone, 'The remuneration of women's services', *Economic Journal*, 27 (March 1917), pp. 61, 64—5.
27. E. Rathbone, *The Disinherited Family* (1924), p. 253.
28. ibid., pp. vii—viii.
29. ibid., pp. ix, 13.
30. ibid., p. 20.
31. ibid., p. 27.
32. ibid., pp. 56, 68, 88.
33. ibid., pp. 256—7, 268—74.
34. ibid., pp. 312—14.
35. A Family Endowment Society existed briefly in 1836; an insurance scheme under that name was set up to cover the cost of bringing

up children. Family Endowment Society, *Observations Explanatory of the Principles and Practical Results of the System of Assurances Proposed by the Family Endowment Society* (1836).

36. Stocks, op. cit., p. 84.
37. K. D. Courtney *et al.*, *Equal Pay and the Family* (1918), pp. 18, 35–41, 48. The scheme would have cost about £240 million.
38. *Report of the War Cabinet Committee on Women in Industry: Appendices, Summaries of Evidence, etc.*, Cmd 167 (1919), pp. 46–7.
39. *Report of the Family Endowment Society for 1925*, p. 1.
40. E. Rathbone, *The Ethics and Economics of Family Endowment* (1927), p. 9.
41. *Report of the Family Endowment Society for 1925*, p. 1. and *for 1930*, pp. 4–5.
42. Rathbone to W. H. Beveridge (20 and 26 May 1924), Beveridge Papers, IIb. 23 (pt 3).
43. Murray was Professor of Greek at Oxford; Slesser was a Labour MP from 1924–9 and Solicitor-General in 1924; Balfour had a number of public posts (for example, a Kensington Borough Councillor, 1924–9).
44. *Reports of the Family Endowment Society for 1925–30.*
45. For example, the Gilbert Murray Papers contain no evidence of any active involvement by Murray in the Society's affairs in the 1920s and 1930s.
46. Mary Stocks, *My Commonplace Book* (1970), pp. 1–140, 148–64.
47. Stocks, op. cit. (1949), pp. 58, 92–3, 109; interview with Baroness Stocks.
48. Diana Hopkinson, *Family Inheritance: A Life of Eva Hubback* (1954), pp. 28–126.
49. Interview with Marjorie Green.
50. For example, at the time she went to Cambridge Eva Hubback 'had no need to earn her living, nor . . . any intention of doing so'. Hopkinson, op. cit., p. 48.
51. *Report of the Family Endowment Society for 1930*, p. 6; Stocks, op. cit. (1949), p. 101.
52. In the 1920s and 1930s the Society changed its headquarters five times, but always remained in London SW1.
53. *Reports of the Family Endowment Society, 1925–30* and *Family Endowment Society Monthly Notes*. Much of this work was carried out by the leaders: 'The burden of expense and the exhausting

work of speaking continue to fall on a few individuals', complained the *1926 Report* (p. 2) and other reports made frequent pleas for more contributions and active campaigning by members.

54. M. Stocks, *The Case for Family Endowment* (1927), p. 41.
55. ibid., pp. 36–9; E. Rathbone and M. Stocks, *Why Women's Societies Should Work for Family Endowment* (1925).
56. National Union of Societies for Equal Citizenship pamphlet, *National Family Endowment* (1920).
57. Minutes of Economic Independence of Women Sub-Committee, 1920–1, and Status of Wives and Mothers Sub-Committee, 1921, National Union of Societies for Equal Citizenship Archives, box 342. (Fawcett Collection).
58. Stocks, op. cit. (1949), pp. 115–18.
59. E. Rathbone, *Memorandum on Widows', Orphans' and Old Age Contributory Pensions Bill* (1925), p. 10.
60. Rathbone, op. cit. (1924), p. 294.
61. Family Endowment Society pamphlet, *Will Family Allowances Mean Lower Wages?* (*c*. 1925).
62. E. Rathbone, letter to the *Liverpool Evening Express* (14 November 1922), Eleanor Rathbone Papers, XIV. 3. 90.
63. E. Rathbone, *Family Endowment in its Bearing on the Question of Population* (Family Endowment Society pamphlet, 1924).
64. Olga Vlasto, 'Family allowances and the skilled worker', *Economic Journal*, 36 (December 1926), pp. 577–85.
65. H. N. Brailsford 'The state and family allowances', in W. H. Beveridge (ed.), *Six Aspects of Family Allowances* (1927), pp. 17–20.
66. Rathbone, op. cit. (1924), p. 265.
67. Stocks, op. cit. (1927), p. 37.
68. *Family Endowment Society Monthly Notes* (February 1925).
69. *Report of the Family Endowment Socety for 1925*, p. 2; *Hansard*, vol. 173 (7 May 1924), cols. 417–18, and vol. 176 (17 July 1924), cols. 716–24.
70. *Report of the Family Endowment Society for 1925*, p. 2; *Hansard*, vol. 176 (28 July 1924), col. 1781.
71. For example, Eleanor Rathbone's letter to *The Times* (17 July 1924), on the 1924 Housing Bill.
72. 'My practice was always to make up my mind what was the most I had the chance of getting and to ask for first that or perhaps 20 per cent more, to leave a margin for bargaining'. Letter from Rathbone to Nehru (28 August 1941), quoted in Stocks, op. cit. (1949), p. 360.

73. Hopkinson, op. cit., p. 96.
74. Speech for Family Allowances Reception (13 November 1945), Eleanor Rathbone Papers, XII. 7.
75. Cutting from *Liverpool Daily Post* (18 October 1924), Beveridge Papers, XII. 7.
76. Beveridge, epilogue in E. Rathbone, *Family Allowances* (1949), p. 270.
77. Correspondence of May and June 1924 between Rathbone, Hubback and Beveridge, Beveridge Papers, IIb. 23 (pt 3).
78. Correspondence between Steel-Maitland and Beveridge (21 and 22 July 1924), Beveridge Papers, V. 1.
79. Family Endowment Society pamphlet, *Memorandum on Family Allowances in the Teaching Profession* (1932); W. H. Beveridge, *The London School of Economics and its Problems, 1919–37* (1960), pp. 46–7.
80. Memoranda by Beveridge: 'Family Allowances, Points for Discussion' (11 June 1924), and 'Report of a Discussion on Family Allowances' (17 June 1924), Bev. Coll. Misc. 9.
81. Beveridge envisaged his scheme as redistributing income within the income group covered by insurance, leaving the rest of society untouched. Beveridge to Australian Royal Commission on Child Endowment (1 June 1928), Beveridge Papers, IXb. 14.
82. Rathbone to Beveridge (2, 12 and 15 December 1924), ibid.
83. Apart from Beveridge, the speakers were Professor R. A. Fisher (the statistician and active member of the Eugenics Society), V. H. Mottram (Professor of Physiology at the University of London), H. N. Brailsford, Joseph Cohen (a member of the International Labour Office) and John Murray (Principal of University College, Exeter).
84. Correspondence between Olga Vlasto and Beveridge (6 and 12 January 1928), Beveridge Papers, IXb. 14; Rathbone to Beveridge (22 May 1930), Bev. Coll. Misc. 9.
85. Correspondence between Vlasto and Beveridge (18 and 29 October 1929), Bev. Coll. Misc. 9.
86. Beveridge Papers, IXb. 19.
87. Correspondence in Bev. Coll. Misc. 9.
88. Bev. Coll. T. vol. X., 'Coal Commission, 1925–6', p. 130.
89. 'Memorandum of evidence by Miss Eleanor Rathbone, on behalf of the Family Endowment Society, to the Royal Commission on the Coal Industry' (1925), pp. 2–9 (contained in ibid., pp. 112–19).
90. op. cit., pp. 279–80.

91. *Report of the Family Endowment Society for 1925*, p. 3.
92. ibid., *for 1926*, p. 2.
93. ibid., *for 1927*, p. 2.
94. Beveridge to Rathbone (19 October 1925), Beveridge Papers, IIb. 24 (pt 2).
95. Rathbone to Beveridge (21 October 1925), ibid.
96. 'Memorandum on family allowances and minimum wage in coal mining industry' by Beveridge, Bev. Coll. T. vol. X, pp. 132–3; Lord Beveridge, *Power and Influence* (1953), pp. 220–1.
97. Beveridge to Rathbone (2 December 1925), Beveridge Papers, VIII. 2.
98. Beveridge to Rathbone (30 November 1925), ibid; 'Memorandum on family allowances and minimum wage in coal mining industry – statistical basis', Bev. Coll. T. vol X, p. 145.
99. ibid., p. 147.
100. *Report of the Royal Commission on the Coal Industry, 1925*, Cmd 2600 (1926), pp. 160–3.
101. Memorandum, 'Revision of wages agreement' (25 June 1925), SRO CB 7/5/28 (Scottish Record Office).
102. Memorandum of 1 August 1925, ibid.
103. Finlay Gibson (secretary, South Wales and Monmouthshire Coalowners' Association) to Robert Baird (secretary, Scottish Coalowners' Association) (15 April 1926), ibid.
104. Rathbone to Beveridge (12 May 1926), Beveridge Papers, VIII. 3.
105. Extract from letter from Family Endowment Society organizer in mining districts (8 August 1927), Bev. Coll. Misc. 9.
106. See, for example, speech by A. J. Cook in the 1930 TUC debate on family allowances, *Trades Union Congress Annual Report for 1930*, pp. 391–3.
107. *Report of the Family Endowment Society for 1930*, p. 3.
108. Family Endowment Society pamphlet, *Memorandum on Family Allowances Presented to the Royal Commission on the Civil Service* (1930).
109. ibid.
110. Family Endowment Society, *The Case for Family Allowances Among the Clergy* (c. 1933).
111. Marjorie Green, 'Family allowances in the teaching profession', *Family Endowment Chronicle*, 1 (January 1932), pp. 31–3.
112. Mary Stocks, 'The future of family allowances', ibid., 2 (May 1932), pp. 8–9.
113. ibid., 3 (July 1933), p. 3.
114. ibid., pp. 1–2.

3   Family Poverty Arguments

Throughout the interwar years the most powerful argument put forward for family allowances was the 'family poverty' one. Under the existing wage structure, it was claimed, mothers and children belonging to large families in poor working class areas were suffering severe undernourishment and poor health, since wages took no account of family needs. In support of this argument there was produced a vast amount of evidence which was repeatedly presented to the government. This chapter will examine the nature of this evidence, and what effect it had in advancing the cause of family allowances.

For most of the nineteenth century, government concern over the health of its citizens was confined to permissive 'environmental sanitration' legislation, with the 1875 Public Health Act the most notable expression of this.[1] By the beginning of the twentieth century, however, the focus of attention was shifting onto the physiology of the individual and the concept of minimum human needs. There it was to remain throughout the 1920s and 1930s, giving rise to bitter and protracted controversies over whether the state had a duty to ensure that all its citizens were living above 'subsistence level'.

The main reason for this change was the concern, increasingly felt by businessmen and politicians after the 1870s, over national fitness. Growing international economic competition forced into public debate the question of how physically efficient (and hence productive) the industrial workforce was, and after the military humiliations of the Boer War this concern also took on national defence implications. The Boer War medical inspection scandal revealed that on average three out of every five soldiers attempting to enlist in the British Army were physically unfit, and in the ensuing public debate much attention was focused on the health of the nation's children.[2] Repeatedly, witness after witness testified to the 1904 Interdepartmental Committee on Physical Deterioration that most of the major defects causing men to be rejected from the army (bad teeth, poor eyesight, retarded growth, general anaemia, heart disease) had originated early in life.[3] A year earlier the Royal Commission on Physical Training (Scotland) had reported that almost one-third of Edinburgh children had not enough to eat, with over ten thousand in urgent need of medical attention; in 1909 the Report of the Royal Commission on the Poor Laws confirmed this gloomy picture; and the First World War produced yet more evidence.[4]

It was against this background that there were introduced three reforms which were to play an important part in the controversy over family poverty in the interwar years: the 1906 Education (Provision of Meals) Act (and subsequent legislation) empowered local education authorities to provide meals for 'necessitous' schoolchildren on condition that no private funds were available (or if available, were inadequate); the 1907 Education (Administrative Provisions) Act set up a system of medical inspection of schoolchildren, again run by local education authorities; and in 1919 there was established the Ministry of Health, which liaised with the Board of Education on the question of the health of schoolchildren, and had overall responsibility for infant and maternal welfare.

The atmosphere in which these reforms were introduced had a profound influence on how they subsequently operated. In the first place, it must be remembered that the concept of 'national health' that emerged from most of the early twentieth-century discussions was only really meaningful in terms of military and industrial efficiency. For example, J. F. Maurice's famous *Contemporary Review* articles[5] were based on the contention that unless a society had enough fit men to defend it, it would perish: 'in some way or other', he wrote, 'if our complicated social organism is to work out its own improvement in security, there must be provided an adequate supply of those who are to protect it'.[6] Maurice, in common with other writers on the subject, also warned of the financial wastage that resulted from national deterioration: if, for example, after two years of service only two out of every five men wishing to enlist remained in the army as effective soldiers, then an 'alarming proportion' of recruits 'had involved the State in considerable expense, but had given no return'.[7] Thus it is hardly surprising that in the interwar years, when this militaristic fervour had waned and a vast army of unemployed provided a pool of surplus labour, there was less immediate concern over the health of future generations.

Secondly, these 'financial wastage' arguments were the dominant ones behind the introduction of school meals and medical inspection, and meant that both were seen as *educational* rather than anti-poverty measures. It was thought to be a waste of educational resources if children were too hungry or ill to concentrate on their lessons. This was the line taken by nearly all the witnesses to the 1904 Interdepartmental Committee,[8] by the very influential National League for Physical Education and Improvement,[9] and by the British Medical Association who approached the problem 'from the point of view that every child, so far as he is hampered by physical defects and thereby unable to obtain proper advantage from the educational opportunities offered him by the community, should be put in the condition to receive that education'.[10]

Although it is possible that Sir Robert Morant, the enormously powerful Permanent Secretary at the Board of Education (1903–11), and to a lesser extent Sir George Newman, the Board's Chief Medical Officer (1907–35), took a wider view at the time and also saw medical inspection and school meals as a method of medical treatment,[11] there is no doubt that the narrow 'educational' view became the dominant one. Throughout the interwar years both the Ministry of Health and the Board of Education insisted that the school medical and dental services existed only to remove those health defects that prevented children from learning.[12] Milk and meals were only to be provided for children in extreme need who were 'unable by reason of lack of food to take full advantage of the education provided for them' and both departments 'always resisted the suggestion that the [Provision of Meals] Act should be used to relieve poverty as such'.[13] Both departments thus refused to accept any responsibility for child poverty in general, and insisted that this was the province of the Poor Law Boards of Guardians (later the Public Assistance Committees) or the Unemployment Assistance Board.

Government concern for the health of children in the interwar years was thus deliberately limited by very restricted terms of reference. In addition, the department with prime responsibility for exercising that concern was the Ministry of Health, and for the twenty years after its foundation the Ministry of Health remained a very weak body, with limited powers of compulsion over local authorities.[14] Action on any particular point tended to be confined to the issuing of an advisory circular, and there was no guarantee that local authorities would take such advice. For example, in 1933, when discussing the appallingly poor condition of children's teeth and ways of improving the situation, the ministry's Advisory Committee on Nutrition felt very frustrated that so little could be done to compel local authorities to introduce better dental treatment.[15] The standard approach of the ministry was thus 'to get a little new money, and then ginger them [the local authorities] up as much as we can by a circular and any other possible way'.[16] These limited powers were often a serious obstacle to policy implementation; but, as will be shown later, they also provided the highly conservative senior civil servants in the ministry with an easy excuse whenever the government was criticized on the issue of child poverty.

Along with the growing concern over national fitness there was occurring the rapid development of the science of nutrition. Until almost 1900 studies of nutrition (or metabolism, as it was more commonly called) had been limited to energy requirements, with an emphasis solely on proteins, fats and carbohydrates. But with the discovery of vitamins, amino acids and mineral elements, analysis of food composition became more sophisticated; and research began to uncover a growing list of 'deficiency diseases' caused by faulty diet.[17] The process of discovery was immensely speeded up during the First World War, which demonstrated the importance of food intake for military efficiency and provided case-studies in the effects of prolonged malnutrition on people subject to economic blockade and disrupted food supplies.[18]

By the early 1930s this 'newer knowledge of nutrition', as it was quaintly called, was attracting a vast amount of research in numerous journals; one authority estimated that in 1933 alone five thousand papers describing the results of original work appeared in the world's literature.[19] Much of this work carried far-reaching social and economic implications: medical scientists now realized the prime importance of food intake as a measure of preventive medicine since, as one eminent nutritionist put it,

> many of the commoner physical ailments and defects could be reduced or even eliminated by proper feeding. Indeed, it is probably no exaggeration to say that proper feeding of the population of this country would be as revolutionary in its effect on public health and physique as was the introduction of cleanliness and drainage in the last century.[20]

The political implications were obvious: if nutrition was the most important factor in public health, then it followed that the best weapon in public health was to ensure proper feeding — from which stemmed the further ominous implication that this could only be achieved if low-income groups, such as the unemployed, had enough money with which to buy the necessary food.

Gradually, nutritional research in the 1920s and 1930s began to show that a large number of important human activities could be profoundly affected by diet. McCarrison and Corry Mann demonstrated the correlation between diet and physique;[21] Seymour and Whitaker showed that young children who ate good breakfasts, high in the 'protective' foods, performed significantly better in intelligence tests that those who did not;[22] Lady Rhys Williams's experiments in the high-unemployment Rhondda Valley area suggested a link between nutrition and maternal mortality,[23] as did the Swedish 'Oslo breakfast' scheme in the case of child mortality;[24] and nutrition was shown to have an influence on tuberculosis rates.[25] Experiments also showed that inadequate nutrition could offset the beneficial effects of environmental improvement, as when a group of slum-dwellers in Stockton-on-Tees were re-housed into a new council estate; rents in the latter were markedly higher, and with less money therefore available for food the re-housed group of tenants experienced a higher mortality-rate.[26] McGonigle and Kirby also argued that much of the work of the school medical service could be undone if children came from low-income households and consequently suffered under-nourishment before their fifth birthday; such children would already be displaying serious health defects by the time they entered school, and thus the school medical service was changed from a preventive agency into one 'mainly concerned with the detection and correction of established pathological conditions'.[27]

As they uncovered more and more of the social implications of nutrition, medical scientists unwittingly began to stray into more and more areas of political sensitivity. In particular, their findings were increasingly applied to the measurement of poverty, and the formulation of a 'scientific minimum subsistence' level of nutrition below which no individual should be allowed to fall. Although it is undoubtedly true that such scientific 'poverty lines' are always ultimately influenced by ideological and cultural factors and can thus be discredited, nevertheless by the 1930s, with three million workers unemployed and many more earning very low wages, the concept of minimum subsistence, backed up as it was by a rapidly expanding volume of research, began to pose a serious political threat to the government.

In his pioneering survey of London's East End, Charles Booth had calculated his poverty line fairly subjectively; for example, he allowed his investigators to use a certain degree of personal judgement in deciding if a family was in poverty.[28] Seebohm Rowntree's 1899 survey of York, however, set the pattern for subsequent poverty investigations by making a precise assessment of minimum nutritional needs (based on the latest research) and then adding estimates of minimum expenditure on such items as rent, clothing, fuel, light, to arrive at his poverty line of 21s 8d for a family of two adults and three children.[29] By the time Rowntree published *The Human Needs of Labour* in 1918, research into nutrition had developed rapidly, and thus his poverty line of 35s 3d for a family of five (at 1914 prices) carried a good deal of scientific authority.[30] Each poverty survey that followed as the depression worsened over the next twenty years used more sophisticated techniques, based on more reliable nutritional indices, and each survey began to reveal disturbing evidence of the extent of child poverty.

Whether this was simply because poverty was being more accurately measured or whether it reflected a worsening of real living standards in the depressed areas is not clear. Certainly the interwar years saw a marked improvement in the *overall* living standards of the British population, as many of the poverty surveys testified. For example, A. L. Bowley and Margaret Hogg showed that in the five towns studied by them (Northampton, Warrington, Bolton, Reading and Stanley) the total number of children in poverty had nearly halved between 1912—14 and 1923—4;[31] the London School of Economics East London survey found that 64·2 per cent of families investigated had incomes of 20s 0d or more above the poverty line;[32] the Bristol survey discovered the average working class family to be enjoying a standard of living that was more than 100 per cent above its minimum needs;[33] and, of course, Rowntree's second survey of York showed the proportion of working class people living in primary poverty to have declined from 15·46 per cent in 1899 to 6·8 per cent in 1936.[34] Boyd Orr reckoned that consumption of productive foods *per capita* rose by nearly 50 per cent between 1919 and 1939, and that whereas in 1930 only one-half of British families were adequately fed, by 1939 this had risen to two-thirds.[35]

What was causing concern in the 1930s, therefore, was not that severe poverty was evenly distributed throughout the working class population without regard to age, sex or location, but that it was mainly confined to mothers and children in large families in the depressed areas where unemployment was high and wages tended to be low. Bowley and Hogg's 1924 study found that 8 per cent of working class families in the week of investigation were living below the poverty line, and this included 11·3 per cent of all children under 14 years; however, they calculated that if their survey had been extended over several years, then the proportion of children passing through poverty at some point in their lives would have been nearer 16·6 per cent.[36] The East London survey showed that in the week of investigation 11 per cent of families and 16 per cent of children were in poverty.[37] The Southampton survey found 21 per cent of working class households below the poverty line, and just over 30 per cent of a sample of schoolchildren.[38] In 1934 was also published Caradog Jones's Merseyside survey, which revealed that nearly one child out of four in the working class families surveyed was living in an overcrowded home, and a similar proportion in poverty.[39] Two years later Boyd Orr published his claim that half the population of Britain lived on a diet incapable of producing perfect health; he deliberately set his nutritional standard at an optimum rather than a minimum level, but even when he divided the population into six groups according to family income the result indicated that about 20–25 per cent of the child population was in the lowest group, receiving a diet that was inadequate in all respects.[40] Two more surveys were published in 1938: in Liverpool, the Pilgrim Trust found that of the 97 families studied who had two or more children under 14 years of age, 83 were in poverty;[41] and the Bristol survey found that 44·3 per cent of all persons in poverty were children, concluding that 'if any form of remedy could be devised to raise a higher level those families which contain three or more children and fall below the [poverty] line . . . 76% of child poverty would be abolished'.[42] Finally, in his 1936 York survey Rowntree discovered that nearly half of the persons in primary poverty were children under 14 years of age, and of these, 61 per cent were in families where there were more than three children.[43]

These poverty surveys were just a tiny fraction of all the research carried out in the interwar years; all in all, there was a vast number of investigations by doctors, medical officers, social scientists and nutritionists into the health and diets of infants, schoolchildren and mothers, particularly in the depressed areas. This 'family poverty lobby', as it can conveniently be called, mostly consisted of individuals acting in an unco-ordinated way, but was also spearheaded by several organizations. Many of the poverty surveys already mentioned were sponsored by universities. Often research bodies provided funds: for example, Margaret Balfour and Joan Drury's investigation of motherhood and nutrition in Tyneside and Durham was financed by Lloyd George's Council of Action for Peace and Reconstruction,[44] and Boyd Orr carried out his 1936 investigation under the auspices of the Rowett Research Institute in Aberdeen and the Ministry of Agriculture's

Market Supply Committee. Some belonged to political groups: Dr Somerville Hastings, who carried out his own inquiry into the nutrition of London schoolchildren[45] was president of the Socialist Medical Association. In addition, minimum nutritional levels were drawn up by bodies like the League of Nations, International Labour Office and Medical Research Council. But what characterized the family poverty lobby most of all was that it was composed of vastly different types of people. At one end of the scale were private individuals like the young Richard Titmuss, working in an insurance office by day and in the evenings collecting the statistical information on poverty, nutrition and mortality that was eventually published in *Poverty and Population* (1938).[46] At the other end were eminent authorities like V. H. Mottram, Professor of Physiology at the University of London, who used his knowledge of nutrition to arrive at a minimum wage figure of 41s 8d for a family of five in 1927.[47] In between was a vast number of ordinary medical officers of health, doctors, and others, who witnessed every day in the course of their work the serious effect that the economic depression was having on mothers and children, and voiced their concern in journals like *The Lancet, The Medical Officer*, the *Journal of Hygiene, Public Health* and the *British Medical Journal*. Indeed, it was hardly possible to open one of these journals in the 1930s without seeing somewhere a discussion of child malnutrition.

Two pressure groups were particularly important. In March 1934 a group of doctors met in London and formed the Committee Against Malnutrition to publicize the problem and bring it to the government's attention. The Committee was convinced

> that there exists in this country widespread undernourishment among the families of the unemployed and low paid workers; that this must inevitably lead to a steady deterioration in the physical standards and health of the population, and of this deterioration there are already signs; that the last thing upon which a community must economize is the nutrition of its working class.[48]

Throughout the 1930s the Committee campaigned for higher unemployment allowances, more thorough medical inspection of schoolchildren, a better supply of free milk and meals for schoolchildren, family allowances and a national food policy, and its predominantly left-wing membership included F. le Gros Clark, Professor J. B. S. Haldane, Sir F. Gowland Hopkins, Sir John Boyd Orr, Dr G. C. M. McGonigle, Professor V. H. Mottram, Professor Julian Huxley, Professor

J. R. Marrack and Professor S. J. Cowell.[49] The other important pressure group, the Children's Minimum Council, will be examined in detail later.[50]

What particularly concerned the family poverty lobby was the situation in the chronically depressed parts of Britain where whole communities had been dependent upon a single industry; with the decline of that industry had come mass unemployment, and large numbers of families having to live on unemployment pay for extended periods. When compared with nutritionally-assessed poverty lines, these unemployment benefit and assistance levels were shown to be seriously inadequate in relation to the needs of large families. Caradog Jones, for example, illustrated the income shortfall as in Table 3.1.[51]

Table 3.1. The relationship between the poverty line, unemployment benefit and assistance levels (1929-30)

Man, wife and no. of children	Poverty line	Unemployment benefit	Liverpool public assistance scales
1 infant	27s 7d	28s 0d	22s 0d
1 infant 2 schoolchildren	37s 7d	32s 0d	29s 0d
2 infants 3 schoolchildren	46s 2d	36s 0d	35s 0d

Clearly, if a family containing more than three children was subject to long-term unemployment its members would be in real danger of suffering some degree of malnutrition. In addition, there were many families in which the employed wage-earner brought home an income little higher than these amounts, or in some cases even lower. Bowley estimated that in 1931 nine million male workers had incomes below £125 per annum;[52] many occupations (for example, coal mining, textiles, unskilled labouring) paid wages of 40s 0d to 50s 0d per week in the 1930s; and the Pilgrim Trust found examples of weekly wages as low as 24s 0d (window cleaner) and 20s 0d (night watchman).[53]

The family poverty case for family allowances was thus based on the contention that widespread malnutrition existed among working class mothers and children in large families and that one important remedy for this was an alteration of the wage system in accordance with family needs. The remainder of this chapter will examine in detail how this evidence of malnutrition was presented to the goverment (and, in particular, the Ministry of Health) and how the government reacted.

From the outset, the whole debate over child poverty in the interwar years was clouded by a failure on all sides to define accurately just what constituted malnutrition. At one extreme, Boyd Orr chose an optimum level that would produce 'a state of well-being such that no improvement can be effected by change in diet', and found half the population below this level.[54] At the other extreme, a leading medical journal could publish a paper purporting to show that a man could live on only 960 calories per day.[55] Between these extremes were many shades of opinion. Rowntree, in the second edition of *The Human Needs of Labour* (1937), put his minimum at 3400 calories per day for a man, 2800 for a woman and 2210 for a child under 14 years.[56] This was also the figure reached by the British Medical Association, the Medical Research Council and the League of Nations.[57] Yet the *Week-End Review's* 1933 'Hungry England' committee of experts came out with a figure 400 calories lower.[58] The army's peacetime ration for soliders was just over 3000 calories, yet convicts on normal heavy labour received 4200 calories.[59] The daily diet of a group of monks was found to produce 2914 calories, yet a typical West End club's menu contained 5148 calories for the three meals of the day – twice as much as would have been needed by its sedentary members.[60]

Many doctors refused to commit themselves to such rigid definitions, believing that malnutrition, like 'health', was a relative concept, varying from person to person and from day to day. If there was 'primary' malnutrition due to faulty diet then there was also 'secondary' malnutrition which arose from other causes (such as diseases of the respiratory, circulatory or endocrine systems).[61] The counting of calories had become a 'fetish' maintained Professor E. P. Cathcart, and took no account of the many physical and psychological factors which affected the body's ability to absorb food.[62]

Much research was therefore undertaken into methods of assessing an individual's nutritional state. Blood haemoglobin could be measured;[63] Quetelet's formula used height divided by weight, expressed as a percentage, and when applied to existing school medical inspection statistics it showed a definite correlation;[64] Emerson's 'zone of weight' used optimum weights for different heights as a standard of normality;[65] the American 'A.C.H.' method measured arm, chest and hip width;[66] and numerous physical efficiency tests were tried, such as the Romberg test (where children had to stand steadily for fifteen minutes with their eyes closed).[67] Yet these clinical tests were all open to criticism if one took the view that nutrition was dynamic, not static, and varied from person to person. Height-weight indices, for example, would produce an incorrect result in the case of a protein-starved, carbohydrate-surfeited child whose bulky, flabby body would pass as normal but who might in fact be malnourished.[68]

Not surprisingly, the Ministry of Health steadfastly denied that malnutrition was purely a matter of food intake, or that it could be clinically tested.[69] Faced with the growing challenge from the family poverty lobby, ministry officials did everything they could to disprove any connection between malnutrition and low income. Thus Sir George Newman insisted that nutrition was not solely the product of dietary deficiency, and that in any case it could not be measured: 'no simple test has been found', he wrote, '. . . the nutrition of an individual is a process, a variable clinical syndrome, not a static, fixed or measurable feature'.[70] Newman's successor as Chief Medical Officer, Sir Arthur MacNalty, also took this line: nutrition, he maintained, depended as much on secondary 'exogenous' factors ('adequate sleep, proper and uncrowded housing, sunlight, fresh air, exercise and even happiness') as on the primary 'endogenous' ones which could be clinically tested.[71] Since no accurate clinical tests existed, therefore, schoolchildren were given medical inspections not on the basis of 'a hypothetical or academic standard of nutrition but whether the child's nutrition was such as debarred it from receiving full advantage from its education'.[72] This insistence that malnutrition could not be precisely measured had the effect of defusing some of the criticisms of the family poverty lobby — but obviously raised the question: if malnutrition could not be measured, then how could the Ministry of Health be sure that it did not exist?

In answer, the ministry pointed to the official school medical inspection figures. These certainly gave the impression of a child population unharmed by the effects of the economic depression: for example, in 1935–7 the proportion of schoolchildren classified as suffering from 'bad nutrition' (the official term for malnutrition) was said to be a mere 0·6–0·7 per cent.[73] But the family poverty lobby maintained that the inspection methods used by school medical officers were so perfunctory, and their criteria so subjective, that by basing official statistics on them the Ministry of Health was practising a form of deception, wilful or otherwise. They pointed to the fact that each child had only three six-minute medical examinations during its school-life, and that medical officers were often so overworked that their judgement was careless: they tended to fix their standard of 'normality' in accordance with what was the average for the area, and thus 'normal' in prosperous Richmond would be a much higher standard than in depressed Jarrow.[74] Research showed that different medical officers investigating the same group of children produced wildly differing results,[75] and there were a number of incidents where a medical officer moved from a prosperous area to a depressed one and, applying his former standards, produced child malnutrition figures so alarming that special inquiries had to be made.[76] As early as 1911 the British Medical Association had complained of the 'exceedingly inadequate' school medical inspection methods, insisting that 'probably at least one-half of the defects which exist are certainly over-looked'.[77] Yet this system remained in force throughout the 1930s, and its short-comings cast grave doubts on the official child malnutrition statistics.

The ministry's next line of defence was to maintain that in the absence of accurate clinical tests, other indicators should be used — such as death-rates, which showed marked improvement over the years. For example, in the House of Commons, Sir Hilton Young, Minister of Health, pointed out that 'the general death-rate of the nation shows an encouraging downward tendency, and that downward tendency is the best proof positive we could have of the general maintenance of national health and physique', and went on to emphasize the steady fall in infant mortality.[78] But, said critics, if *standardized* death-rates were examined then there were grounds for serious unease: the difference in death-rates between the depressed areas and the rest of the country was greatest in the case of children;[79] since 1900 the decline in mortality-rates from tuberculosis (a disease associated with malnutrition) among adolescents and young adults had been much slower than for other age-groups;[80] there was a definite correlation between low incomes and high death-rates;[81] and these regional death-rate variations were reflected in the medical inspection statistics of recruits to the army: while the rejection rate of men from the home counties was 32 per cent, it was 58 per cent for men from depressed East Lancashire.[82]

Thirdly, the Ministry of Health insisted that if malnutrition did exist, it was not related to low income. The ministry's Permanent Secretary, Sir Arthur Robinson, was convinced that 'malnutrition is ignorance quite as much as insufficient resources and it is the ignorance on which I want to organize the attack'.[83] Similarly, one of the ministry's advisors, Dr H. E. Magee, maintained that the basic problem was that many people 'did not know how to buy the right type of food and, what was equally important, did not know how to prepare and cook it';[84] thus for Magee the most effective policy to combat malnutrition was a programme to educate the public in food values.[85]

Critics, however, argued that such an approach was both unpleasantly moralistic and intentionally misleading. It 'cast an undeserved slur upon the capacity of the working-class housewife', said McGonigle, and was designed to obscure the fact that in families where the breadwinner was unemployed or earned low wages there was simply not enough money for food.[86] What advice the ministry did offer housewives was usually impossible to follow. For example, in 1937 its Advisory Committee on Nutrition recommended that every nursing or pregnant mother should have two pints of milk per day, and children one and a half pints; for a family of five this would have cost about 14s 0d per week – which few working class families could have afforded:[87] Titmuss calculated that if they followed this advice some 22 million people would not have sufficient money left with which to purchase other essential foods.[88] Interesting results emerged whenever critics tested the validity of these official explanations of malnutrition. For example, the Board of Education was adamant that the greatest obstacle preventing more working class children consuming milk was parental indifference and the children's dislike of its taste; experiments showed, however, that children from poor families put forward such reasons to conceal the fact that their parents could not afford the milk, or to avoid the stigma of being judged 'necessitous' and thus eligible for free milk: when milk was offered free, nearly all the children drank it.[89] Finally, critics pointed to the fact that these official pronouncements on the public's ignorance of food values had to be set against a background of widespread government-organized food destruction, undertaken in order to stabilize prices and benefit the food-producing industries. As Leff put it, 'one Government department was educating and advising the public to make a wise and wide choice of foods, while another was restricting the production and entry of foods in the country'.[90]

When under attack by the family poverty lobby the Ministry of Health did not remain solely on the defensive, however. From about 1930 onwards its senior officials conducted a counter-campaign to disprove the allegations of its critics. Leading this campaign was Sir George Newman, Chief Medical Officer until 1935. Newman was a remarkable civil servant, with an enormous array of acquaintances in public life.[91] 'No living man has done more to improve these [public health] conditions than you have', Lloyd George told him,[92] and on his retirement he received glowing tributes from the medical profession.[93] He brought to the fairly mundane subject of public health an imaginative approach and flair for public relations (for example, writing official reports in an interesting way),[94] and in his early years seems to have had very radical ideas on the subject of preventive medicine, on which he had been much influenced by the Webbs.[95] However, by the 1930s Newman was at the end of his career: originally a bacteriologist, he was clearly out of touch with the new developments in nutrition, and, more importantly, realized that at all costs the Ministry of Health must never announce an official poverty line in cash terms. Thus Newman was adamant that mass unemployment was having no detrimental effect on national health, particularly in the case of children, and reacted bitterly to the criticisms of the 'socialistically inclined' Dr George McGonigle, considering them little more than 'stunts'.[96]

Newman's attitudes were shared by senior civil servants in the Ministry of Health, who did everything they could to stop public discussion of malnutrition. In 1933, for example, they threatened McGonigle and Boyd Orr with suspension from the Medical Register if they went ahead with a radio discussion on the extent of malnutrition and the need for a better food policy; since he had no intention of ever practising medicine again Boyd Orr ignored the threat, but later civil servants tried to prevent the publication of his damning book, *Food, Health and Income.*[97] But much more importantly, in the 1930s the Ministry of Health conducted several investigations wholly or partly designed to prove that malnutrition caused by poverty was not widespread.

There was much controversy, for example, over whether malnutrition was affecting infant and maternal mortality-rates. Infant mortality-rates had fallen continuously, from 142 deaths per 1000 live births in 1881—90 to 56 per 100 in 1936—8 (England and Wales), a success story that was hailed by Newman as 'one of the greatest single achievements in Preventive Medicine which have marked modern times'.[98] Maternal mortality-rates, however, showed no corresponding fall: in 1881—90 the annual rate had been 4·7 maternal deaths per 1000 live births; it had fallen to 3·90 in 1921—5, but rose thereafter to 4·60 in 1934, declining to 3·08 in 1938 (figures for England and Wales).[99] There were a number of unanswered questions, such as why maternal mortality was higher in women of social class II than those of social class V,[100] and successive Ministers of Health expressed bewilderment that the rate was not falling significantly.

Many in the family poverty lobby argued that if mothers were better fed then maternal mortality-rates would fall more rapidly. They pointed to evidence that seemed to demonstrate this, such as Lady Rhys Williams's experiments in South Wales, where mothers receiving extra diets had shown far lower maternal mortality-rates,[101] and Dr Kathleen Vaughan's conclusion that mothers with properly-shaped pelvises (a result of adequate nutrition in girlhood) were less at risk in childbirth.[102] In reply, the Ministry of Health set up a number of maternal mortality inquiries, all of which played down the importance of malnutrition caused by poverty.

In 1932 two such reports were published. The first, into areas with high maternal death-rates, admitted that nutrition played 'a more important part in maternal morbidity than is generally realised. Some degree of malnutrition is fairly widespread among all women in these towns', but insisted that such malnutrition was 'due mainly to ill-balanced dietaries and ignorance of food values'; among the many recommendations made (such as educating the public, improved ante-natal services, better training of girls in the rules of hygiene) nowhere was there a suggestion that the economic status of the mother should be raised.[103] Similarly the final report of the Departmental Committee, although attributing the low maternal mortality-rate in Holland to better pelvic development in Dutch women, and admitting that in high-mortality areas of Britain poverty and unemployment were severe, nevertheless concluded that 'malnutrition and the indirect effects of poverty do not in themselves explain the high maternal death rate which has in fact persisted in these areas for many years during periods of prosperity as well as adversity, for well-nourished as well as for ill-nourished women'.[104]

From 1934 onwards the controversy intensified. The TUC and Labour Party began to attack the government on the issue,[105] and Ministry of Health officials realized that, together with the Conservative Central Office, they should prepare effective 'counter-propaganda' in reply.[106] Sir Arthur Robinson accordingly set up yet another investigation into maternal mortality, under the leadership of Sir Comyns Berkeley, a distinguished consultant obstetrician of conservative views; Berkeley made it clear to his team of investigators that 'in view of the political situation' what was wanted was a quick preliminary report showing that malnutrition and bad housing had no effect on maternal mortality and that if evidence of this could be obtained in the very near future 'the Minister would not worry much about the time taken thereafter'.[107] Not surprisingly, Berkeley's report found no evidence of malnutrition, and although it agreed that 'where means are straitened it is the mother who denies herself for the sake of the children', it suggested that where women did not obtain sufficient food for their needs this was due 'in some cases to ignorance of the resources available, to shiftlessness, or to pardonable pride'.[108] This confidential report remained unpublished, but information from it went towards two further reports published in 1937, one for certain areas of England and the other for Wales. Both repeated the standard arguments: such experiments as had been conducted on nutrition and death-rates were too unrepresentative for general conclusions to be drawn; facilities existed for the supply of extra nourishment to expectant mothers, but many mothers did not utilize them; a precise assessment of malnutrition in pregnant women was impossible, but if it existed it was not caused by insufficient food.[109]

This evasive approach dominated every venture by the Ministry of Health into the malnutrition controversy. For example, in 1934–5 an official inquiry was made into health conditions in Sunderland and Durham, following allegations made to *The Times* by a Sunderland doctor, G. F. Walker, that a 'substantial and progressive' deterioration in public health was taking place; Walker accused the Ministry of Health of complacency, and severely criticized Newman. Further controversy arose in the Press, questions were asked in the House of Commons, and the Ministry of Health was forced to act.[110] In April 1935 the results of the inquiry were published as a White Paper: not surprisingly, Walker's allegations were strenuously denied by the ministry who pointed out that 'clinical observations' revealed only 2·2 per cent of children in Sunderland to be under-nourished, and only 1·3 per cent in Durham.[111]

However, the ministry's method of investigation had simply been to use the vague and (as it admitted) inaccurate school medical inspection techniques; the White Paper conceded that

> our investigation has been extensive rather than intensive, and our conclusions, other than those based on official statistics, should, therefore, be regarded as approximate rather than as of scientific accuracy: for example, where numbers and percentages relating to conditions of nutrition are given, it is unlikely that any two observers would arrive at precisely the same figure.[112]

The team of investigators spent only seventeen days inspecting 4600 people, which must have meant an average of less than five minutes per person — a fact which, said critics, 'sheds some light on the mentality and methods acceptable to the Ministry of Health and Board of Education, but none on the health of the people of Durham'.[113]

In fact, beneath this official optimism there was considerable private unease among some Ministry of Health and Board of Education officials. For example, in early 1934 yet another investigation had been made into conditions in Tyneside, County Durham, Lancashire and South Wales, the impetus for which had once again come primarily because public pressures had made such an investigation 'politically necessary', as Sir Arthur Robinson put it, rather than because either department felt there was genuine cause for concern.[114] By July 1934 the results were complete, and after reading them Sir Hilton Young admitted in a meeting with the Board of Education and the Ministry of Labour that

> the reports as a whole, and especially that of South Wales, seemed to him to give cause for grave disquiet. They indicated that the effects which were to be expected as the result of a long depression were beginning to be shown. In particular, there was cause for anxiety about the state of nutrition of children and young persons, especially boys, between the ages of fourteen and eighteen.[115]

The condition of infants was found to be 'disquieting' and it was noted that in South Wales the death-rates in the 15—25 age-group had actually increased.[116] The results of these investigations, however, were never published. Again, in private some of the Ministry of Health's medical advisors were very uneasy about the validity of the school medical inspection figures upon which the government's confident statements were based.

> We have for a long time been very doubtful as to the value of the statistics of malnutrition received annually from SMOs [one of them wrote in 1933], . . . the returns for the whole country are published in the CMO's Reports and attract considerable attention, but we know that they are compiled from individual figures which will not bear detailed examination.[117]

Perhaps the best example of this private unease beneath the public confidence is to be found in the Ministry of Health's Advisory Committee on Nutrition. The idea of a committee of eminent nutritionists to furnish expert advice had emerged in the late 1920s,[118] and eventually on 28 January 1931 the first meeting of such a committee was held.[119] Its object was to disseminate information to the public, investigate the problem of how to measure malnutrition, draw up minimum nutritional levels, and advise the government on particular problems. From the start, however, severe restrictions were imposed by the ministry. The Committee's membership was deliberately chosen from personalities who were likely to clash and produce disagreement.[120] More importantly, the ministry placed a veto on any discussion of minimum subsistence in cash terms: and thus the Committee's first publication, *The Criticism and Improvement of Diets* (1932), merely gave suggestions for suitable minimum diets on the level of 3000 calories per man per day. The pamphlet was fairly innocuous, but the issues raised by it caused dissension within the Committee: on the one hand the conservative Professor E. P. Cathcart warned that 'the diet recommended . . . is something much better than the average working man can afford' and that 'if it is embodied in an official document it may be seized upon by transitional beneficiaries and others as a yard stick to measure what their allowances should be';[121] yet on the other hand more liberal members like Greenwood and Mellanby felt deeply uncomfortable about having to work under such constraints, 'like the "scientists" of the comic papers, i.e. only being interested in a subject so long as it *is* of no practical importance'.[122] Greenwood believed that existing indicators were insufficiently sensitive to measure malnutrition and that the ministry's optimism was wholly unjustified;[123] likewise, in Committee meetings Mellanby maintained that malnutrition *was* widespread, quoting such evidence as a recent examination of a thousand London schoolchildren which revealed that 70 per cent had widespread dental caries.[124]

These internal tensions came to a head in the winter of 1933—4. In November 1933 the British Medical Association's Committee on Nutrition published a report in which it recommended 3400 calories plus 50 grammes of protein per man per day as a level of minimum requirements.[125] A year earlier, the Ministry of Health's Advisory Committee had recommended 3000 calories plus 37 grammes of protein as its minimum,[126] and immediately a fierce controversy arose. The BMA report was widely publicized in the Press, and much of the comment was adverse: newspapers carried reports of interviews with housewives who claimed that the suggested diets were monotonous and unrealistic.[127]

In particular, controversy centred on the fact that the BMA Committee had translated its specimen diets into cash terms — exactly what the ministry's Committee had been forbidden to do. It was doubly unfortunate for the ministry that the BMA report appeared just when the 1934 Unemployment Bill was being discussed in Parliament and unemployment benefit and assistance rates were the subject of much public debate. Critics thus pointed to the fact that according to the BMA a man, wife and three children needed to spend £1 2s 6½d per week on food alone — yet the maximum rate of unemployment benefit for such a size of family was £1 9s 3d, leaving a manifestly inadequate margin of 6s 8½d for a week's rent, coal, lighting, clothing, etc.[128]

Within the Ministry of Health there was near panic. Newman urged Robinson to prevent any meeting between the two bodies, as this would 'involve the Ministry in a far-reaching economic issue, which is most important to avoid — an issue which might easily affect wages, cost of food, doles, etc';[129] both men maintained that the BMA Committee members were not true experts in nutrition, and that its report had been engineered by that 'promising labour politician', McGonigle.[130] Sir Hilton Young, however, decided that a meeting would have to be arranged, but issued a stern warning to Dr Mellanby, who was to attend it, that 'there can be no discussion of the translation of diets into money values or of the application in practice of the scientific principles at issue', on the intriguing basis that 'these are administrative and not scientific questions'.[131]

In February 1934 the two sides met,[132] and quickly agreed on a face-saving formula whereby different calorie levels would apply to different types of people (that is, from an adult man on heavy work down to a child).[133] But the incident did irreparable damage to the ministry's Committee, and eventually led to Greenwood's resignation: he had been deeply unhappy about the restrictions placed on the Committee, about the ministry's refusal to allow him to co-opt some economists to investigate family budgets and about the criticisms voiced in the Press — many of which he must have agreed with.[134]

In May 1935 a new Ministry of Health Advisory Committee on Nutrition was formed, partly in response to pressure from the Economic Advisory Council. Once again the ministry made sure it worked within very limited terms of reference: research was undertaken into family budgets, but households of the long-term unemployed were excluded, and the Committee was carefully diverted from the question of malnutrition and low income.[135]

Thus throughout the interwar years the Ministry of Health and Board of Education successfully fended off the challenges of the family poverty lobby and carefully avoided being drawn into the debate on malnutrition and income. Both departments clearly understood the far-reaching consequences that would result if they ever announced publicly an official minimum subsistence level in cash terms, stating that all those receiving incomes below such a level were likely to be malnourished. For this would lay the government wide open to demands that unemployment benefit and assistance levels should be brought up to that level and, more importantly, that there should be introduced some form of statutory minimum wage, possibly including family allowances. To a Conservative-dominated National Government, dedicated to free-market solutions and fiscal retrenchment, this was something to be avoided at all costs.

Given this determined opposition within the government to all the evidence of malnutrition, particularly in the case of children, it is hardly surprising that the main child poverty pressure group of the 1930s, the Children's Minimum Council (CMC), achieved very little.

The CMC was founded in early 1934, holding its first public conference on 15 February, and had close connections with the Family Endowment Society. Eleanor Rathbone was the main driving force behind it, Eva Hubback was also actively involved, and most of the administrative and propaganda work was carried out by Marjorie Green. From the start, the CMC's tactics bore all the hallmarks of an Eleanor Rathbone campaign. Important public figures were made vice-presidents with their services (and money) being requested whenever most appropriate. The Council's leadership included MPs such as Francis Acland, Robert Boothby, R. D. Denman, Sir Edward Grigg, Harold Macmillan and Duncan Sandys, and nutritionists such as Boyd Orr, Sir Frederick Gowland Hopkins, Sir Robert McCarrison and Dame Janet Campbell (who had retired from service with the Ministry of Health in 1933).[136] Numerous other organizations were affiliated to it — for example, the Save the Children Fund, the Nursery Schools' Association of Great Britain, the Catholic Social Guild, the National Association of Schoolmasters — and thus Eleanor Rathbone could claim with justification that it represented several million supporters.[137]

The CMC had both short-term and long-term aims. On the one hand, it put pressure on government departments during the implementation of the 1934 Unemployment Act to ensure that unemployment benefit and assistance (particularly in the case of large families) would be calculated in accordance with the BMA minimum standard. On the other hand, the Council aimed at securing official recognition of the extent of child poverty, and the introduction of appropriate remedial measures.

This latter aim contained a number of proposals, the most important of which was that the Ministry of Health should announce an official minimum needs scale, which would then be used as a basis for unemployment allowances, and any wage-earning household living below this level should have milk and meals provided for its children. In addition, there were demands for higher child allowances, for the unemployed, rent rebates proportional to family size, free milk for infants and expectant or nursing mothers, free milk for children in state-aided schools, and an end to the situation where, in the midst of widespread poverty, the food-producing industries had a surplus of such valuable foods as milk, bacon, eggs, fish, and were destroying large quantities of them in order to keep up prices.[138]

The Family Endowment Society's involvement was natural, since apart from aiming to raise the family allowance component in unemployment benefit and assistance, the CMC was also demanding 'family endowment in kind'. If unemployment child allowances could not be raised to realistic levels without overlapping on wages, then family assistance should be granted in kind, not cash. Eleanor Rathbone pointed out that 'the provision of supplementary nourishment, given whenever it is needed, would safeguard the health of the mothers and children without disturbing the relationship of wages and unemployment pay'.[139] By avoiding the sensitive issue of low wages she evidently hoped to achieve more success with the government.

But from the start the attitude of ministers and senior civil servants was one of hostility. The Ministry of Health received an invitation to the Council's February 1934 opening conference, and sent Lord Balneil as an observer; in a sardonic memorandum Balneil summed up the proceedings as 'a number of disappointed spinsters representing "many millions of mothers" advocated all the old demands for free milk, etc., for nursing mothers, etc., etc.'[140] Indeed, the only point of concern to the ministry was that one of the conference speakers was a London County Council Assistant Medical Officer who should be quietly told not to involve herself in such a campaign.[141]

Soon after this conference the CMC requested an audience with the Prime Minister, Ramsay MacDonald, and when permission was given, submitted four demands: that a daily ration of clean, fresh milk should be made available to all children attending state-aided schools; that it should be made compulsory for local authorities to provide free school meals for needy children; that unemployment child allowances should be substantially increased; and that rent rebates should be granted where family income was insufficient to meet minimum needs.[142]

The deputation met MacDonald on 12 March. But two days earlier, via internal memoranda, the Ministry of Health had already rejected their demands. Compulsory school meals for needy children would cost over £4 million per annum as compared with existing expenditure of about £560 000 and such an increase could only be contemplated if widespread child malnutrition could be proved to exist – which school medical inspection returns of only 1·07 per cent malnourished in 1932 clearly did not; besides, officials insisted, 'much malnutrition is due to delicacy, not poverty'. Criticism of the 2s 0d unemployment child allowance on the grounds that this sum was well below the actual cost of a child was mistaken, they announced; since a child was maintained not on its own, but as part of the family, it was the family income that mattered – and in most cases public assistance scales compared favourably with the BMA minimum. Finally, on the question of rent rebates the ministry pointed out that since housing was essentially a local authority responsibility the government could adopt no other position than one of 'benevolent neutrality'.[143]

In the face of this determined opposition the CMC deputation achieved nothing. Sir Edward Grigg and Eva Hubback initiated the proceedings; Sir Francis Acland then made out the case for higher milk consumption, beneficial both to children and to British agriculture; Mrs Eleanor Barton insisted that mothers everywhere in the country knew malnutrition was widespread; and Robert Boothby accused the government of negligence in not attempting to discover the true situation. In the course of an evasive and rambling reply the Prime Minister assured his visitors that he shared their concern; promising them that the matter was under consideration, he urged them to take their specific demands to the relevant government departments where they would be sympathetically listened to. MacDonald then abruptly left, and civil servants from the Ministry of Health and Ministry of Labour gave verbal versions of the pre-arranged replies.[144]

The first department to be lobbied was the Ministry of Health on 23 March 1934. Eleanor Rathbone requested that an official minimum needs level in cash terms be declared and that her rent rebate scheme be considered; and Eva Hubback suggested legislation compelling local authorities to provide free or cheap milk to mothers and young children. The case for higher allowances for the children of the unemployed was put to the Ministry of Labour three days later. But the response of both departments was negative.[145]

Despite this discouraging start, the Council expanded its activities and for the rest of the 1930s led the family poverty campaign. In Marjorie Green it possessed an extremely energetic and imaginative secretary, and under her and Eleanor Rathbone's direction the CMC did everything it could to influence public opinion. Numerous pamphlets were published, letters and articles were sent to the Press, influential public figures were converted, and meetings were held throughout the country.[146] A typical example of the CMC's methods was the 'fivepenny lunch' held at the London School of Economics on 30 March 1938. Guests included Lord Horder, fifteen MPs, a bishop, several doctors, and the menu was based on the BMA minimum scales.[147] One particularly interesting speaker at the meeting was a Mrs Yates, wife of an unemployed labourer, who spoke of the impossibility of keeping herself, husband and child on unemployment assistance of £1 18s 0d per week; 'to me and thousands like me this meal is a luxury', she declared, adding that it was 'such a heavy meal — I feel I want to go and sleep'.[148]

The Council submitted numerous memoranda throughout the period 1934–9, but nothing was achieved. On 21 July 1936 the Council wrote to the Prime Minister, yet again pointing out the need to raise unemployment child allowances; the reply they received merely referred them to a recent House of Commons debate on the Unemployment Assistance Board regulations.[149] On 25 February 1937 Eleanor Rathbone led a deputation (including Duncan Sandys, Eva Hubback, Lady Juliet Rhys Williams and Dr Margaret Balfour) to the Ministry of Labour, on the need for extra milk and meals for mothers and children in the depressed areas; civil servants replied by insisting that the local authorities were doing all they could and that 'the strong Advisory Committee on Nutrition were continuing their labours and would no doubt advise the minister from time to time as they found themselves able to reach conclusions'.[150] Later in that year, on 27 July, yet another deputation was sent to the Ministry of Health on the need for a national cheap milk scheme for low income families; Kingsley Wood's only concession was a promise to remind local authorities of the value of milk as a protective food.[151] Finally, on 27 March 1939 there was an equally fruitless deputation to the Board of Education.[152]

One of the few actions taken by the government in the 1930s positively to improve the nutrition of the nation's children was the 1934 'milk in schools' scheme, whereby schoolchildren in grant-aided schools could purchase one-third of a pint of milk at a cost of 0½d per day. Yet this and other efforts to improve milk consumption in the 1930s were not in response to pressure from groups like the Children's Minimum Council but were primarily aimed at assisting the milk-producing industry. After its establishment in 1923 the National Milk Publicity Council realized that the expansion of the milk market was largely dependent on greater consumption by children,[153] and it therefore used the growing volume of nutritional research to persuade local authorities to provide more milk for children.[154] By the 1930s there had developed a complex system of government subsidies through the Milk Marketing Board, whereby surplus milk was sold to schools cheaply and at the same time producers were guaranteed a market price.[155] Undoubtedly the Ministry of Health and the Board of Education were fully aware of the appallingly low consumption of milk in Britain (0·385 pints per head per day)[156] and of the consequences of this for public health; also they were faced with the difficult problem that the areas where children were most in need of milk were the ones least able to raise the necessary money in rates.[157] But throughout the 1930s both departments judged suggestions for improving the situation primarily on the criterion of whether they would assist the milk producers, and the only solutions contemplated were ones that would adjust market forces slightly by means of the price mechanism.[158] Fully one-third of the milk produced in England was sold to industry for manufacturing purposes at the extremely low price (through the government subsidy) of 5·39d per gallon, whereas schools wishing to participate in the 'milk in schools' scheme had to pay 1s 0d per gallon.[159] In addition, the Board of Education took action against any local authority that tried to provide free milk for all schoolchildren in families living below a certain income, insisting that the only criterion permissible was that of medical inspection.[160]

Much the same attitude was displayed by the government towards CMC requests that surplus food should not be destroyed but should instead be diverted towards a free school meals scheme for low-income children. There appears to have been some interest shown within the Ministry of Agriculture and Fisheries towards a scheme in the USA whereby people on relief could exchange vouchers for food which would otherwise have been destroyed. But this interest centred on the fact that the scheme was designed more to help American farmers than to improve the nutrition of the unemployed.[161] In any case, strong opposition came from the Unemployment Assistance Board on the grounds that such a scheme in Britain would be administratively problematic, might cause resentment between the low-income employed and the unemployed, and would be an open admission that the Board's scales were inadequate.[162] Thus suggestions by the Children's Minimum Council that free milk and meals should be provided for low-income families were never taken seriously.

The failure of the Children's Minimum Council is an appropriate point at which to conclude this survey of the family poverty case for family allowances. This chapter has shown how the evidence of poverty and malnutrition in large families slowly grew in the interwar years, reaching a peak in the mid-1930s. This evidence was repeatedly presented to the government and was backed up by a wealth of nutritional and medical data. Yet the government steadfastly denied that there was any pressing need to raise the economic status of mothers and children. There were a number of superficial reasons for this: the difficulty of defining malnutrition, and the question of whether it was related to low income; the narrowly 'educational' view of the school medical service; the post-1931 constraints on public spending; the autonomy of the local authorities; and so on. But beneath these superficial reasons lay the fundamental explanation, which was that the government was clearly determined not to announce a minimum needs level in cash terms, for to do so would open the way to demands that a large section of the working class, whether unemployed or receiving low wages, should have their incomes brought up to such a level. This was something to be resisted at all costs, and resisted it indeed was up to the outbreak of the Second World War. Perhaps in conclusion it is appropriate to quote the revealing incident that took place when Sir John Boyd Orr was summoned to meet Kingsley Wood just prior to the publication of *Food, Health and Income*: the Minister of Health

> wanted to know why I was making such a fuss about poverty when, with old age pensions and unemployment insurance, there was no poverty in the country. This extraordinary illusion was genuinely believed by Mr Wood, who held the out-of-date opinion that if people were not actually dying of starvation there could be no food deficiency. He knew nothing about the results of the research on vitamin and protein requirements, and had never visited the slums to see things for himself.[163]

Notes and References

1. J. M. Mackintosh, *Trends of Opinion about the Public Health, 1901–51* (1953), p. 6.
2. Bentley B. Gilbert, *The Evolution of National Insurance in Great Britain* (1966), pp. 83–9.
3. 'Summary of evidence', PRO ED 24/106.
4. S. and V. Leff, *The School Health Service* (1959), p. 24; *Report upon the Physical Examination of Men of Military Age by National Service Medical Boards, 1917–18*, Cmd 504 (1920), p. 4.

5. 'Miles' (J. F. Maurice), 'Where to get men', *Contemporary Review*, 81 (January 1902), pp. 78—86; and 'National health, a soldier's study', ibid., 83 (January 1903), pp. 41—56.
6. ibid. (1903), p. 50.
7. ibid., p. 41.
8. 'Summary of evidence', op. cit.
9. 'Note of deputation' (27 February 1906), PRO ED 24/279.
10. 'Minute of a deputation from the BMA on medical inspection of schoolchildren in London' (27 June 1911), PRO ED 24/282.
11. Argued by Gilbert, op. cit., pp. 123—6.
12. *Annual Report of the Chief Medical Officer at the Board of Education: the Health of the School Child, 1931*, p. 6, and ibid., *1932*, p. 51.
13. 'Memorandum on milk in schools' (13 December 1933), PRO ED 24/1367.
14. Political and Economic Planning, *Report on the British Health Services* (1937), pp. 29—30.
15. Minutes of 4th meeting of Advisory Committee (12 February 1934), PRO MH 56/52.
16. Memorandum by Dame Janet Campbell (4 October 1930), PRO MH 55/272.
17. Henry Sherman, *The Nutritional Improvement of Life* (1950), p. 15.
18. John Burnett, *Plenty and Want* (1966), p. 224; *Bulletin of the Committee Against Malnutrition* (May 1934), p. 9.
19. F. C. Kelly, 'Fifty years of progress in nutritional science', *The Medical Officer* (16 February 1935).
20. Memorandum by Dr E. Mellanby (Secretary of the Medical Research Council) (19 March 1934), PRO ED 24/1374.
21. Robert McCarrison, 'Problems of nutrition in India', *Nutrition Abstracts and Reviews*, 2 (July 1932), pp. 1—8; H. Corry Mann, *Diets for Boys During the School Age* (1926).
22. A. H. Seymour and J. E. Whitaker, 'An experiment in nutrition', *Occupational Psychology*, 12 (Summer 1938), pp. 215—23.
23. Children's Minimum Council pamphlet, *Special Areas Bill* (February 1937), p. 6.
24. Sir John Boyd Orr, *Not Enough Food for Fitness* (1937), p. 8.
25. *Bulletin of the Committee Against Malnutrition* (May 1934), pp. 10—11.
26. G. C. M. McGonigle and J. Kirby, *Poverty and Public Health* (1936), pp. 108—29.

27. ibid., p. 81.
28. The criteria used by Booth are discussed in T. S. and M. B. Simey, *Charles Booth, Social Scientist* (1960), pp. 184–9.
29. B. S. Rowntree, *Poverty, a Study of Town Life* (1902 edn), ch. 4.
30. B. S. Rowntree, *The Human Needs of Labour* (1918), pp. 123–9.
31. A. L. Bowley and M. Hogg, *Has Poverty Diminished?* (1925), p. 18.
32. H. Llewellyn Smith, et al., *The New Survey of London Life and Labour*, Vol. 3 (1932), p. 91.
33. H. Tout, *The Standard of Living in Bristol* (1938), p. 24.
34. B. S. Rowntree, *Poverty and Progress* (1941), p. 120.
35. Sir J. Boyd Orr, 'Nutrition and the family', in Sir James Marchant (ed.), *Rebuilding Family Life in the Post-War World* (1945), p. 43.
36. Bowley and Hogg, op. cit., pp. 17–18, 24–5.
37. Llewellyn Smith, op. cit., pp. 83, 89.
38. P. Ford, *Work and Wealth in a Modern Port* (1934), pp. 120, 200.
39. D. Caradog Jones, *The Social Survey of Merseyside*, Vol. 1 (1934), pp. 172–3.
40. J. Boyd Orr, *Food, Health and Income* (1937 edn), p. 27.
41. Pilgrim Trust, *Men Without Work* (1938), p. 111.
42. Tout, op. cit., pp. 39–40.
43. Rowntree, op. cit. (1941), pp. 115, 117.
44. M. Balfour and J. Drury, *Motherhood in the Special Areas of Durham and Tyneside* (1935), p. 3.
45. Hastings examined 53 children of unemployed fathers and judged 33 to be under-nourished and 31 to be under-weight. Letter to *The Lancet* (25 March 1933).
46. Margaret Gowing, 'Richard Morris Titmuss', *Proceedings of the British Academy*, 61 (1975), pp. 403–4.
47. V. H. Mottram, 'The physiological basis of the minimum wage', *The Lancet* (22 October 1927).
48. *Bulletin of the Committee Against Malnutrition* (March 1934), p. 1.
49. ibid., 1934–9.
50. Other less important organizations were the Save the Children Fund, the Ten Year Plan for Children and the Next Five Years Group.
51. Caradog Jones, op. cit., p. 150.
52. A. L. Bowley (ed.), *Studies in the National Income* (1942), pp. 70–1.

53. Pilgrim Trust, op. cit., p. 202.
54. J. Boyd Orr, *Food, Health and Income*, op. cit., p. 11.
55. A. F. Dufton, 'Food for thought', *The Lancet* (26 December 1936).
56. Rowntree, op. cit. (1937), p. 70.
57. See, for example, British Medical Association, *Report of a Committee on Nutrition* (1933), p. 8.
58. *Week-End Review* (1 April 1933).
59. Rowntree, op. cit. (1937), p. 71.
60. ibid., pp. 75—6; Ministry of Health unpublished report, 'Minimum food requirements: an investigation into the diet of an enclosed monastery', by H. E. Magee (1934), PRO MH 56/41.
61. See, for example, Dr Robert Hutchinson in *British Medical Journal* (23 March 1935).
62. E. P. Cathcart, 'Nutrition and public health', *Public Health*, 48 (May 1935), p. 286.
63. H. E. Magee to J. C. Carnwath (18 October 1933), PRO MH 56/53.
64. Victor Freeman, 'Weights, heights and physical defects in school children', *The Medical Officer* (18 August 1934).
65. C. E. McNally, *Public Ill-Health* (1935), pp. 80—1, 83—5.
66. *The Medical Officer* (24 February 1934).
67. *Proceedings of the Royal Society of Medicine*, 28 (1935), p. 717.
68. *The Medical Officer* (20 January 1934).
69. See, for example, *The Health of the School Child, 1937*, op. cit., pp. 20—1.
70. Sir George Newman, *The Building of a Nation's Health* (1939), p. 336.
71. *The Health of the School Child, 1935*, op. cit., pp. 13—14, 27.
72. Newman, op. cit., p. 334.
73. *The Health of the School Child, 1937*, p. 12.
74. F. le Gros Clark analysed medical officers' criteria of 'normality' and found that the majority took this to mean 'average'. F. le Gros Clark (ed.), *National Fitness* (1938), pp. 127—30.
75. ibid., pp. 132—4. R. Huws Jones, 'Physical indices and clinical assessments of the nutrition of schoolchildren', *Journal of the Royal Statistical Society*, 100 (1938), pp. 1—52.
76. McNally, op. cit., p. 29.
77, 'Minute of a deputation from the BMA', op. cit.
78. *Hansard*, vol. 291 (20 June 1934), cols. 391—2.
79. *New Statesman* (23 November 1935).
80. *Bulletin of the Committee Against Malnutrition* (May 1934), p. 5.
81. McGonigle and Kirby, op. cit., p. 273.

82. R. M. Titmuss, *Poverty and Population* (1938), p. 224.
83. Robinson to Sir Hilton Young (18 December 1933), PRO MH 56/53.
84. *Public Health*, 48 (May 1935), p. 291.
85. Memorandum by Magee (29 August 1933), PRO MH 56/53.
86. G. McGonigle, *Nutrition: the Position in England To-Day* (1936), p. 10.
87. J. Boyd Orr, *Not Enough Food for Fitness* (1937), p. 5.
88. Titmuss, op. cit., p. 247.
89. Marjorie Green, *School Feeding in England and Wales* (Children's Minimum Council pamphlet, 1938), pp. 18–19.
90. S. Leff, *The Health of the People* (1950), pp. 132–3.
91. Letters in Newman Papers.
92. Newman Diaries (8 February 1933).
93. For example, press cutting from *The Medical Officer*, ibid. (30 November 1935).
94. See his interesting 'incrementalist' account of the development of social policy in *The Health of the School Child, 1932*, p. 6.
95. Bentley B. Gilbert, *British Social Policy, 1914–1939* (1970), ch. 3.
96. Memorandum by Newman (17 January 1934), PRO MH 56/56.
97. Lord Boyd Orr, *As I Recall* (1966), pp. 115–17. *Food, Health and Income* was published by Macmillan, whose chairman was Harold Macmillan, MP for Stockton-on-Tees, where McGonigle was medical officer of health.
98. Newman, op. cit., p. 312.
99. ibid., pp. 282, 307, 311.
100. Ministry of Health unpublished report, 'Maternal mortality investigation' (1935), PRO MH 55/264.
101. Titmuss, op. cit., pp. 153–4.
102. Kathleen Vaughan, 'Maternal mortality and its relation to the shape of the pelvis', *Proceedings of the Royal Society of Medicine*, 23 (November 1929 to April 1930), pp. 191–6, and other papers in PRO MH 55/687.
103. Ministry of Health, *Reports on Public Health and Medical Subjects, No. 68: High Maternal Mortality in Certain Areas* (1932).
104. Ministry of Health, *Final Report of Departmental Committee on Maternal Mortality and Morbidity* (1932), pp. 60–1, 92–8.
105. Sir Walter Citrine to Sir Hilton Young (30 November 1934), PRO MH 55/217.
106. A. N. Rucker to Sir Arthur Robinson (15 November 1934), PRO MH 55/265.

107. Berkeley to Dr B. Macewen (5 April 1935), PRO MH 55/264.
108. Report, 'Maternal mortality investigation', ibid.
109. *Ministry of Health: Report of an Investigation into Maternal Mortality*, Cmd 5422 (1937), pp. 121, 123–4; *Ministry of Health: Report on Maternal Mortality in Wales*, Cmd 5423 (1937), pp. 93–4.
110. Press cuttings of December 1934 in PRO MH 61/9.
111. *Report of an Inquiry into the Effects of Existing Economic Circumstances on the Health of the Community in the County Borough of Sunderland and Certain Districts of County Durham*, Cmd 4886 (April 1935), p. 41.
112. ibid., p. 3.
113. *Bulletin of the Committee Against Malnutrition* (July 1935), pp. 39–40.
114. Robinson to Newman (21 February 1934), PRO MH 79/331.
115. Note of meeting (12 July 1934), PRO MH 79/337.
116. Typescript report, contained in ibid.
117. Memorandum by C.W.M. (9 November 1933), PRO MH 56/53.
118. Memorandum by Newman (6 December 1927), PRO MH 56/43.
119. Correspondence in ibid. The chairman was Professor Major Greenwood, and the members were Dr G. F. Buchan, Professor E. P. Cathcart, Sir Frederick Gowland Hopkins, Miss Jessie Lindsay, Professor E. Mellanby and Professor V. H. Mottram.
120. I owe this point to Dr Derek Oddy.
121. Statement by Cathcart, reported in J. C. Carnwath to Newman (1 December 1931), PRO MH 56/51.
122. Memorandum by Greenwood (15 July 1933), PRO MH 56/48.
123. Memorandum by Greenwood (12 December 1932), PRO MH 56/52.
124. Minutes of 4th meeting of Advisory Committee (12 February 1933), ibid.
125. British Medical Association, *Report of Committee on Nutrition* (1933), p. 8. The chairman was Dr E. le Fleming, and its membership included Sir Robert Hutchinson, Professor V. H. Mottram, Dr. G. P. Crowden and Dr G. McGonigle.
126. Ministry of Health Advisory Committee on Nutrition, *The Criticism and Improvement of Diets* (1932), pp. 5–7.
127. *British Medical Journal* (9 December 1933).
128. Speech by Arthur Greenwood, *Hansard*, vol. 283 (30 November 1933), col. 1110.
129. Memorandum by Newman (17 January 1934), PRO MH 56/56.

130. ibid.; Robinson to Young (11 January 1934), ibid; note of meeting (11 December 1933) PRO MH 56/43.
131. Young to Mellanby (11 January 1934), PRO MH 56/56.
132. Note of meetings (6 and 27 February 1934), ibid.
133. Ministry of Health, *Nutrition: Report of a Conference between Representatives of the Advisory Committee on Nutrition and Representatives of a Committee appointed by the British Medical Association* (1934), p. 6.
134. Letter of resignation from Greenwood to Young (11 July 1934), PRO MH 56/40. A typical criticism was that of the *Daily Herald* (press cutting of 11 January 1934 in PRO MH 56/56) which pointed out that the Advisory Committee had recommended 4s 6½d as the weekly cost of feeding a child in a Poor Law Children's Home, yet unemployment insurance child allowances were only 2s 0d. The newspaper strongly attacked Greenwood for tolerating this anomaly.
135. For a fuller account, see J. Macnicol, 'The Movement for Family Allowances in Great Britain, 1918–45' (University of Edinburgh PhD thesis, 1978), pp. 167–72.
136. Invitation to the Children's Minimum Council inaugural conference, PRO MH 55/275. Initially it was called the Children's Minimum Organising Committee.
137. Full list of affiliated organizations in letter to Prime Minister (27 February 1934), ibid.
138. Invitation to conference, op. cit; *British Medical Journal*, (4 January 1936).
139. Children's Minimum Council pamphlet, *Special Areas Bill* (1937), p. 8.
140. Balneil to A. N. Rucker (15 February 1934), PRO MH 55/275.
141. Rucker to Robinson (16 February 1934), ibid.
142. Letter to MacDonald (27 February 1934), and summary of proposals, ibid.
143. Ministry of Health memoranda (n.d., probably 10 March 1934), PRO PREM 1/165.
144. Note of deputation (12 March 1934), ibid.
145. Note of deputation (23 March 1945), PRO MH 55/275; Eleanor Rathbone Papers, XIV. 3. 6.
146. For example, a conference was held in Cardiff in December 1937. Marjorie Green Papers. Letters asking the help of various public figures are contained in Eleanor Rathbone Papers, XIV. 2.7 (11).

147. Invitation, menu, etc., in PRO MH 55/688.
148. Press cuttings of *Manchester Guardian* (31 March 1938), *Daily Sketch* (31 March 1938), and *News of the World* (3 April 1938), Marjorie Green Papers.
149. Correspondence in PRO MH 55/688.
150. Note of deputation (25 February 1937), ibid. The Council's evidence was published as a pamphlet, *Special Areas Bill: Memorandum on Proposed Provision for Additional Food, etc., for Mothers and Children in Distressed Areas* (1937).
151. Note of deputation (27 July 1937), ibid.; Children's Minimum Council pamphlet, *Memorandum on Milk for Mothers and Children Under Five* (1937).
152. Eleanor Rathbone Papers, XIV. 2. 7(12).
153. Board of Education memorandum, 'Provision of milk for schoolchildren' (April 1934), PRO ED 24/1367.
154. F. le Gros Clark, *A Social History of the School Meals Service* (1964), p. 43.
155. For a full account of the system, see Marjorie Green, *School Feeding in England and Wales* (Children's Minimum Council pamphlet, 1938); *Bulletin of the Committee Against Malnutrition* (March 1936), pp. 1—8, and (January 1939), pp. 57—9.
156. ibid.
157. Children's Minimum Council pamphlet, *Special Areas Bill* (1937), pp. 11—12.
158. Memoranda in PRO ED 24/1367.
159. Children's Minimum Council pamphlet, *Memorandum on Milk for Mothers and Children Under Five* (1937), p. 11; M. Green, *School Feeding in England and Wales* (1938), p. 16.
160. ibid. (1938), p. 8.
161. Memoranda in PRO MAF 38/318.
162. Sir George Reid (Unemployment Assistance Board) to D. E. Vandepeer (Ministry of Agriculture and Fisheries) (19 June 1939), and memo of 22 May 1939, ibid.
163. Lord Boyd Orr, *As I Recall* (1966), p. 115.

4   Demographic Arguments

In addition to the family poverty case, the movement for family allowances in the interwar years rested on another pillar of support — the demographic arguments. Although less important than the former,[1] the idea that family allowances would encourage parents to produce more children was an important feature of the campaign, particularly in the late 1930s and early 1940s. In the public mind pro-natalist arguments have always been closely associated with family allowances, and this is more than simply a legacy of the Speenhamland System applying to Britain alone, since it occurs in all advanced industrialized countries where concern over falling birth-rates coincided with the introduction of family allowance systems.

Many supporters of family allowances as a measure of child welfare have deeply regretted this pro-natalist emphasis.[2] George and Walley have even suggested that the indifference shown by successive British governments towards family allowances since 1945 can be attributed to the disappearance of these erroneous demographic arguments as fears of population decline likewise disappeared.[3] Yet so influential have these pro-natalist misconceptions been that modern writers have also felt it important to discuss them, and try to disprove them. Studies made of Canada and the Soviet Union have shown that despite predictions to the contrary, family allowances have had no measurable influence on birth-rates.[4] The whole question of how far economic inducements can 'bribe' parents to produce more children is an extremely complex one, but most authorities have agreed that such small payments as are made under existing family allowance systems can have little effect.[5]

Still, despite the lack of any firm evidence either way, there remain legitimate hypothetical questions: if family allowances were higher, and represented the full cost of maintaining a child, would the birth-rate then be affected? Even if they do not raise birth-rates, might not family allowances prevent a decline? Might they also not contribute to population growth indirectly by lowering infant and maternal mortality? Since the subject of population growth is so full of uncertainty and speculation, it is hardly surprising that the demographic arguments on family allowances are extremely difficult to disentangle. Essentially, the real question to be answered in a historical study is not whether family allowances have affected birth-rates, but how one is to 'measure' the pervasive influence of the erroneous belief that they do. Bearing that in mind, this chapter will attempt to disentangle the confused jumble of claims and counter-claims — many of them resting on the flimsiest of evidence — that made up the demographic case for family allowances in Britain in the interwar years.

Between the late 1870s and the early 1940s Britain, along with most other European countries, experienced a progressive fall in her annual birth-rates. In the late 1870s the annual average rate of population growth was 1·30 per cent; in the early 1900s it was 0·98 per cent; and by the 1930s it had fallen to 0·44 per cent.[6] The crude fertility-rate (the birth-rate per 1000 population) fell from 35·3 in 1876—80 to 28·3 in 1901—5 and 15·3 in 1931—5, which meant that the average number of children per family fell from just under 6 in the 1870s to 2·2 in the 1930s.[7] Of course, at no time did there take place an actual decline in numbers: the population of Great Britain increased from 23·1 million in 1861 to 46·6 million in 1941. But by the late 1930s the declining birth-rate was beginning to arouse considerable alarm among social scientists and demographers, since it appeared likely that very soon the population would not be replacing itself: the natural increase (the excess of births over deaths) had fallen steadily from 4·6 million in 1901—11 to 1·2 million in 1931—41.[8]

The statistics, familiar to every social historian, caused great puzzlement in the 1930s because the fall in fertility had taken place alongside great improvements in diet, sanitation, medicine, housing and real wages — which from a Malthusian point of view should have produced a rising birth-rate. Even today there is much uncertainty among demographic historians over the exact causes of the post-1870s fall in fertility. There is general agreement that the explanation must lie in the overall 'demographic transition' thesis: briefly, that the late nineteenth-century 'great depression' first implanted in the minds of middle class parents the desire to reduce family size in order to make the economies necessary if their overall standards of living were to be preserved; that thereafter, for middle class parents expenditure on educating their children rose as entry into the professions increasingly came to be by competitive examination, and for working class parents restrictions on child labour and the introduction of compulsory elementary education turned their children from producers of wealth into passive consumers.[9] But within this general explanation lie many uncertainties: did contraceptive knowledge pass 'sideways' or 'downwards' through the social scale? How much importance must be attached to the 1877 Bradlaugh-Besant trial? If the explanation relates to a certain stage of industrialization, why did France, with a predominantly agricultural economy, experience a decline probably as early as the 1770s? The existence of so many puzzling problems makes the whole question of the fall in fertility one that must be approached with great caution.

If today's demographers are still baffled by aspects of the decline in the birth-rate, then those of the 1920s and 1930s were many more times so. Immediately after the First World War there was a brief period when fear of over-population was in vogue: J. M. Keynes had popularized this in his book *The Economic Consequences of the Peace* (1920) and for a time the theory held a certain attraction as a convenient explanation of mass unemployment.[10] However, in 1933 the birth-rate reached its lowest-ever point, and thereafter there began to develop growing concern over the long downward trend.

Essentially, the 'population panic' of the 1930s centred on three main fears. First, there was the prospect of an actual decline in total numbers setting in at some not-too-distant date. Dr Enid Charles caused considerable alarm by her prediction that if fertility- and mortality-rates continued to fall as they had done in the past, the population of England and Wales would be reduced to one-tenth of its existing size over the next century; and even if fertility and mortality remained constant at 1933 levels, the population would be halved in this time.[11] Other demographers of a less pessimistic outlook still produced alarming figures: David Glass, for instance, forecast that the population would fall to 15 per cent of its existing size in just over two centuries.[12]

Of course, had the British birth-rate remained at its pre-1870 level even more horrifying prospects would have been in store: by the year 2100 the population would have reached the astronomic figure of 460 million.[13] But the 1930s were years of growing international tension and emerging colonial independence movements, and thus most concern centred on the prospect of a British Empire unable to defend itself through insufficient manpower. Duncan Sandys, the Conservative MP, warned in 1937 that

> unless the population trend in Great Britain and Western Europe alters, the Dominions, in order to maintain their population, may be forced to seek emigrants from Asiatic and Eastern European

countries where the decline in population is not so imminent. Apart from the cultural aspect and the weakening of Imperial ties it would involve them in all the difficulties consequent upon the importation of cheap labour accustomed to a substantially lower standard of life . . . A great Empire whose population is not only declining but is also on an average growing older is particularly vulnerable to attack.[14]

These fears were not only the province of those on the political right: even a left-wing scientist like Lancelot Hogben could warn that 'sooner or later any Government, Socialist or otherwise, will have to face the task of raising fertility or to accept a downward retreat to racial extinction',[15] and Beveridge declared that soon the question would have to be faced of 'how far the unequal adoption of birth control by different races will leave one race at the mercy of another's growing numbers, or drive it to armaments and perpetual aggression in self-defence'.[16]

This gave rise to a second fear — that a continuing fertility decline would alter the age-distribution of the population so that an increasing proportion of old people would have to be supported by a declining proportion of producers (those aged between 15 and 65 years). Dr Enid Charles estimated that whereas in 1935 64·30 per cent of the population of England and Wales was aged between 15 and 59 years and 12·45 per cent 60 and over, by the year 2000 these proportions would have changed to 49·63 per cent and 46·49 per cent respectively.[17] Such an imbalance would bring about many changes detrimental to economic growth: in particular, taxation would have to be enormously increased to pay for enlarged social services to old people (for example, more hospitals and old age pensions).[18]

The third major cause for concern was the phenomenon of differential fertility. The decline in the birth-rate began in the upper-middle class and slowly permeated down the social scale, with the result that fertility became inversely related to social class. Thus the 1911 Census for Scotland showed that the average number of children for certain occupations was: crofters, 7·04; coal miners, 7·01; general labourers, 6·29; clerks, 4·38; teachers, 4·25; physicians and surgeons, 3·91.[19] From such statistics on fertility distribution it appeared that the population was increasingly being recruited from the lowest social classes and if, as many eugenists argued, the lowest social classes were also the least intelligent, then obviously 'national intelligence' was declining. Raymond Cattell maintained that it was just such a process that had caused the decline of the Roman and Greek civilizations, and calculated that on present trends in three hundred years' time half the British population would be mentally defective.[20] Sir Bernard Mallet (president of the Eugenics Society) claimed that between 1906 and 1929 the number of mental defectives had increased by 35 per cent while the population had only increased by 14 per cent.[21] Others argued that society was becoming increasingly burdened with an ever-expanding 'social problem group' of unemployables, lunatics, criminals, caused by the growth of 'bad stock'.[22]

It is hardly surprising that in this atmosphere of alarm and pessimism many mistaken theories were put forward to explain past population trends and predict future ones. The more extreme of these suggested that mysterious and deep-seated biological changes had taken place in the physiology of individuals in industrialized societies, caused by such factors as the increased use of artificial fertilizers, preservatives in food, soap, and so on; so pervasive had these theories become by the 1940s that the Royal Commission on Population felt it necessary to appoint a special Biological and Medical Sub-Committee to look into the question of whether reproductive capacity had declined.[23] However, most commentators realized that the fall in fertility had been voluntary: as early as 1905–6 the Fabian Society had conducted an investigation of 316 middle class marriages, and had found that in 242 of them birth-control was being practised.[24] It was the cause of this voluntary limitation that was so baffling. Professor Raymond Pearl, a biologist, drew an analogy with the behaviour of fruit-flies and suggested that human beings also slowed down their breeding when a certain degree of overcrowding was reached.[25] The eminent economist G. Udny Yule attributed it to changes in price levels.[26] In a debate on the subject in the House of Commons an MP blamed the increasing number of women entering public life, 'like lambs straying out into the jungle'.[27] Beveridge quite wrongly suggested that after 1880 contraceptives were more available and reliable.[28] Others invented their own causes, like Dr John Brownlee's 'race physiology' or Raymond Cattell's 'social melancholia',[29] until by the end of the 1930s two population experts could list many bizarre 'explanations' that had been put forward at various times:

> fear of another world war; the inadequate wages paid to the working man; the cost and difficulty of obtaining domestic servants; the craze for amusement and pleasures; the 'pace' of modern life; over-indulgence by the modern girl in athletics; the danger of dying in childbirth; the increase in homosexuality among men; the selfishness of the modern girl; the demoralising influence of towns.[30]

Of course, many experts and non-experts in the interwar years realized that the explanation lay in the general 'rising standard of living' argument later developed by J. A. Banks in *Prosperity and Parenthood* (1954), and that reversing the trend was probably outwith man's control.[31] Nevertheless, in this generally alarmist atmosphere it was inevitable that family allowances should be seized upon as a possible means of raising the birth-rate. The remainder of this chapter will outline the pro-natalist arguments for and against family allowances as expressed by eugenists, population experts and Family Endowment Society leaders. Finally, the response of the government will be considered.

The eugenics movement in Britain grew directly, if slowly, out of Social Darwinism and owed much to the pioneering work of Francis Galton. Galton was a cousin of Charles Darwin, and after the publication of the latter's *Origin of Species* in 1859 he began to apply his mind to the possibility of substituting social controls for natural selection in shaping human evolution. From his experiments into such areas as the pedigrees of famous families, Galton concluded that by selective breeding the innate qualities of a nation could be improved or, for that matter, impaired.[32] In the last quarter of the nineteenth century Galton's ideas began to attract a growing band of disciples, and the eugenics movement took on the two features that were to characterize it over the next half-century — a profound pessimism and a highly conservative outlook.

A full explanation of why the eugenics movement became increasingly pessimistic would need to be lengthy and complex. For the purpose of this study, however, it is worth remembering that the eugenics movement was essentially an upper-middle class movement, and reflected the growing insecurity felt by that section of society in the face of new threats from the 1880s onwards — increasing international economic and military rivalry, the appearance of colonial independence movements and, most of all, the rise of socialism. Thus the generation of eugenists after Galton claimed with growing alarm that, thanks to differential fertility, the British race was not only losing its stock of 'great men' but was becoming increasingly burdened with a 'social problem group' or 'residuum' at the bottom who bred recklessly and made up the bulk of paupers, criminals, lunatics, deaf mutes, alcoholics and feeble-minded.[33]

Thus according to A. F. Tredgold, between one-fifth and one-quarter of the total workhouse population were 'mentally affected and quite unfitted to be at large'; at least 20 per cent of the criminal population were mentally defective; and of all the feeble-minded in the country, no less than two-thirds were being supported by the general public.[34] The social problem group was viewed as a considerable burden on the community (costing fully £48 million per annum, Leonard Darwin estimated in 1914),[35] and one which was expanding through abnormally high birth-rates.[36] Eugenists quoted such statistics as the fact that of the 122 000 certified idiots and lunatics in England and Wales officially registered on 1 January 1906, 91 per cent were paupers,[37] and argued that if such 'bad stock' was not allowed to breed, the 'fit' members of society would gain enormously through reduced taxation, higher wages and increased industrial efficiency.[38]

By the early twentieth century eugenics was attracting the interest of a wide spectrum of political opinion — although generally conservative and opposed to state intervention, it nevertheless attracted some socialists like Sidney Webb[39] — and the question of how the 'desirable' sections of society could be encouraged to raise their birth-rates was being increasingly discussed. Ironically, the aim of eugenists was to reverse the doctrine of 'the survival of the fittest' by replacing it with 'the survival of the highest social classes' since, as Professor R. A. Fisher put it, now the problem was 'that the biologically successful members of our society are to be found principally among its social failures, and equally that classes of persons who are prosperous and socially successful are, on the whole, the biological failures, the unfit in the struggle for existence'.[40] Thus Sidney Webb saw the task of eugenists as 'deliberately to manipulate the environment so that the survivors may be of the type which we regard as the highest',[41] while others went further and suggested that such agents of upward social mobility as scholarships and competitive entry into the professions should be abolished.[42]

Inevitably, the idea of family endowment was suggested. By the time the Family Endowment Society began its campaign, a number of proposals had been made. For example, the Whethams wanted 'a satisfactory system of selective public endowment of parenthood' for those in all social classes who produced healthy and strong offspring, to be administered by trustees 'who should look solely to the probable quality of the offspring', with greatly extended tax relief for families,[43] and the psychologist William McDougall suggested that the state should introduce a family allowance system for its 'best elements' such as senior civil servants.[44]

By the 1920s, however, this interest among eugenists was being tempered with a good deal of caution. In that decade the eugenics movement became increasingly conservative, with the concept of a 'social problem group' enjoying renewed popularity with the appearance of mass unemployment. Few eugenists went as far as Professor E. W. MacBride, who suggested that parents on public assistance should be compulsorily sterilized,[45] but most agreed that the long-term unemployed were, as the *Eugenics Review* put it, 'a standing army of biological misfits'.[46] Great alarm was expressed over the apparent increase in the number of mental defectives in England and Wales to a total of 300 000 by the late 1920s; over half of these, it was claimed, owed their condition to heredity, and if they could be prevented from having children then in three generations the number of mental defectives would be halved.[47] A number of attempts were made to prove conclusively the existence of such a 'social problem group', such as E. J. Lidbetter's laborious project, spread over twenty-five years, which investigated the pedigrees and case-histories of Poor Law applicants and purported to show that their pauperism was caused by hereditary weakness.[48] By the late 1920s and early 1930s voluntary sterilization was attracting considerable support among eugenists as the most effective way of tackling this problem.

Not surprisingly, therefore, many eugenists saw a universal family allowance scheme as thoroughly dysgenic. Leonard Darwin warned that such a scheme would not appreciably raise the living standards of the highest social classes and would encourage the lowest classes to produce even more children.[49] The economist Professor A. C. Pigou warned that since the First World War there had been an unfortunate narrowing of income differentials between the professions and the working class, and claimed that universal family endowment would only exacerbate this.[50] Thus whenever the topic was mentioned in the *Eugenics Review* in the early 1920s it tended to be viewed with hostility. The New South Wales scheme, for example, received sarcastic condemnation because it did most for poor working class families: 'the "cult of incompetence" could hardly go further!' was the *Review*'s verdict.[51]

However, eugenists *were* keenly interested in family allowances for the higher social classes and, despite their suspicion of state intervention, they wanted the government to introduce social policies to counteract differential fertility.[52] Within the Eugenics Society in particular there was discussion of how this might be achieved, and three main suggestions emerged: a system of family allowances proportional to parental income so that the 'best stock' would receive most (the Society included this in its statement of aims, published in 1926); generous extensions of income tax child rebates, for which the Society campaigned throughout the interwar years; and occupational family allowance schemes for the professions, such as Beveridge's London School of Economics system.[53] Provided that a proposed scheme contained sufficient safeguards, therefore, eugenists tended to approve of it: for example, William McDougall declared that

> family allowances are so obviously just, so economically expedient, so politically advantageous, so powerful to promote the aims of the humanitarian and the feminist, that in a world racked with economic distress and discontents, a world of rapidly falling birth-rates, a world deeply concerned to effect radical change in its economic system, we may confidently expect to see them universally instituted in one form or another in the immediate future.[54]

Thus when Eleanor Rathbone delivered a talk to the Eugenics Society[55] on 12 November 1924 she was not unfavourably received. Well aware of her audience's prejudices, she suggested that a graded family allowance system related to parental income would be best.[56] In reply Leonard Darwin (the Society's president) strongly supported this, and urged his fellow eugenists to become involved in the campaign for family allowances 'to insure that the tiller of maternity is turned in the right direction' away from any scheme that might encourage fertility among the 'least efficient types'.[57]

Within the Eugenics Society there were a number of enthusiastic supporters of this type of family allowance scheme. Professor R. A. Fisher, for example, was a member of both it and the Family Endowment Society. Soon after its publication he gave *The Disinherited Family* a very warm welcome in the *Eugenics Review*,[58] and in many subsequent speeches and writings he advocated family allowances as a eugenic measure.[59] In 1932 he even appears to have organized a short-lived Family Allowances Sub-Committee, under the auspices of the Eugenics Society, with a membership that included Eva Hubback, Professor Julian Huxley and Dr C. P. Blacker (the Society's general secretary).[60]

The eugenics movement in Britain probably reached a peak of social conservatism in the early 1930s, with quite a number of eugenists casting approving eyes at European fascism,[61] but thereafter it retreated from this position. By the mid-1930s the full implications of Nazi eugenic policies were beginning to be understood, the science of nutrition was suggesting new analyses of poverty, and the movement came

under savage attack from left-wing scientists like Professors Lancelot
Hogben and J. B. S. Haldane who ridiculed its claims to scientific
accuracy while employing such terms as 'dregs', 'social misfits' and
'unsound stock'. Hogben, in his brilliantly sardonic style, called eugenics
'the pastime of decking out the jackdaws of class prejudice in the peacock
feathers of biological jargon . . . It has drawn its personnel and funds
from the childless rentier — twentieth century Bourbons who have earned
nothing and begotten nothing.'[62] This more tolerant trend in the eugenics
movement was assisted by the influx of a number of liberal social scientists into the Eugenics Society like Richard Titmuss, David Glass and
Francois Lafitte, who viewed the Society merely as a convenient organization through which to publicize the quantitative population problem:
these writers took an active part in the Society's affairs and wrote articles
for the *Review* in which a radical–liberal analysis of social problems
would be somewhat ingenuously cloaked in mildly eugenic language.[63]
As a result of these combined influences the Society's attitudes softened.
In 1938, for example, it co-operated with the research organization
Political and Economic Planning to form a Population Policies Committee 'for the purpose of surveying the social and economic conditions
which discourage the replacement of eugenically sound stocks'[64] — the
sort of 'environmentalist' approach that would have been unthinkable
ten years earlier.

By the mid-1930s, in fact, the eugenic case for and against family
allowances had merged into the general pro-natalist case which was being
put forward with increasing urgency by social scientists, economists
and demographers. Faced with the prospect of a declining population,
this section of opinion tended to stress the need for quantitative rather
than qualitative change, and had no fears that a flat-rate universal
scheme would 'encourage the poor to breed recklessly'.

In the 1920s little interest had been shown by population experts
towards family allowances; since much of the discussion in that decade
centred on the wages question, birth-rate arguments were of minor
importance. Some concern was expressed that family allowances might
exacerbate the 'over-population problem' of the early 1920s: Paul
Douglas, for example, mentioned this as a possible objection, maintaining that 'the great problem for Western civilisation, and Eastern too
for that matter, is how to limit population, and not how to expand it'.[65]
But mostly there were doubts over whether family allowances would
really influence the birth-rate either way: J. H. Richardson approved of
the principle for the lowest paid, but pointed out that 'its value in the
case of other groups of workers depends to a large extent on its effect

on population, regarding which there is at present little satisfactory evidence'.[66]

However, by the mid-1930s the quantitative pro-natalist case for family allowances was attracting more and more support. Probably the start of this new interest can be fixed at the year 1936 when there were published three important books warning of the population problem — D. V. Glass's *The Struggle for Population*, R. R. Kuczynski's *Colonial Population* and A. M. Carr-Saunders's *World Population*.[67] In the following year the *Sociological Review* devoted an issue to the declining birth-rate, and in its pages G. F. McCleary expressed the view increasingly held by social scientists that 'the public is at last beginning to realize that the population question is of such importance, that compared with it most of the topics that fill the newspapers sink into insignificance'.[68]

The most important practical expression of this concern was the formation of two independent committees of experts to investigate the population problem and suggest remedies. The first was the Population Investigation Committee, founded in 1936 under the chairmanship of Professor A. M. Carr-Saunders, with David Glass as research secretary; this Committee used the offices of the Eugenics Society, and received a grant from it, but was technically an independent body. Some informal co-operation was obtained from relevant government departments, but that was all. The Committee's aim was to co-ordinate research into the population problem and investigate possible economic inducements to parenthood — among which family allowances were included.[69]

In 1938 another research body was launched — the Population Policies Committee, jointly sponsored by the Eugenics Society and Political and Economic Planning. This had close connections with the Population Investigation Committee, and it also considered family allowances as a possible pro-natalist policy, but one that could only work if it existed along with other family policies — higher income tax child allowances, the removal of job discrimination against married women, better maternity services, improved child nutrition.[70] 'Family endowment in the sense solely of cash allowances cannot be regarded as a panacea for the population problem', wrote Francois Lafitte, the Committee's secretary: 'A clearly thought-out population policy will probably include cash allowances in some shape or form among its measures, but it will include them as one element in an integrated system of measures rather than as the main plank of its programme'; such a population policy, he insisted, should be accompanied by social reforms to ensure that 'every child that is brought into the world is guaranteed an adequate basic minimum of food, clothing, shelter and medical care'.[71]

By the late 1930s, therefore, the quantitative pro-natalist case for family allowances had overtaken the qualitative eugenic case (for and against), and was frequently being expressed in the same breath as the family poverty case by reformist social scientists who viewed the population problem as part of a much wider social problem needing drastic economic remedies. Glass pointed out that nowhere had European family allowances by themselves produced a rise in birth-rates,[72] and declared that 'no action is likely to have a permanent influence unless it provides conditions in which the working-class is able to bring up children without thereby suffering from economic and social hardship';[73] Carr-Saunders called for future social policies to be much more family-oriented;[74] and Hogben maintained that only a new socialist approach to the family would achieve an upturn in fertility.[75]

These writers strongly denied that family allowances would by themselves be pro-natalist. Indeed, in common with most supporters of family allowances as a measure of child welfare, they appear to have found the pro-natalist arguments rather abhorrent. Yet by presenting the family poverty case for family allowances in the context of the population problem they may well have unintentionally been giving these pro-natalist misconceptions a new lease of life.

In the interwar years, therefore, the demographic case for and against family allowances was presented in a bewildering variety of ways, from a wide spectrum of political opinion, and frequently via statements that were confused, contradictory and based on pure speculation. All discussions foundered on the lack of reliable census data. Until the 1938 Population (Statistics) Act birth registration did not include the age of the mother, the duration of the marriage and the birth order of each child; specific fertility-rates were thus only obtainable from limited studies. Most of the pro-natalist claims and counter-claims were based on the flimiest evidence; eugenists were particularly prone to vague, unscientific language that at times bordered on the absurd.[76] Again, the decline in the birth-rate could be 'analysed' in many different ways, according to one's political predilections: thus Richard and Kay Titmuss could interpret it as an indictment of capitalism,[77] yet delegates to the 1937 Conservative Party conference discussed it in imperialistic, 'national defence' terms.[78] Many participants in the debate were highly inconsistent in their attitudes; for example, when

Beveridge first discovered family allowances in 1924 he viewed them as a demographic measure,[79] later maintaining that the aim of his London School of Economics scheme had been 'to remove some of the obstacles to academic infertility'[80] — indeed, he even boasted to William McDougall that by 1933 the scheme had helped produce forty 'little economists', a remark no doubt made in jest, but taken seriously by McDougall;[81] yet in the 1942 Beveridge Report the pro-natalist arguments were said to be relatively unimportant.[82] Finally, statements on family allowances and the birth-rate were usually highly ambiguous, a typical example being the declaration by Professor R. A. Fisher that family endowment was 'the only agency which seems at all capable of checking the present tendency of many European peoples to decline in numbers; although its power of doing so must still be regarded as doubtful and, if effective, its action will certainly be slow'.[83] Because of all this confusion it was then, as now, extremely difficult to trace any thread of consistency running through the many claims and counter-claims that were made.

If this creates great problems for the modern researcher, it inevitably created even greater ones for the leaders of the Family Endowment Society. Acutely conscious of the need to attract as wide a range of support as possible, they felt obliged to alter their viewpoint according to whatever audience they were addressing. When applied to the pro-natalist arguments this approach only served to confuse issues even further.

The 'Equal Pay and the Family' group of 1917—18 considered the population question and decided that family endowment could only have a beneficial effect: it would redress differential fertility by raising the birth-rate of the professional and artisan classes, and lowering it among 'those classes of the community where there is at present no check but the physical capacity of the parents'.[84] This tended to be the attitude of the FES leaders throughout the 1920s. Family allowances, they argued, would raise the economic status and self-respect of the lowest classes, and thereby raise them out of the sort of mentality that produced large unplanned families; in any case, the lowest social classes were having the maximum number of children that was practically possible, and therefore cash payments would not make them any more prolific; and, finally, the birth-rates of the middle and upper classes might be raised.[85] Thus when addressing the Eugenics Society in 1924, Eleanor Rathbone mentioned the known connection between overcrowding and high fertility and suggested that family endowment, 'by making it more possible for families to obtain accommodation proportionate to their size, might then be expected to reduce the birth-rate among the slum dwellers'.[86] As a final point, the Society tended to emphasize that since its aim was to get the *principle* of family endow-ment accepted, any criticism over the possible effects on the quality and quantity of population growth should result in the adjustment of any proposed scheme (for example, from a universal flat-rate one to one with graded payments) rather than a complete abandonment of the basic principle.[87] As in other aspects of their campaign, the Society's leaders were very careful not to alienate any one section of opinion on the birth-rate issue.

Eleanor Rathbone, however, displayed a marked fondness for eugenic arguments, no doubt because of her underlying conservatism. In 1917 she deplored the fact that the lowest social classes were producing the most children, warning that 'hence we are as a nation recruiting the national stock in increasing proportion from those who have sunk into the lowest strata because they are physically, mentally or morally degenerate'.[88] In *The Disinherited Family* she claimed to disagree with the eugenists' concept of 'bad stock' yet still could declare that 'on the whole the elements in the working class who are restricting their families (in whatever way they do it) represent the cream, and those who are not practising restriction the dregs'.[89] Again, in a letter to *The British Weekly* in 1924 she declared it impossible to say whether family allowances would raise the quantity of the population, but then said that its quality would be improved 'by encouraging the thrifty, ambitious artisan and professional classes to have more children and by making possible to the unskilled workers those higher standards with regard to housing, orderly living and the status of women, which are the best antidote to excessive and dysgenic breeding'.[90]

By the mid-1930s the other Family Endowment Society leaders were increasingly stressing the qualitative and quantitative pro-natalist arguments. This was in part a product of their decision to campaign for limited occupational schemes in the aftermath of the 1931 economic crisis; family allowances in the teaching profession, civil service and clergy were seen as necessary in order 'to preserve the qualities of eugenic value in the salaried and professional classes'.[91] But it was also an attempt to espouse what they considered were increasingly popular ideas. By 1936 Eleanor Rathbone even went so far as to say that 'the factor most likely to force the adoption of family allowances will be the approaching steady and steep decline in the population, which threatens to become a menace to white civilization and especially to the Anglo-Saxon races'.[92] Typical of this increasingly pro-natalist eugenic line was that put forward by Professor R. A. Fisher in the Society's *Family Endowment Chronicle* in 1931: Fisher agreed that family allowances in France had had no effect on the birth-rate, but still maintained that they were 'the most powerful available means of preserving among civilised peoples those innate qualities which make civilisation possible'; he declared that since, in his opinion, differential fertility was caused by the social promotion of the less reproductive strains in society, family allowances given to any class in society 'will tend progressively to raise the birth-rate of all classes above it, by preventing the preferential promotion into these classes of relatively infertile strains; and will tend in like manner to lower the birth-rate of all classes below it by preventing the preferential demotion of the more infertile'.[93] Clearly, arguments were now becoming hopelessly confused.

In common with others who pronounced on the subject, the Family Endowment Society leaders tended to make very equivocal statements. Thus at no point in her *Family Allowances* (1938) did Marjorie Green openly state that family allowances would raise the birth-rate; but at the same time she maintained that a declining population would be one of the consequences of a wage-system that took no account of family needs.[94] Again, in one article she could give much more prominence to the child malnutrition arguments than the birth-rate ones,[95] yet in another, entitled 'Cash allowances for families: scheme to check fall of the birth rate', she could suggest occupational family allowance schemes for the professions on the grounds that 'the real danger threatening us is not class war but class suicide. How, without unwarrantable interference with private liberty, can the people who make the best parents be persuaded to have the most children?'[96] All this was understandable political opportunism, of course, and usually the Society's leaders insisted that the child poverty arguments were more important.[97] But inevitably these pro-natalist arguments were taken up by other family allowances supporters and misinterpreted, as when Viscount Samuel confidently declared in the House of Lords that a family allowance scheme would be 'the principal measure that can be adopted on the economic side to deal with this problem of the decline in parenthood'.[98] Without fully intending to, the Family Endowment Society's leaders had helped perpetuate the growing misconception that cash allowances would raise the birth-rate.

Finally, there must be considered the extent to which the demographic case for family allowances was accepted by the government in the period 1918—39. As far as can be ascertained, eugenic ideas made little impression. Despite the fact that those who joined the Eugenics Society shared the same social and educational background as those who became senior civil servants or Conservative politicians, there appears to have been little inclination on the part of those in positions of power to regard eugenics as anything other than a very esoteric science, and one which aroused too much controversy. Perhaps the best illustration of this can be seen in the official response to the cause that eugenists probably campaigned most actively for — voluntary sterilization.

Throughout the 1920s voluntary sterilization for mental defectives attracted strong support from eugenists as the only effective way of checking the growth of the 'social problem group' they feared so much; voluntary sterilization, they claimed, would enable defectives to lead more normal lives instead of having to be segregated in asylums, and in time the financial, administrative and social burden imposed by them on the rest of society would be reduced.[99] In 1928 the Eugenics Society and some other interested organizations decided to lobby the government and request that some sort of official commission be set up to investigate the possibility of voluntary sterilization legislation, the Society even going so far as to publish a draft Bill in the *Review*.[100] In 1929 the Society set up a special Committee for Legalising Eugenic Sterilisation; propaganda pamphlets were published; and in 1931 a private member's motion was unsuccessfully introduced into the House of Commons.[101] In June 1932 the government appointed a Departmental Committee on Sterilisation under the chairmanship of L. G. Brock, Chairman of the Board of Control.[102] The Brock Committee's recommendation — hardly surprising, given its membership — was that, subject to certain safeguards, voluntary sterilization should be made legally available for mental defectives and for people suffering from transmissible hereditary disorders.[103]

The Ministry of Health, however, strongly resisted the ensuing pressure from eugenists to implement the Brock proposals. There was some sympathy towards eugenic ideas within the ministry; Sir Arthur Robinson, for example, found it

> repugnant to common sense that, if a mentally deficient parent
> or parents on the average produces or produce similar children,
> the State should allow them to continue to do so and thereby
> throw on the next generation problems of segregation or super-
> vision which this generation has conspicuously failed to solve.[104]

But ministry officials were well aware of the strength of opposition in certain sections of public opinion. The churches were suspicious, with the Roman Catholic Church steadfastly opposed to what it saw as 'immoral, unnatural and inhuman' proposals.[105] The Labour Party viewed voluntary sterilization as a red-herring issue, obscuring the real problem of bad socio-economic conditions, and maintained that in practice such a policy would only be used on the poor.[106] A large number of other organizations were also opposed, and made their feelings known to the Minister of Health.[107] Significantly, when a private member tried to introduce a motion in the House of Commons in favour of voluntary sterilization, it was defeated by 167 votes to 89 after a crushing speech by the Labour MP, Dr H. Morgan.[108] Ministry of Health officials thus trod very carefully whenever the subject was under discussion, and when a deputation came to the Minister of Health in 1935, requesting that the Brock proposals be implemented, they were firmly told that too large a section of public opinion was against them, and that accordingly there was absolutely no possibility of a government-sponsored Bill in the near future.[109]

From the available evidence it would seem that civil servants and ministers were also disinclined to be swept along by the tide of alarm over the prospect of a declining population. One of the few expressions of official interest was an exchange of views between Lord Eustace Percy, Minister Without Portfolio, and S. P. Vivian, Registrar-General. In early 1936 Percy composed a long memorandum on the population problem, several drafts of which were circulated to other departments. In it he referred to Enid Charles's pessimistic forecasts and pointed out that on present trends, after twenty years had elapsed there would begin a serious decline in the male age-group aged 20–44 'representing the main military and industrial strength of the nation'. He discussed a number of possible remedies – improved maternity and child welfare services ('politically speaking, the essential "sweetener" to any publicity campaign in favour of larger families'), propaganda to make large families more fashionable, policies to give greater security of employment to young adults, better housing – and then considered possible extensions of the family endowment principle, though he admitted that income tax child allowances had had no measurable effect on middle class birth-rates.[110] Vivian's reaction, however, was typical of most other civil servants: he cautiously agreed that there might be some cause for concern, but insisted that no economic inducements to parenthood could be introduced until the exact causes of the decline in fertility had been identified.[111]

One of the few practical steps taken by the government was the introduction of the 1938 Population (Statistics) Act which extended the scope of birth-registration information. Certainly, this was a response to Ronald Cartland's House of Commons motion of February 1937 expressing concern over the fall in fertility, and in the 'Financial Memorandum' which accompanied the Bill it was admitted that the additional information was now needed 'for the practical consideration of the problems in regard to the future population of Great Britain to which the decline in the birthrate has given rise'.[112] Yet the private exchange of views among civil servants and ministers in preparation for the House of Commons debate contained no expressions of deep concern. The standard official response was to regard the predictions of demographers such as Enid Charles as scaremongering, to emphasize that the exact causes of the decline in fertility were still unknown, and to view the pro-natalist arguments for family allowances with profound scepticism.[113] This attitude appears to have been shared by the Cabinet: the only occasion on which the population question was discussed was in January 1935 when the Minister of Health, Sir Hilton Young, suggested that an extra census might be desirable in 1936 'because of its utility as a basis for national planning in such matters as housing' — but this idea was summarily rejected on grounds of economy.[114]

Some historians have suggested that evidence of government concern over the falling birth-rate can be found in the periodic raising of income tax child allowances in the interwar years.[115] For most of the 1920s these stood at £36 per annum for the first child and £27 each for subsequent children, amounting in 1927—8 to more than £39·5 million.[116] In his 1928 budget the Chancellor of the Exchequer, Winston Churchill, raised them to £60 and £50 respectively, justifying this on the grounds that 'the burden of bringing up a family of young children weighs very heavily upon the smaller class of Income Tax payer . . . the notable decline in the birth rate since the War is a convincing witness of the burden upon parents who have young children depending upon them'. Churchill went on to state that 'the expenses of maternity are a serious problem for all small Income Tax payers', but evidently he did not consider these expenses so serious a problem for the low wage-earner, for in a panegyric on the family endowment principle (citing with approval the ancient Roman system) he made no mention of the desirability of family allowances for all.[117] As in 1909, this form of family endowment was welcomed unquestioningly by MPs; only Hugh Dalton expressed the hope that some day child allowances would be enjoyed by all income groups.[118]

In 1931 these allowances were cut to £50 for the first child and £40 each for subsequent children, but no mention was made of the birth-rate until 1935, when Neville Chamberlain fixed them at £50 for all children, and justified this by saying:

> I must say I look on the continued diminution of the birth-rate in this country with considerable apprehension . . . I have a feeling that the time may not be too far distant . . . when the countries of the British Empire will be crying out for more citizens of the right breed, and when we in this country shall not be able to supply that demand.[119]

Allowances were yet again increased the following year to £60 for each child, and such comments as MPs made on the subject tended to reflect the growing concern over the birth-rate.[120] By 1939 the total paid out in child tax rebates was almost £87·5 million per annum — more than half as much again as the 1945 family allowances scheme was to cost.[121]

However, it is likely that these pro-natalist sentiments were little more than a convenient and fashionable rationalization for measures primarily designed to woo the middle class electorate. Whenever both Houses of Parliament discussed the possibility of family allowances for all, government spokesmen tended to view the demographic arguments with scepticism. Repeatedly, Eleanor Rathbone's supporters asked for an official inquiry into universal family allowances, and each time they encountered a wall of indifference.[122] Some ministers like Kingsley Wood did at times voice concern over the population problem,[123] but the government's firm view in the late 1930s was that family allowances would have as little effect on the British birth-rate as they had had on European ones,[124] and that only when more was known about the exact causes of the fall in fertility could the question of economic inducements to parenthood be considered.[125]

By 1939, therefore, the demographic case for family allowances had been presented in a bewildering multitude of ways. It was part of a much wider debate on the causes and consequences of the qualitative and quantitative decline in fertility, and like many of the arguments in this debate, the demographic case for family allowances often rested on the flimsiest of evidence, and more often on pure speculation. The pro-natalist case for family allowances tended to be discussed within a tiny social and intellectual elite,[126] often in esoteric journals; yet the leaders of the Family Endowment Society felt obliged, partly

for tactical reasons, to participate in it, and in doing so helped perpetuate the myth that allowances would raise the birth-rate. Whatever
the confusion surrounding the pro-natalist case for family allowances
in the interwar years, however, one thing stands out clearly: at no
time did the government pay the slightest attention to it.

Notes and References

1. For example, Beveridge insisted that his advocacy of family allowances in 1942 was 'almost entirely' on economic grounds as opposed
   to demographic. W. H. Beveridge, 'Children's allowances and the
   race', in *The Pillars of Security* (1943), p. 14.
2. For example, James C. Vadakin, *Family Allowances, an Analysis
   of their Development and Implications* (1958), p. 91.
3. V. George, *Social Security, Beveridge and After* (1968), p. 193;
   Sir John Walley, *Social Security: Another British Failure?* (1972),
   pp. 183—7.
4. Bernice Madison, 'Canadian family allowances and their major
   social implications', *Journal of Marriage and the Family*, 26 (May
   1964), pp. 139—43; James C. Vadakin, *Children, Poverty and
   Family Allowances* (1968), pp. 95—101; Joseph Willard, 'Some
   aspects of family allowances and income redistribution in Canada',
   Public Policy, 4 (1954), pp. 190—232; D. Heer and J. Bryden,
   'Family allowances and fertility in the Soviet Union', *Soviet
   Studies*, 18 (October 1966), pp. 153—63.
5. For example, Vincent Whitney, 'Fertility trends and children's
   allowance programmes', in Eveline Burns (ed.), *Children's Allowances and the Economic Welfare of Children* (1968), pp. 123—9;
   Judith Blake, 'Are babies consumer durables?', *Population Studies*,
   12 (March 1968), pp. 5—25.
6. *Current Trend of Population in Great Britain*, Cmd 6358 (May
   1942), p. 3.
7. ibid., p. 8.
8. *Report of the Royal Commission on Population*, Cmd 7695
   (June 1949), pp. 8, 9, 25.
9. For detailed accounts, see ibid., pp. 33—43; Neil Tranter, *Population Since the Industrial Revolution* (1973), pp. 108—29; J. A.
   Banks, *Prosperity and Parenthood* (1954).
10. See controversy between Keynes and Beveridge on this point in
    the *Economic Journal*, 33 (December 1923), pp. 447—86; and

Economica, 4 (February 1924), pp. 1–20.

11. Enid Charles, 'The effect of present trends in fertility and mortality upon the future population of Great Britain and upon its age composition', *London and Cambridge Economic Service, Special Memorandum, No. 40* (August 1935), pp. 18–19. Dr Charles also made considerable impact with her book *The Twilight of Parenthood* (1934).

12. David Glass, 'The population problem and the future', *Eugenics Review*, 29 (April 1937), p. 41.

13. *Report of the Royal Commission on Population*, p. 9.

14. *Hansard*, vol. 320 (10 February 1937), col. 494.

15. L. Hogben, 'Planning for human survival', in G. D. H. Cole, *et al., What Is Ahead of Us?* (1937), p. 172.

16. *Economic Journal*, 33 (December 1923), p. 474.

17. Charles, op. cit. (1935), p. 14.

18. For a full discussion, see J. M. Keynes, 'Some economic consequences of a declining population', *Eugenics Review*, 29 (April 1937), pp. 13–17; G. F. McCleary, *Population: Today's Question* (1938), pp. 168–9; R. M. Titmuss, *Poverty and Population* (1938), pp. 19–32; W. B. Reddaway, *The Economics of a Declining Population* (1939).

19. J. C. Dunlop, 'The fertility of marriage in Scotland: a census study', *Journal of the Royal Statistical Society*, 77 (February 1914), pp. 275–7.

20. R. B. Cattell, *The Fight for Our National Intelligence* (1937), pp. 1–3, 43.

21. Mallet to Neville Chamberlain (18 February 1929), PRO MH 58/103.

22. For a discussion of this concept, see C. P. Blacker (ed.), *A Social Problem Group?* (1937).

23. *Report of the Royal Commission*, pp. 1, 31–2. No evidence was found of this. If anything, such dietary and other changes would be more likely to improve reproductive capacity.

24. Sidney Webb, *The Decline in the Birth-Rate* (1907), pp. 10–12.

25. G. F. McCleary, *Race Suicide?* (1945), p. 45.

26. G. Udny Yule, *The Fall in the Birth Rate* (1920), p. 39.

27. Speech by R. A. Pilkington, *Hansard*, vol. 320 (10 February 1937), col. 504.

28. W. H. Beveridge, 'The fall of fertility among European races', *Economica*, 5 (March 1925), p. 20.

29. J. Brownlee, 'The present tendencies of population in Great

Britain with respect to quantity and quality', *Eugenics Review*, 17 (July 1925), p. 75; Cattell, op. cit., pp. 146—58.

30. C. P. Blacker and D. V. Glass, *Population and Fertility* (1939), p. 6.

31. For example, F. Lafitte, 'The work of the Population Policies Committee', *Eugenics Review*, 31 (April 1939), pp. 49—53.

32. For the origins of the eugenics movement, see Nicholas Pastore, *The Nature—Nurture Controversy* (1949), pp. 20—8; Mark Haller, *Eugenics* (1963), pp. 8—20; L. C. Dunn, 'Cross currents in the history of human genetics', in Adela S. Baer (ed.), *Heredity and Society* (1973), pp. 18—24; C. P. Blacker, *Eugenics, Galton and After* (1952), pp. 19—126.

33. Again, a proper explanation of the 'social problem group' concept would need to be very lengthy. It was a concept that appeared in much of the literature on social problems in the late nineteenth century (for example, Charles Booth's plan for labour colonies) and can be traced through to modern 'cycle of deprivation' theories.

34. A. F. Tredgold, 'The feeble-minded', *Contemporary Review*, 97 (June 1910), p. 719.

35. L. Darwin, *An Address on Practical Eugenics* (1914), p. 13.

36. Mrs R. J. Hawkes, *What Is Eugenics?* (1910), p. 4.

37. George Whitehead, *Socialism and Eugenics* (1911), p. 10. This is explained by the fact that lunacy was officially registered on only a very few occasions, application for Poor Law relief and criminal arrest being two of them. Upper class lunatics would be hidden away in private hospitals.

38. L. Darwin, *Eugenics and National Economy* (1913), pp. 13—14.

39. Sidney Webb, 'Eugenics and the Poor Law' (1909).

40. R. A. Fisher, *The Genetical Theory of Natural Selection* (1930), p. 222.

41. Webb, op. cit. (1909), p. 5.

42. W. C. D. and C. Whetham, *The Family and the Nation* (1909), pp. 190—4.

43. ibid., pp. 202, 215—16.

44. W. McDougall, 'A practicable eugenic suggestion', *Sociological Papers, 1906* (1907), pp. 74—80.

45. J. B. S. Haldane, *Heredity and Politics* (1939), pp. 119—20.

46. 'Notes of the quarter', *Eugenics Review*, 25 (April 1933), p. 5.

47. Pamphlet from the Committee for Legalising Eugenic Sterilisation (n.d., prob. 1929), PRO MH 58/103; Parliamentary Committee on Sterilisation, 'The Sterilisation of Mental Defectives' (1932),

p. 12, PRO MH 58/104A.

48. E. J. Lidbetter, *Heredity and the Social Problem Group*, Vol. I (1933); and 'The social problem group as a public charge', in C. P. Blacker (ed.), *A Social Problem Group?* (1939), pp. 152–61.

49. Darwin, op. cit. (1914), p. 10; and 'Some birth rate problems', *Eugenics Review*, 12 (January 1921), pp. 283–4.

50. A. C. Pigou, 'Eugenics and some wage problems', in *Essays in Applied Economics* (1923), pp. 80–91.

51. 'Endowment of motherhood' by E. I. C., *Eugenics Review*, 14 (July 1922), p. 134.

52. Leonard Darwin, 'Population and civilisation', *Economic Journal*, 31 (June 1921), p. 195.

53. 'An outline of a practical eugenic policy', *Eugenics Review*, 18 (July 1926), p. 98; 'Notes of the quarter', ibid., 20 (July 1928), p. 75; R. A. Fisher, 'Income-tax rebates', ibid., p. 81.

54. William McDougall, 'Family allowances as a eugenic measure', *Character and Personality*, 2 (December 1933), p. 114.

55. The Society was founded in 1907, and the *Review* launched in 1909. A brief but interesting history of the Society is contained in the *Eugenics Review*, 60 (September 1968), pp. 142–75.

56. E. Rathbone, 'Family endowment in its bearing on the question of population', ibid., 16 (January 1925), pp. 274–5. The speech (pp. 270–5) was also published as a Family Endowment Society pamphlet.

57. ibid., pp. 277–8.

58. ibid. (July 1924), pp. 150–3.

59. For example, two pamphlets by Fisher in Eugenics Society Library File A 11/1: *The Overproduction of Food* (1929), pp. 56–60; and *The Social Selection of Human Fertility* (Herbert Spencer Lecture), (1932), pp. 24–31.

60. *Eugenics Society Annual Report for 1932–3*, p. 2. No evidence of this committee's activities has survived.

61. The *Eugenics Review*, while condemning the persecution of the Jews, approved of Hitler's opposition to the Roman Catholic Church in Germany, which it considered 'subversive' for opposing Nazi eugenic policies; op. cit., 25 (July 1933), pp. 77–8.

62. L. Hogben, *Dangerous Thoughts* (1939), pp. 53–4, 57. See also J. B. S. Haldane, op. cit., esp. pp. 104–27.

63. For example, the article by Titmuss and Lafitte in the *Eugenics Review*, 33 (January 1942), pp. 106–12, which was entitled 'Eugenics and poverty', was in fact an enthusiastic review of

Rowntree's *Poverty and Progress*, and mentioned heredity not at all. Two more liberalizing influences were Dr Maurice Newfield, who edited the *Review* from 1933 to 1949, and Dr C. P. Blacker, who was general secretary of the Society from 1931 to 1952.

64. ibid., 30 (April 1938), p. 4.
65. Paul Douglas, 'Some objections to the family wage system considered', *Journal of Political Economy*, 36 (October 1924), p. 691.
66. J. H. Richardson, *A Study on the Minimum Wage* (1927), p. 121.
67. On 28 and 29 September 1936 *The Times* carried two articles on the population problem that aroused much interest.
68. Review by G. F. McCleary, *Sociological Review*, 29 (July 1937), p. 310.
69. Membership included Lord Horder, Dr C. P. Blacker, Eva Hubback, Professors Julian Huxley, Lancelot Hogben and T. H. Marshall. The Eugenics Society donated £500 in 1937. Other prominent donors were Lawrence Cadbury (£200 for two years) and Seebohm Rowntree (£50). 'Population Investigation Committee: First annual report', *Eugenics Review*, 29 (January 1938), pp. 240—3. The Population Investigation Committee had been briefly preceded by a Positive Eugenics Committee sponsored solely by the Eugenics Society.
70. Political and Economic Planning unpublished memorandum, 'Population Policies Committee: Scope of investigation' (25 May 1938). In its memo on the development of family allowances the Committee stressed the family poverty arguments more than the pronatalist ones. Political and Economic Planning unpublished memorandum, 'Population Policies Committee: Family allowances as a population policy (17 October 1938).
71. F. Lafitte, 'The work of the Population Policies Committee', *Eugenics Review*, 31 (April 1939), pp. 49, 55.
72. For a full discussion, see D. V. Glass, *The Struggle for Population* (1936), esp. pp. 87—8.
73. ibid., p. 91.
74. A. M. Carr-Saunders, *World Population* (1936), pp. 256—7.
75. Hogben, op. cit. (1937), pp. 178—92.
76. For example, R. B. Cattell, in *The Fight for Our National Intelligence* (1937), p. 51, attributed the instability of South American governments to 'the low average mental capacity in South American half-breeds'. Replete with such statements, this work earned its author a D.Sc. from the University of London.
77. R. and K. Titmuss, *Parents Revolt* (1942), esp. pp. 116—23.

78. *Conservative Party Annual Conference Report for 1937*, pp. 37–43.

79. Press cutting from the *Manchester Guardian* (16 December 1924), Beveridge Papers, XII. 7.

80. Beveridge to Sir John Clapham (23 March 1937), ibid., IXb. 24.

81. McDougall, op. cit. (1933), p. 101.

82. *Social Insurance and Allied Services*, Cmd 6404 (1942), pp. 8, 154.

83. R. A. Fisher, *The Overproduction of Food* (1929), p. 60.

84. K. D. Courtney, *et al.*, *Equal Pay and the Family* (1918), pp. 31–4.

85. For an outline of this view, see M. Stocks, *The Case for Family Endowment* (1927), pp. 73–83.

86. E. Rathbone, *Family Endowment in its Bearing on the Question of Population* (1924), p. 2.

87. E. Rathbone, *The Disinherited Family* (1924), p. 232.

88. E. Rathbone, 'The remuneration of women's services', *Economic Journal*, 27 (March 1917), p. 66.

89. *The Disinherited Family*, p. 239.

90. Press cutting of 17 February 1924, Beveridge Papers, XII. 6.

91. Eva Hubback and Marjorie Green, 'Family endowment: a proposal for constructive eugenics in England', *Eugenics Review*, 25 (April 1933), p. 34.

92. 1936 'Circular to constituents', p. 3, Eleanor Rathbone Papers, XIV. 3. 4.

93. R. A. Fisher, 'The biological effects of family allowances', *Family Endowment Chronicle*, 1 (November 1931), p. 21.

94. op. cit., pp. 20–2.

95. M. Green, The case for family allowances', *Social Service Review*, 20 (February 1939), pp. 45–8.

96. Press cutting from *News Chronicle* (8 January 1937), Marjorie Green Papers. Admittedly, the emphasis in the title was probably the work of a sub-editor.

97. See, for example, E. Rathbone, *The Case for Direct Provision for Dependent Families through Family Allowances* (Family Endowment Society pamphlet, 1936).

98. *Hansard* (Lords), vol. 113 (21 June 1939), col. 612.

99. The *Eugenics Review* saw voluntary sterilization as 'an added liberty, a humane and honourable alternative for hereditarily afflicted men and women who to-day have no choice except between celibacy or the risk of transmitting their defect', op. cit.,

26 (April 1934), p. 3. The Eugenics Society was always opposed to compulsory sterilization.

100. ibid., 20 (October 1928), pp. 166–8. Letters from various organizations to Neville Chamberlain, Minister of Health, in PRO MH 58/103.
101. C. P. Blacker, 'The sterilisation proposals', *Eugenics Review*, 22 (January 1931), p. 240; pamphlets in PRO MH 58/103; *Hansard*, vol. 255 (21 July 1931), cols. 1250–6.
102. Material relating to the Committee's appointment in PRO MH 58/104A.
103. *Report of the Departmental Committee on Sterilisation*, Cmd 4485 (1934), p. 57.
104. Robinson to Chamberlain (18 April 1929), PRO MH 58/103.
105. T. Burns (organizing secretary, Catholic Federation) to Chamberlain (28 February 1929), ibid.
106. Labour Party Research and Information Department, Public Health Advisory Committee unpublished memorandum, 'The causes and prevention of mental deficiency' (July 1929), ibid.
107. Letters in PRO MH 58/103.
108. *Hansard*, vol. 255 (21 July 1931), cols. 1250–6.
109. 'Note of deputation' (23 May 1935), PRO MH 58/100.
110. Memoranda by Percy, 'The population problem in England and Wales' (January–February 1936), PRO RG 26/10.
111. Memorandum by Vivian, 'Lord Eustace Percy's Memorandum' (February 1936), ibid.
112. *Parliamentary Papers*, 1937–8, IV, p. 147. A brief but interesting account (based partly on General Register Office papers and partly on personal recollection) of the campaign by demographers for better birth registration, resulting in the 1938 Act, is contained in D. V. Glass, *Numbering the People* (1973), pp. 170–80.
113. Note by Registrar-General's department (February 1937), and Ministry of Health memorandum 'Optimum Population' (February 1937), PRO MH 58/311.
114. Cabinet meeting of 16 January 1935, Cabinet 4(35), PRO CAB 23/81.
115. For example, N. Branson and M. Heinemann, *Britain in the Nineteen Thirties* (1973 edn), pp. 182–3.
116. *Report of the Commissioners of Inland Revenue for 1929*, Cmd 3500, pp. 67, 70.
117. *Hansard*, vol. 216 (24 April 1928), cols. 871–2.

118. ibid., vol. 219 (27 June 1928), cols. 642–4.
119. ibid., vol. 300 (15 April 1935), col. 1634.
120. For example, speech by Sir F. Sanderson, ibid., vol. 320 (9 February 1937), col. 214.
121. *Report of the Commissioners of Inland Revenue for 1939*, Cmd 6099, p. 53.
122. For example, *Hansard*, vol. 337 (29 June 1938), cols. 1893–1900.
123. For example, ibid., vol. 324 (8 June 1937), cols. 1607–11.
124. Statement by Lord Templemore (government spokesman), *Hansard* (Lords), vol. 113 (21 June 1939), cols. 643–4.
125. Statement by R. Bernays (Parliamentary Secretary to the Ministry of Health), *Hansard,* vol. 344 (28 February 1939), cols. 1088–9.
126. Membership of the Eugenics Society was only about 650 in 1938. *Eugenics Review*, 30 (April 1938), p. 11.

5   Family Allowances and Unemployment

Although the family poverty and pro-natalist arguments for family allowances made little impression on the government in the interwar years, there was one area of social policy in which the family endowment principle did become increasingly important. This was in the various income—maintenance policies towards the unemployed, and this chapter will show how the recognition of family needs in unemployment policy gradually developed in the interwar years until it finally pointed to the need for family allowances in wages.

The original scheme of state unemployment insurance took no account of family needs. The 1911 National Insurance Act provided unemployment benefit at the very low rate of 7s 0d per week for adult men and 3s 6d for youths, at a time when poverty-line wages were in the region of 20s 0d per week; only 2¼ million men out of a total male workforce of 10 million were covered, in trades where unemployment was fairly predictable; and numerous restrictions were attached (for example, benefit was payable for only fifteen weeks in any insurance year). The scheme, in short, was firmly based on actuarial principles rather than any concept of need.[1]

During the First World War, unemployment fell to insignificant levels. Thus although the extension of insurance to munitions workers in 1916 nominally raised the number of insured workers to nearly 4 million by July 1918,[2] there was a rapid fall in the amount paid out in benefit — with the result that the insurance fund showed a healthy balance of £15 million at the end of the War.[3] With the ending of the War, however, there came the first rude shocks to the system, and thereafter government policies to maintain the unemployed were plagued with problems.

The full story of the breakdown of unemployment insurance in the period 1918—34 is an infinitely complex one, and has been described in detail by a number of writers;[4] perhaps it is enough to mention that between 1920 and 1934 forty separate unemployment insurance acts were passed. What particularly concerns this study is the way that out of the confused succession of temporary expedients, *ad hoc* solutions and last-minute compromises that constituted unemployment income—maintenance policy in these years there quickly emerged two vitally important principles which, once introduced, proved impossible to remove thereafter and eventually created an anomalous situation for which family allowances were one of two alternative solutions. The first principle was the recognition of family needs in unemployment benefit via the payment of dependants' allowances; the second was the state's commitment to supporting the able-bodied unemployed at some sort of subsistence level separate from the Poor Law.[5]

Both originated in the system of out-of-work donation introduced on 25 November 1918. This had begun as a scheme of relief for ex-servicemen unable to find jobs on demobilization, but with the abrupt ending of the War and in the absence of any comprehensive plan for an enlarged unemployment insurance scheme to ease the transition from war to peace, it was hurriedly extended to civilians as well. The original military out-of-work donation scheme had been based on separation allowances, and thus both it and the civilian scheme included child allowances: in addition to benefits of 29s 0d per week for men and 25s 0d per week for women there were payments of 6s 0d per week for the first child under 15 years of age and 3s 0d per week for each subsequent child.[6] Such amounts were well in excess of what the ordinary unemployment insurance scheme was paying, and the existence of dependants' allowances made the discrepancy even more marked in the case of family men. However, the implications of this were either little understood or else ignored by social administrators in the immediate post-First World War years, and instead of introducing a completely reorganized scheme to meet the needs of all able-bodied unemployed Lloyd George's Coalition Government stumbled through a series of 'temporary' solutions to meet each new crisis as it arose.

There were two main reasons for this policy of expediency. In the first place, there was an understandable lack of appreciation by politicians and civil servants of the way that the War had speeded up long-term economic changes in Britain and was about to usher in two decades of mass unemployment. Out-of-work donation was thus viewed as a purely temporary scheme to bridge the gap from war to peace, and every extension of it tended to be viewed by the Cabinet as 'an emergency and temporary arrangement to meet the altogether exceptional conditions produced by the War'.[7] This view was encouraged by the healthy state of the main unemployment insurance scheme: by the end of 1920 the insurance fund had accumulated a balance of over £21 million, in spite of the fact that benefits had been raised in 1919 without a corresponding increase in contributions.[8] Thus even after the attempt at reorganization via the 1920 Unemployment Insurance Act continuing high unemployment was seen by the Cabinet as 'abnormal, due to exceptional circumstances, and greatly aggravated by the Coal Strike'.[9] As late as 1930 the Cabinet was still convinced by a memorandum from the Minister of Labour that 'the exhaustion of the Unemployment Fund is due to an abnormal and unforeseen increase in unemployment, which is world-wide in character'.[10] Indeed, it was probably only after the 1931 economic crisis that politicians and civil servants fully accepted that mass unemployment was long term.

The second reason for the many extensions of insurance was the political impossibility of throwing destitute unemployed ex-servicemen onto the resources of private charity or the Poor Law. Not to provide a special scheme of insurance for these men might have caused them to express their resentment in violent political demonstrations. Between 25 November 1918 and 31 March 1921 military out-of-work donation was 'temporarily' renewed four times for this reason. It had been due to expire on 24 November 1919, but the Cabinet decided that unemployed ex-servicemen could not be left without any means of subsistence over the winter months, and agreed to a further period at slightly lower rates which were closer to what was being contemplated for the eventual reorganized scheme.[11] Four months later there had to be another extension, until July 1920.[12] By then the situation had actually worsened, and the Minister of Labour, Thomas Macnamara, was being warned by numerous ex-servicemen's organizations not to attempt any cuts in out-of-work donation.[13] Macnamara was well aware that if unemployed ex-servicemen were left destitute they could create the sort of politically volatile situation that would be 'eagerly exploited by the Socialist organizations'; and besides, public opinion would not tolerate these men having to apply for Poor Relief after all they had done for their country.[14] By September Macnamara was warning his Cabinet colleagues that the growing industrial troubles were making the situation even more dangerous.[15] Thus in February 1921 the 330 000 ex-servicemen on the dole were incorporated into the main insurance scheme, but only at the expense of raising all adult men's benefits to 20s 0d per week (the level of military out-of-work donation), thus putting a severe strain on the finances of the insurance fund.[16]

Meanwhile, in the previous August the government had introduced the 1920 Unemployment Insurance Act, which extended coverage to over 11 million workers in all trades except agriculture, private domestic service, railways and certain categories of public employment. This Act formed the basis of subsequent unemployment insurance legislation, and was a somewhat unrealistic re-assertion of 1911 principles: benefits were still designed to be a small 'tiding-over' sum to encourage saving, contributions were to be kept low, and unemployment was envisaged as a short-term phenomenon. Perhaps the most striking illustration of governmental optimism was that the Act made allowance for an unemployment rate of only 5·32 per cent, yet in the years immediately following the annual average rate of unemployment in the insured trades was 12·7 per cent (1922), 11·0 per cent (1923), 10·0 per cent (1924) and 11 per cent (1925).[17] Not surprisingly, within eight months of the Act's passage the solvency of the insurance fund had been destroyed.

It was against this confused background that there occurred in 1921 an event of crucial importance to the development of family allowances — the introduction of dependants' allowances into the main unemployment insurance scheme. Given the policy-making chaos of the years 1918—21, it is not surprising that no clear picture emerges of exactly when it was decided to introduce them. All that can be done is to identify the various factors that led to the establishment of this important family endowment precedent in government policy.[18]

The immediate impetus seems to have come from the Prime Minister, Lloyd George. Throughout 1920—1 the Cabinet had become increasingly concerned about the political and economic consequences of continuing high unemployment. Schemes for reviving trade and providing relief works for the unemployed were under frequent discussion, and ministers were very concerned over the possible political consequences of transferring the unemployed ex-servicemen to the main insurance scheme, which would involve a drastic cut in their benefit levels. A Cabinet Committee on Unemployment was therefore established on 7 September 1920 to monitor the constantly-changing situation.[19]

A year later a crisis point was reached. The Committee realized that something extra would have to be done for the unemployed over the coming winter, and was being pressed to introduce some comprehensive and generous unemployment relief system which would be distinct from the Poor Law yet would not be restricted to those with satisfactory contribution records. The decisive pressure was exerted by a group of Labour mayors from London, who sent a deputation to the Committee on 16 September 1921. They argued that in a period of mass unemployment some alternative to the Poor Law would have to be provided for men who had no entitlement to unemployment benefit; ratepayers in high unemployment areas were bearing the brunt of supporting the unemployed, who were in fact a national problem.[20]

The mayors received little response from Sir Alfred Mond, chairman of the Committee, and therefore decided to visit Lloyd George, who was on holiday at Gairloch in Scotland. The mayors were kept waiting for four days while Lloyd George recovered from a serious tooth infection, and as a result the deputation was fairly acrimonious.[21] The mayors were convinced that the government was doing virtually nothing to help the unemployed, and provided vivid descriptions of the intensity of political feeling among them: the Mayor of Hackney, Herbert Morrison, warned that

> there is a bitter feeling and a sheer lack of faith in the whole of the institutions of the State which is growing among these bands of hungry and desperate men. As time goes on the leadership of unemployed organizations will tend to be rather distinct from the organized Labour Movement, and the leadership may get into hands which cannot be looked upon with ease.

In reply Lloyd George maintained that his government had done more for the unemployed than any previous one, and said a national relief scheme would be impossibly costly; but he agreed that existing rates of unemployment benefit were too low, and promised to give the matter consideration.[22]

Unemployment was discussed at Gairloch over the next ten days (several members of the Cabinet being present), and among a number of proposals eventually agreed upon was one to set up a special temporary distress fund to finance the payment of dependants' allowances in the main insurance scheme: this suggestion was put to the Cabinet Committee on Unemployment by Lloyd George on 6 October, and it was decided to investigate it via a small Relief of Distress Committee under Sir Robert Munro, Secretary of State for Scotland.[23]

The Relief of Distress Committee met in an atmosphere of growing alarm over the political threat posed by the unemployed. Throughout September, while Lloyd George was in Scotland, the Minister of Labour, Thomas Macnamara, was reminding his Cabinet colleagues of the serious situation that lay ahead: the coming winter would see between one and one-and-a-half million unemployed forced to live solely off unemployment benefit — a situation which would give communists 'an opportunity the like of which they have not yet had'.[24] The Home Office was closely monitoring the activities of those who organized demonstrations by the unemployed (even to the extent of opening their mail and infiltrating their organizations) and repeatedly sent warnings to the Cabinet.[25] Thus by early October the Cabinet Committee on Unemployment was well aware that without some positive action 'the Government might find themselves in the position of having alienated the whole of the working class, who might sweep away all parties, put in their own people, and in the first flush of their success undertake experiments which would endanger the life of the community'.[26]

Faced with this urgency, the Relief of Distress Committee took little time in coming to a decision on dependants' allowances. The only alternative discussed was whether the emergency distress provision should be made in kind — for example, by coupons exchangeable for food,[27] or by soup-kitchens run by Boards of Guardians (who would receive government grants).[28] But this would be administratively complex, and would have insufficient guarantees against fraud. Dependants' allowances could simply copy the out-of-work donation system.[29] On 11 October, therefore, the Committee decided to recommend the setting up of a temporary distress fund for six months only, the finance of which would be kept quite distinct from the main insurance fund, with different stamps and cards: contributions of 2d each from employer and employee, and 3d from the state (with reduced rates for women and juveniles) would provide 5s 0d per week for a wife and 1s 0d per week for each dependent child.[30] On 19 October Lloyd George made a long statement to the House of Commons on new unemployment measures, and in the course of it announced the introduction of the allowances.[31]

In the short term, therefore, Lloyd George played a key role. But in the long term it must be remembered that the idea of family endowment in unemployment benefit had been under discussion for some time. Lord Aberconway's Committee of Inquiry into out-of-work donation had discussed it in 1919, as had Ministry of Labour officials.[32] Six months before dependants' allowances were actually introduced Macnamara told the House of Commons that the government had been considering the idea for a long time.[33] And there is evidence to suggest that as early as 1914 the Treasury had considered extending the scope of income tax downwards, using the machinery of the 1911 National Insurance Act, with rebates for wives and children.[34]

Outside the government, demands for higher benefits plus dependants' allowances had been coming from the Labour movement. A special TUC—Labour Party conference in January 1921 had discussed a motion calling for benefits of 50 per cent of average earnings, with an additional 10 per cent for a dependent wife and 5 per cent for each dependent child under the age of 16 years (subject to an income limit), and eventually had recommended benefits of 40s 0d per week for each householder, 25s 0d per week for single men or women with child allowances.[35]

Within the House of Commons, the question of differentiation between married and single unemployed was discussed periodically throughout 1921. In February, Labour speakers pressed hard for a recognition of family needs in unemployment benefit and found the government not unsympathetic: Macnamara agreed it was 'common-sense' for married men to receive more, but insisted that dependants' allowances would destroy the solvency of the insurance fund and would create administrative problems, such as what to do if employers discriminated against married men (who would cost them more in contributions).[36] Macnamara absolutely refused to deviate from the insurance principle, but Labour speakers insisted that in a period of mass unemployment, benefits had to be fixed at 'full maintenance':[37] the government was proposing to pay only 15s 0d per week to an unemployed man, yet was prepared to pay £1 19s 1d to maintain a lunatic in an asylum.[38] Thus when the introduction of dependants' allowances was debated on 1 November 1921 the family endowment principle was little commented on, and the only criticism made by MPs was that the child allowances should have been higher.[39]

The government's original intention had been to keep the finance of dependants' allowances separate from the main insurance fund, so that when 'normal' conditions improved they could be wound up. The 1921 Unemployed Workers' Dependants' (Temporary Provisions) Act had thus stipulated that they should only operate for six months. However, in March 1922 it was decided to continue them for a further temporary period;[40] in April 1922 they were formally amalgamated with the main scheme;[41] and in February 1923 the Cabinet decided to make them permanent.[42] In 1924 the child allowance was raised to 2s 0d per week, and the scope of the scheme was enlarged; the wife's allowance was raised in 1928 to 7s 0d per week, raised again in 1930 to 9s 0d, and lowered in 1931 to 8s 0d, with the child allowance remaining unchanged.[43]

Thus dependants' allowances were introduced into the main unemployment insurance system with little controversy about the precedents and implications. Civil servants appear to have been mainly concerned about the new administrative problems,[44] with the Ministry of Labour finding it simplest to copy the wartime separation allowance regulations.[45] From the government's point of view, dependants' allowances were politically attractive in as much as they prevented hundreds of thousands of families from having to apply to the Poor Law — popular with the unemployed themselves and with ratepayers in high-unemployment areas.[46] But more importantly, they were also a way of holding down main benefit levels: in the autumn of 1921 the insurance fund was paying out over £1·4 million per week and falling badly into debt,[47] yet the government was under great political pressure to raise benefits all round; faced with this situation, the Cabinet realized that the introduction of dependants' allowances would be far cheaper than all-round increases in benefits or special grants to Boards of Guardians.[48] In March 1922 when the continuation of dependants' allowances was being considered within the Cabinet, discussion centred on their attractiveness as a means of holding down or even reducing benefit levels for the unmarried childless unemployed.[49]

Evidently, therefore, the government's desire to keep as many as possible of the able-bodied unemployed (the most politically volatile section of the community) off the Poor Law, plus the tendency to see every new policy as a temporary expedient, meant that the most important implication of dependants' allowances was little discussed in the years 1918–23. This was that they could lead to an erosion of the principle of less eligibility by entitling an unemployed man with a large family to a level of benefit near to, or even more than, he could earn in a wage-system that was not adjusted to family needs. However, in 1923 and 1924 this problem began to be considered by civil servants as part of the 'all-in insurance' discussions of those years, and some interesting views emerged.

The 'all-in insurance' activity of 1923–4 was directed towards a number of aims; the removing of the many anomalies that had developed in social administration;[50] the formulation of some kind of new assistance scheme for those able-bodied unemployed who had no entitlement to insurance benefit, yet one that would not smack of the Poor Law;[51] the examination of the possibility of insurance by industry;[52] and the unification of health and unemployment insurance.[53] These subjects had been discussed inside and outside the government for some time, and with the ending of Lloyd George's Coalition in October 1922 each of the three main political parties began to cast about for social policy reforms that would be electorally popular. A number of committees of civil servants were appointed, the most important of which was the interdepartmental committee under Sir John Anderson, Permanent Secretary at the Home Office.[54]

The members of the Anderson Committee realized that 'as soon as political and industrial conditions permit', a complete reorganization of social services to the unemployed would have to be undertaken.[55] It was impossible to allow a large section of the unemployed to remain semi-permanently on the Poor Law: the unemployed themselves would not tolerate it; in some areas Boards of Guardians were deliberately paying over-generous relief scales and making it financially more profitable for men with large families to remain unemployed; and many Boards of Guardians were demanding that the relief of all able-bodied unemployed should be made a charge on national finances.[56] Yet to solve the problem by endless extensions of insurance benefit would mean that 'the stigma now attaching to the Poor Law Relief might, in course of time, also attach to discretionary unemployment benefit if such benefit were derived from a fund not resting on an independent contributory basis'.[57]

The solution was seen by the Anderson Committee as a classification of the unemployed into three distinct groups. At the top would be those whose contribution record entitled them to unemployment benefit under a new insurance scheme which would be run strictly on actuarial principles, with no extended benefit. Below them, the long-term unemployed would be paid uncovenanted benefits out of a separate 'distress fund', the solvency of which would be guaranteed by the Treasury;[58] applicants to this new scheme would have to prove that they were 'genuinely seeking work and unable to find it', and in dealing with them the Minister of Labour would have new enlarged powers of discretion 'to refuse benefit in order to eliminate "unemployables" and persons to whom benefit is a temptation to remain in idleness'.[59] At the bottom of this three-tier system would be the Poor Law; the future of this was very much under discussion, and there were plans to abolish it, but until then, having had the able-bodied unemployed removed from its scope, it would be left to deal with categories like the old, the sick, widows — in other words, 'that residuum of misfortune, improvidence and unfitness which defies classification'.[60]

This, however, would create a problem. In any such reorganization, the whole relationship between wages, benefit rates and assistance would need to be clearly defined. In answering this problem,

the Anderson Committee evidently had in mind a three-tier classification of the unemployed that would go beyond mere administrative
demarcation and would also have economic and moral components.
A three-tier structure of less eligibility would have to be established,
with each level carrying a different degree of social stigma. Before
the Committee met, T. W. Phillips (Principal Assistant Secretary at the
Ministry of Labour) outlined his department's view that

> a person in receipt of insurance benefit should be less well off
> than a person in receipt of wages and that a person disentitled
> to benefit should be less well off than a person receiving benefit.
> Whereas the old Poor Law held that the condition of the man
> relieved must of necessity be less eligible than that of the man
> maintaining himself, a second intermediate grade, that of the
> insured man, should ultimately be introduced.[61]

Thus if the principle of insurance as a stigma-free payment was to
be preserved, the unemployed man on the proposed new relief scheme
must be made to feel worse off than his insured counterpart.[62] One
way of achieving this might be to introduce a labour test which could
be disguised as re-training, 'but for a large proportion of the applicants
it is essential that it should be unattractive and if possible that it
should be generally regarded as carrying a social stigma'.[63] There was
concern that under the existing system in many economically depressed
areas the unemployed were receiving unemployment benefit and Poor
Law assistance simultaneously, resulting in payments which frequently
came near to, or even exceeded, prevailing low wage rates: without a
careful re-drawing of the boundaries between wages, benefit and
assistance such practices could spread rapidly.[64]

The principle of dependants' allowances appears to have been
accepted unquestioningly by the Anderson Committee. Indeed, it was
even decided that in the new scheme for the able-bodied, child allowances might be raised to 1s 6d per week.[65] However, in the surviving
papers of the Committee there is evidence that the implications of
such a policy were just beginning to be seen: if these child allowances
were raised above 1s 6d, 'the possible interaction of benefit and wages
in low-paid employment would have to be taken into consideration.
It would probably not be possible so to increase dependants' benefit
without at the same time revising the scale of benefits to a man and
wife'.[66]

The evidence left by the all-in insurance activity of 1923—4 is
interesting for a number of reasons, but what concerns this study is

the way that it marks the first expression of concern over the problem
that was to grow in the 1920s and 1930s and eventually point the way
to family allowances in wages –· the impossibility, in a low-wage economy, of preserving less eligibility while public opinion demanded that
benefit and assistance levels take some account of varying family
needs.

For the whole of the 1920s, however, this remained a theoretical
problem, and not a practical one, for the simple reason that even with
dependants' allowances, benefits of 15s 0d per week for men and
12s 0d per week for women were well below low wage levels. In 1923,
for example, Sir Montague Barlow, the Minister of Labour, was questioned on this point and replied that the Ministry of Labour knew of
no cases where earnings for a full week in the insured occupations
were lower than rates of benefit.[67] When Lloyd George had originally
announced the introduction of dependants' allowances he had said
that they would be subject to a maximum limit of 9s 0d per week,[68]
but evidently this was an economy measure rather than one for preserving less eligibility, for in the face of parliamentary opposition
Macnamara later agreed to drop this condition.[69] Three years later,
when looking back on this, Macnamara maintained that the figure
of 1s 0d week per child was 'all we could do at the time', given
the state of the fund, and implied that he would have liked the figure
to be higher.[70] In 1927 the Blanesburgh Committee looked at the question of benefit rates and re-affirmed that a cardinal principle of an
insurance scheme was that 'it should provide benefits definitely less
in amount than the general labourer's rate of wages, so that there may
be no temptation to prefer benefit to work', but went on to discuss
the problem of how far insurance benefits should be needs-related.[71]
Indeed, the only instances of less eligibility becoming a practical
problem in the 1920s are to be found in certain parts of the country
where Boards of Guardians made public assistance payments in excess
of prevailing low wage rates, particularly in the case of large families.[72]

However, by the early 1930s the preservation of less eligibility was
beginning to become a problem. The reason for this was, quite simply,
the rise in the real value of benefits. Between 1920 and 1930 the
amount of unemployment benefit received by an adult man with a
wife and two children doubled, from 15s 0d to 30s 0d; yet at the same
time the cost of living fell by about 43 per cent, and, more importantly,
the money value of wages fell by about 33 per cent.[73] By the early
1930s, therefore, the danger foreseen by the Ministry of Labour in
1923—4 was becoming a reality: an unemployed man with a very

large family could receive in benefit an amount that came close to low wage levels. After the creation of the Unemployment Assistance Board (UAB) and the Unemployment Insurance Statutory Committee (UISC) by the 1934 Unemployment Act this problem grew until by the end of the 1930s it dominated income—maintenance policies to the unemployed.

The 1934 Unemployment Act set up a three-tier system of relief to the unemployed. At the top, the UISC acted as a financial watchdog administering a new, strictly actuarial insurance scheme under which the insurance fund's debt, which had been caused by the endless extensions of benefit entitlement since 1920 and amounted to £105 780 000 in 1934, would eventually be paid off. In the middle was the UAB, another ostensibly independent committee of social policy experts: it ran a new relief scheme according to strictly defined regulations and purported to remove the sensitive question of means-tested, needs-related payments to the long-term unemployed from the arena of local and central party politics; the UAB thus took over the functions of the controversial Public Assistance Committees as regards the able-bodied unemployed, and also dealt with those who had previously been living on 'extended' insurance benefit. At the bottom of this three-tier structure, the Public Assistance Committees provided relief for the miscellaneous categories of destitution (the old, the sick, widows with children). Most historians have attributed the 1934 Act to the complex turmoil of events during 1930—4, but clearly what was established in 1934 was the threefold classification suggested by the Ministry of Labour ten years earlier.[74]

The Unemployment Assistance Board was one of the most controversial bodies in twentieth-century British social policy. Its claim that it was 'taking relief out of politics' and administering means-tested, needs-related relief in a spirit of independence and fairness was ridiculed by critics, who claimed that the Board was in fact a device for removing the politically explosive question of relief from Parliament's influence, that it was designed to impose bureaucratic control over the long-term (and hence potentially more discontented) unemployed, and that its avowed independence was a sham.[75] The Board's members (Lord Rushcliffe as chairman, Sir Ernest Strohmenger, Violet Markham, Professor H. M. Hallsworth, Thomas Jones, M. A. Reynard, and five civil servants)[76] were acutely conscious of their unpopularity over such issues as the household means test, their exact constitutional status, and such incidents as the notorious 'standstill' of January and February 1935.[77]

Probably the greatest area of conflict between the Board and its critics was over its scales of relief. As indicated in previous chapters, it was on this point that Eleanor Rathbone and her supporters drew on the rapidly-expanding volume of nutritional research into minimum human needs, and campaigned vigorously for the Board's scales to be drawn up in accordance with some publicly-announced minimum nutritional standard. These scales were, after all, supposed to be needs-related. Clause 34 of the 1934 Act charged the Board with the promotion of the welfare of the unemployed, and Sir Henry Betterton, Minister of Labour, assured MPs that 'you cannot promote the welfare of a man unless you take into account his physical requirements'.[78] He also stressed that 'we have to provide that there shall be an opportunity for men to keep fit for employment'.[79] A similar assurance was given in the Board's first annual report.[80]

During the passage of the Bill, however, the government remained studiously vague over exactly how these needs would be calculated. To a deputation from the Children's Minimum Council Betterton insisted that he would calculate need in accordance with recent nutritional research,[81] but in Parliament he was less definite. At one point Eleanor Rathbone tried to introduce an amendment to the Bill which would commit the Board to a concept of need that would cover a 'reasonable amount' for rent, plus 'the minimum requirement of healthy physical subsistence' for the applicant and his dependants. 'If every item of the applicant's means and resources is to be taken into account, let every item of his needs be also taken into account', she suggested, and asked that the Board's scales be calculated on 'a basis which is fully worked out and clearly laid down by Parliament'; above all, the meaning of 'need' should be precisely defined.[82]

In reply, Betterton assured her that her amendment was unnecessary: the Board was committed to maintaining the unemployed at a healthy physical subsistence level, and the spirit of her amendment was implicit in the Board's regulations.[83] This reply seems to have satisfied most MPs, for throughout the many debates on the 1934 Bill there was little mention of this point again. Some speakers realized that the assistance scales would have to be lower than insurance benefit (which the government admitted to be below subsistence, since it was still based on the 1911 concept),[84] but most critics concentrated their attacks on the household means test and the Board's immunity from parliamentary control. Eleanor Rathbone, however, was far from satisfied. As already indicated in previous chapters, she began an intensive campaign through the Children's Minimum Council to influence the Board's members while they were still discussing proposed scale rates: in addition to deputations to government departments, the CMC sent many requests to the Board asking that it announce publicly the scientific basis for its scales,[85] and made sure that this campaigning received maximum publicity.[86]

But all this activity elicited virtually no response whatsoever from the Board's members, save for a feeling of mild irritation.[87] In their private discussions they began to grope towards the only definition of 'scientific minimum subsistence' that was open to them. Like the Ministry of Health, they well realized the consequences that would follow if they assessed minimum needs too highly, and thus it was decided that science would have to take second place to three all-important criteria — Treasury limitations, unemployment benefit levels and, most important of all, low wage rates.[88] At the fourth meeting of the Board, on 22, 24 and 25 July 1934, Wilfred Eady (the Board's secretary and a Ministry of Labour official) quickly warned of the wages problem: although they could supplement insurance benefit in exceptional cases, they must not touch on wages, since 'it would obviously have been a very dangerous principle if the Board had accepted any responsibility for the subsidy of low wages to wholly employed persons'. Sir Ernest Strohmenger followed by maintaining that even if under-nourishment existed in Britain, particularly among children, there was little evidence that it was confined to the households of the unemployed: 'in other words, under-nourishment might well prove to be a matter not so much of inadequate allowances as of bad use of income. It was very important that the Board should have this clearly in mind because they could not accept responsibility for general malnutrition'.[89]

Thereafter, discussion centred on the question of exactly how far below wage rates the Board's scales should be. One suggestion, for example, was that they should be anchored just below the levels of unskilled wages recognized by local Trades Councils. All members 'recognised that where there was a large family the scale came very near to, if it did not exceed, the earnings of low paid workers', and that therefore the problem was essentially one of keeping these 'overlap' cases to a minimum by arriving at the most appropriate scale levels. As Sir Ernest Strohmenger warned, to provide large children's allowances 'on the lines suggested by Miss Rathbone leads to the dilemma of either cutting across wage levels or of establishing a very low scale for childless couples'.[90] Eventually, the Board decided on the latter, and cut the married couple's allowance from 24s 0d to 22s 0d.[91]

This, therefore, was how the UAB calculated scientific minimum subsistence: 'the provision of allowances to meet need must be conditioned by wages'.[92] Professor Hallsworth warned his fellow members of the dangers of touching on wage levels; the Board's scales

> would be taken as representing the official standard of minimum subsistence over the whole country. The Board would be operating largely in areas whose wages are subject to world conditions. It would be a grave matter if the scale prevented any adaptation of the wage level which economic circumstances might require.

In other words, fixing the scales too high might make it impossible for industry to impose wage-cuts in the future if these became necessary. Eady firmly told the other members that there was 'no scientific standard for the calculation of all the needs to be covered by the Board; the matter was one of social convention and expediency. The Office had therefore proceeded on the principle of less eligibility'.[93] Previously, he had circulated two memoranda on this point, warning of the 'mischievous social consequences' if wage levels were exceeded, and reassuring his colleagues that the government had foreseen this problem: the Act's stipulation was that scales should be calculated 'by reference to' and not 'in accordance with' the applicant's needs – a legalistic difference that was designed to overcome this very difficulty and shield the Board from adverse criticism.[94] Low wages had to be accepted as an unavoidable feature of industrial life; to make the unemployed better off than the employed 'would be resented not only by employers but, more strongly, by other workpeople'.[95] In any case, the Ministry of Labour claimed, by the standards of most nutritional research the Board's scales *were* adequate for households with fewer than three children.[96]

Given this method of assessing need, it was hardly surprising that the Board refused to take up the challenges of the Children's Minimum Council. When answering its critics it claimed on the one hand that its scales were based on the findings of the BMA, the Ministry of Health Advisory Committee on Nutrition, the Merseyside Survey and the New Survey of London; yet on the other hand it was careful to qualify this by asserting that there was as yet 'no absolute criterion or scientific basis of need'.[97]

When the Board eventually published its scales and put them into operation they were criticized fiercely by groups such as the CMC as being manifestly inadequate, and a betrayal of Betterton's original promises in Parliament.[98] In 1936, for example, the CMC pointed out

that using the BMA nutrition standard, the Merseyside Survey's estimate of expenditure on clothing, light and fuel, and the Board's own
basic rent scale, the following comparison could be made.[99]

*Table 5.1. The relationship between minimum needs, unemployment
benefit and UAB scales (1936)*

Man, wife and no. of children	Minimum needs	Standard unemployment benefit	UAB scale
1 child	29s 0½d	29s 0d	28s 0d
3 children	40s 0d	35s 0d	34s 6d
5 children	52s 3d	41s 0d	40s 6d

To empirical criticism such as this the Board either refused to reply,
or else invented the most convenient excuse. For example, in discussion
with the CMC it defended its policy of reducing allowances for children
in households of more than five members (by the sum of 1s 0d each)
by maintaining that with such an increase in numbers there was not an
equivalent increase in costs: for instance, clothes could be passed on to
younger children.[100] But in private its members admitted that

> the scaling down of children's allowances where there are three or
> more children is desirable because the graduated scale for children
> originally proposed, if allowed to operate fully, would quickly
> produce for the family of normal size allowances in excess of the
> wage rate, and thus necessitate the application of the 'stop'
> clause . . . too frequent application of this clause is likely to
> create dissatisfaction.[101]

The Board's position was hopeless. Having decided to follow the
principle of less eligibility, all that could be done in the face of hostile
criticism was to retreat along prepared lines, and its members were
instructed on what these should be. Critics should first be told that
no scientific calculation of minimum needs was possible. Then, if they
persisted, they should be told that if malnutrition did exist it was
not confined to the households of the unemployed. The final defence
against criticism such as Rowntree's contention, that a family of
five needed 53s 0d a week for the maintenance of health and efficiency,
was for the Board to wash its hands of all responsibility: 'the best
line of reply', members were told on this point, 'is probably that if
this were true, the Unemployment Assistance Board is a relatively

small member of a good company and that in order to bring this doctrine about the general wage structure of the country would have to be revolutionized'.[102]

It was precisely such a wage revolution that Eleanor Rathbone and her supporters believed they were campaigning for, and having had no success in forcing the Board to raise its scales during 1934 and 1935 they changed their line of attack: from 1935 onwards the Family Endowment Society and the Children's Minimum Council, realizing the Board's quandary, began to campaign for the whole problem to be tackled at the wages end by family allowances.

This new approach elicited a more favourable reaction from the Board's members, for now the problem of overlap with wages was beginning to exacerbate a situation about which they felt growing unease. As the economy began to pick up after 1934 the problem of the long-term unemployed assumed increasing importance. Would these men be able and willing to return to work once the economy had completely recovered? Would they refuse to enter jobs with wages only slightly higher than they had been receiving from the Board? Unemployment began to fall steadily from 1936, and in the following year the Board estimated that nearly 20 per cent of its male applicants had settled down to life on the dole.[103] 'What cumulative consequences are likely to pile up for the nation in a few years time', warned Violet Markham, 'if the dole habit spreads and grows and the theory of money for nothing becomes an established practice amongst the younger generation'?[104]

What the Board feared was not so much the numerical incidence of these overlap cases as their disproportionate effect on the work ethic of future generations. After all, in 1937 only about 6 per cent of the Board's applicants received allowances within 4s 0d of their normal wages; and only 1·3 per cent of male and 3·5 per cent of female applicants received allowances equal to or above their normal wages.[105] But since these cases occurred chiefly in households with a large number of children, evidently the Board's members feared that an increasing number of young married unemployed would regard large families as a way of maximizing their income and also pass on the 'dole habit' to their children.

From 1935 onwards, the Board's annual reports began to display a growing obsession with this problem. After only a year of operation, it was claimed that men with large families showed 'little disposition to take work or hold it when it is given to them'. The whole problem of the relationship between wages and assistance raised 'wider issues' which the Board felt 'should be examined on the widest basis in the near future'.[106] In 1938 there came an even stronger statement about the difficulties caused by this, difficulties which had 'far reaching implications and obviously raise questions of very serious social consequences which go beyond the problems which the Board alone are in a position to solve'.[107]

Furthermore, there was another serious long-term problem. By industrial standards, many of the Board's applicants were relatively old: 45 per cent of those in the age-range 18–64 were over 45 years old, as compared with only 27 per cent of claimants to insurance benefit, and thus it would be extremely difficult for these men to be re-absorbed into industrial life once prosperity returned.[108] This had been exacerbated by the changing age-distribution of the British population: in 1901, out of every 1000 people 149 had been aged between 44 and 65 years, but by 1935 this proportion had risen to 223. The Board's annual report for 1936 contained a passage on this very theme, reflecting the 'population panic' of the 1930s and warning that these older men would need a long period of re-training and industrial acclimatization before they became efficient workers. In a situation like this, any reluctance on the part of the younger, fitter men to return to work would be disastrous.[109]

Of course, those with a first-hand knowledge of the plight of the unemployed found exactly the opposite to be the case. Bakke, for example, discovered no evidence that the will to work was being destroyed, and gave as an example the instance of a job advertised in Birmingham for two men with their own bicycles, with wages of only £2 per week: nearly one thousand men tried to apply for it.[110] Admittedly, the hopeless task of searching out work when none was available often caused the long-term unemployed man's state of mind to progress 'from optimism to pessimism, from pessimism to fatalism', as Beales and Lambert put it.[111] But this usually happened only after months or years of fruitless searching: Max Cohen, for example, tramped the streets daily from nine to five o'clock in his 'compelling desire to find work'.[112]

However, by the late 1930s those in the upper strata of British society were evidently thinking differently, and were sharing the Board's fears. In the House of Lords the Bishop of Winchester was warning about the erosion of work-incentives[113] and during a debate on population problems the Archbishop of York talked of 'the obvious evil in the recruiting of the population largely from the unemployed ranks, and from those who are content to remain unemployed'.[114] Again, in 1938 *The Times* asserted that

> there are hundreds and thousands of young men who do not
> show any disposition to bestir themselves to get out of unem-
> ployment into employment . . . there is a slackness of moral
> fibre and of will as a muscle . . . salutory action is beyond dispute
> . . . the breakdown of morale can only be made good by applying
> compulsion.[115]

What forms of compulsion should be used? A number were discussed and tried — such as the stopping of an allowance if an applicant
refused to enlist in a re-training programme[116] — and eventually the
members of the Board began to realize that family allowances in wages
could be the answer. In May 1938 the Children's Minimum Council
submitted a memorandum making out the case for family allowances
as the only way of solving the overlap problem without having to
resort to 'the negative and inhuman device of keeping down unemployment pay'.[117] In reply, Violet Markham admitted that the memorandum stated 'very clearly a problem with which we are all familiar',[118]
and such evidence as can be gleaned from her private papers suggests
that her mind was working along these lines. For her, the problem of
the unemployed was part of the general problem of the low-wage
group, and she felt particular concern over 'the employed man with a
large family and a low wage who is obliged to struggle on without any
assistance from the State'.[119] In the face of this, she told Paul Cadbury,
'many of us who are concerned with unemployment are feeling more
and more than whatever differences of opinion there may be in the
method of application, the principle of family allowances is the only
way out of the morass in which we find ourselves'.[120]

Officially, the Board had no power to recommend anything as
drastic as family allowances, being a supposedly independent body
with limited terms of reference.[121] In fact, since the Board was pretty
closely controlled by the Ministry of Labour and the Treasury it is
likely that when it opened a file on family allowances in June 1938[122]
and began gathering information, the ground was being prepared for
possible future schemes based on the European equalization-fund
method. In September 1938 the Board began writing to firms in Britain
that already operated their own family allowance schemes, asking for
information.[123] Exactly what was being planned remains a mystery.

This gradual acceptance of the need for family allowances by the
UAB was at the same time being mirrored in the experiences of the

Unemployment Insurance Statutory Committee. The Committee's prime task was to pay off the unemployment insurance fund's debt at a rate of £5 million per annum. Its members were required to report on the condition of the fund not later than February each year (or at any other time, if necessary) and having reviewed the financial situation they could recommend any changes in benefit and contribution levels and ways of paying off the fund's debt.[124] In arriving at a decision, the Committee sought advice on the likely level of future unemployment from the Economic Information Committee of the Economic Advisory Council (represented by H. D. Henderson), and then received deputations from interested organizations like the National Confederation of Employers' Organisations, the TUC and — inevitably — the Children's Minimum Council.

Ostensibly, the Committee was an impartial body independent of direct government control, with its actions being dictated solely by the state of the fund. In practice, however, its independence was as much of a myth as the UAB's and, as with the latter, there was the usual remarkable coincidence between what the government wanted and what the Committee finally recommended. Like the UAB, it was designed to shield the Minister of Labour from the embarrassing task of resisting parliamentary and public pressure for higher benefit rates, and in addition was as much at the mercy of the Treasury as were conventional government departments. For example, the reduction in 'waiting time' from six days to three (introduced in 1937) was designed to cut the number of applicants who might apply for unemployment assistance during this period of no income (which could be up to a fortnight in practice, since benefit was paid at the end of the week), and thus widen the scope of insurance (33 per cent Treasury-financed) over assistance (100 per cent Treasury-financed).[125]

However, having Beveridge as chairman undoubtedly prevented the UISC from falling completely under Treasury and Ministry of Labour influence, since he was well versed in the tactical nuances of intra-governmental politicking.[126] In addition, direct pressure from government departments was less of a problem for the Committee than the indirect effect its actions had on other areas of social policy. It was here that the problem arose. When it was first established, the Committee's main worry seemed likely to be the repayment of the fund's debt; but owing to the decrease in unemployment each year the reverse happened, and the problem was how to dispose of a growing surplus.

Essentially, the Committee's task was to steer a path through a very tricky middle ground. On the one hand, it had to keep benefit levels above assistance scales; apart from being in line with Treasury policy of avoiding supplementation by the UAB, there was the political necessity of ensuring that applicants to a contributory scheme should always be better off than those receiving means-tested, tax-financed, discretionary payments. As a true 'insurance man', Beveridge charac- teristically saw this as a cardinal principle, 'not because he thought the applicant for assistance was a less deserving case but because the recipient of benefit had contributed for it', and the rest of the Com- mittee agreed.[127] However, this posed great problems. The govern- ment still adhered to the 1911 principle that insurance benefit was a supplement to savings, and should not represent full maintenance. Any criticism of benefit levels met with this response: they were dictated by the solvency of the fund, not the needs of the individual.[128] Yet at the same time benefits had to be kept above the UAB's scales — which the government insisted *were* needs-related. This contradiction was further heightened every time the UAB raised its scales, for on these occasions the Committee had to do likewise, all the time maintaining the fiction that such increases were solely due to the fund's improved financial condition.

On the other hand, benefits had to be kept below wages. Again Beveridge justified this in 'insurance' terms: 'unemployment benefit was intended to be an insurance against loss of wages, and in other forms of insurance it was never the practice to over-insure', he fre- quently reminded his colleagues on the Committee.[129] However, this vital principle that 'the indemnity should never be allowed to exceed the loss'[130] proved increasingly difficult to uphold. As the fund annually displayed a continuing surplus it became impossible for the Committee to resist pressure for higher benefits — which in turn made it harder and harder to keep benefits below wage levels. The fact that this occurred exclusively in families with a large number of children pointed to an obvious solution — the adjustment of wages to family size.

The first report of the Committee, for the year 1934, was very cautious. With benefits at 17s 0d per week for a man, 15s 0d per week for a woman, and dependants' allowances of 9s 0d for a wife and 2s 0d for each child, a surplus of almost £12½ million had been achieved, but the Committee felt it was too early to make any changes.[131] It merely outlined five possible ways this surplus could be disposed of: a reduction in contributions (favoured by the National Confederation of Employers' Organisations), an increase in child allowances (favoured by the TUC and the Children's Minimum Council), an increase in the adult man's benefit rate, an extension of the period of entitlement to benefit, and a reduction in the fund's outstanding debt.[132] These were generally the options throughout the 1930s, and deciding between them was by no means easy.

Beveridge was, of course, a staunch supporter of Eleanor Rathbone, and with Mary Stocks on the Committee the question of family endowment was obviously going to get sympathetic consideration. However, Beveridge was aware of the problems of introducing too great an element of needs-assessment into insurance; unemployment benefit he regarded as 'an extension of wages', and since 'the composition of the family is not taken into account in determining rates of wages . . . it was, therefore, a question whether it should be taken into account in determining rates of benefit'.[133] Higher child allowances were being strongly demanded by both the TUC and CMC, and thus in its special mid-year report of July 1935 the Committee attempted a compromise: a rise of 1s 0d per week in the child allowance was to be subject to an upper benefit limit of 41s 0d per week (equivalent to the rate for a man, wife and five children). This, the Committee maintained, was vital. Without it, cases of overlap would become much more common: an unskilled labourer with a wife and six children, normally earning 40s 0d per week, would be 4s 0d better off when unemployed. A wage-stop might be a better idea, but since contributions took no account of differing wage levels then neither should benefit. Families with more than five children could receive supplementation from the UAB — but only if they underwent the Board's means test and proved they had no resources.[134]

This upper limit was rejected by Ernest Brown, Minister of Labour, on the grounds that such a recommendation was outside the Committee's terms of reference,[135] and thereafter the problem of overlap began to loom larger and larger. In its report for 1935 the Committee called for a thorough investigation of the relations between wages, benefits and assistance, and in its first hint at family allowances it warned that 'the growing direct provision for families, under unemployment insurance and assistance, is beginning to raise acutely the general problem of dependency under a wage system which makes no similar provision'.[136]

In their private discussions, the Committee members were beginning to grasp the magnitude of their problems. By the end of 1935 the fund was making an embarrasingly healthy profit of £290 000 per week, and every indication was that this would continue. How should it be spent?

The easiest way out would be to leave benefits alone and concentrate on extending the scope of insurance as against assistance. Naturally, both the Treasury and the Ministry of Labour saw this as the best course, but both departments realized that it would not be possible to spend rather more than £17 million in this way over the next seven and a half years. Similarly, it would be politically very unpopular to devote the growing surplus solely to a reduction in the debt repayment period: such an action would benefit not the workers of the 1930s but their sons.[137]

Throughout 1936 and 1937 the Committee tried to find a way out of these difficulties, with no success. When asked its opinion, the TUC General Council pressed for child allowances of at least 5s 0d per week (being quite willing to see contributions raised to finance this), rejected the idea of differentiation between insurance and assistance (which they saw as divisive) and took the line that the real issue was not that benefits were too high but that wages were too low. They agreed that it would probably be wrong if benefit exceeded a man's normal wages, but opposed a wage-stop; in short, they could offer no solution, given existing low wage levels.[138] Similarly, a long meeting with three members of the UAB in November 1936 produced no answers.[139]

As in the case of the Board at this time, there now began to creep into the Committee's discussions fears about the possible long-term effects of this situation on work-incentives: as Mary Stocks put it, 'a man might find that he could do his duty to his family better by losing his job'.[140] A number of inquiries were made by the Ministry of Labour, all of which showed that reluctance to seek work because of high benefit was not widespread: job refusal, when it occurred, was caused more by factors such as the type of work or its location than by the size of the applicant's family.[141] As with the UAB, the problem of overlap was statistically very insignificant: families with more than five children made up only one-nineteenth of total claims; average benefit rates for men, including dependants' allowances, were only two-fifths of median wage rates — 24s 6d as against 55s 6d; thus only 2·3 per cent of men and 5·2 per cent of women were as well or better off when on benefit than when in employment. But, again, like the Board, it was a problem that the Committee felt would have dangerous long-term repercussions. Of the men on 41s 0d benefit, 10 per cent were as well or better off than when in employment, but of those on 50s 0d benefit the proportion was over one-third. The Committee was being pressed on all sides to raise child allowances by 1s 0d per week, but to do this would increase the incidence of overlap by one-third; and in the case of large families, by even more: at the 41s 0d rate of benefit it would rise from 10 per cent to 25 per cent.[142]

To Beveridge, this was complete anathema. Repeatedly, he expressed his dislike of 'over-insurance', and in the 1937 report finally suggested that there were only two possible remedies — a wage-stop or else family allowances in wages. The former had been rejected by the Minister of Labour in 1935. A recommendation of the latter was way outside the Committee's terms of reference; but nevertheless recommend them it did, on the grounds that 'if the wage system made allowance for dependency, the main objection to further increases in rates of benefit would be removed'.[143] The issue could no longer be dodged: with a growing surplus in the fund, benefits would have to be raised sooner or later, and the whole question of family dependency considered *in toto*.

In the event, the Committee did manage to avoid the problem for another year. Despite pressure from the TUC for further increases, the 1938 report simply recommended that the annual surplus be used to reduce the outstanding debt by £6 million per annum instead of £5 million.[144] The following year the Committee relented and raised child allowances to 4s 0d per week each for the first two children and 3s 0d for every other.[145] By then, however, the outbreak of war had changed everything.

By the late 1930s, therefore, both government bodies dealing with the able-bodied unemployed had come round to a virtual recommendation of family allowances. The family endowment principle had merged into unemployment insurance for a number of reasons: hurried administrative expediency in the case of the out-of-work donation; the political threat posed by the unemployed in the case of the 'temporary' introduction of dependants' allowances in 1921; and thereafter, family-adjusted benefits were seen as a relatively inexpensive way of mitigating the worst hardship, since such a system was cheaper than across-the-board benefit rises. By the 1930s, however, the rise in the real value of benefits turned into a reality that some civil servants in the early 1920s had discussed in theory — the problem of preserving less eligibility in the case of unemployed men with large families in a low-wage economy. By the late 1930s both the UAB and the UISC were urgently insisting that the problem could only be solved at the wages end.

This, however, raised acutely controversial issues and brought to head the two conflicting and irreconcilable attitudes that have always marked the history of family allowances. To those on the political left, this call for family allowances by the UAB and UISC merely obscured the real issue, which was that many industries were paying grossly substandard wages. Both bodies, they maintained, had followed a policy of less eligibility for fear of provoking a confrontation with industry. If rates of benefit and assistance were raised to nutritionally-defensible levels then the resultant enormous number of cases where it was more profitable to be unemployed than in work would simply demonstrate how many wage rates were below minimum human needs. If industry claimed it could not afford to pay adequate rates, then it should be reorganized on socialist lines and made more efficient; existing wage levels were a crushing indictment of capitalism. This was the line taken by most Labour MPs present in the Commons on 25 March 1938 when unemployment insurance was discussed.[146] Aneurin Bevan accused the UISC of being a body 'which regards it as its first duty to protect the wage system', and said it was very serious that many workers were receiving wages lower than insurance benefit, which everybody admitted was inadequate; rates of benefit had been fixed low for agricultural workers, for instance, because if they were higher then agricultural wages would have to be raised. Another Labour MP, George Tomlinson, said that if the Lancashire cotton industry continued to decline, then the majority of weavers there (numbering between 90 and 100 000 adults) would soon be on a wage less than unemployment benefit.[147]

One economist who investigated this point was Juergen Kuczynski. Using official Ministry of Labour figures for 1935, Kuczynski compared wage levels with Rowntree's 1937 'Human Needs' standard of 53s 0d per week for a man, wife and three children, emphasizing that in arriving at this figure Rowntree had pared down minimum needs to a most Spartan level and had allowed for no luxuries. The result showed that, for example, about two-thirds of the weavers in the cotton industry needed a rise in weekly full-time earnings of 33 per cent or more in order to come up to Rowntree's minimum. The proportion of workers in various industries who earned wages below this level was: coal mining, 80 per cent; railways, 25 per cent; building, 50 per cent; textiles, 40 per cent of men and 50 per cent of women; clothing, 12 per cent of men and 35 per cent of women. In all, 4 million adult male workers and 2 million adult female workers earned less than the Rowntree minimum which, including their dependants, made a total of 10 million people. Yet, maintained Kuczynski, although in the period 1931—8 unemployment benefit in real terms had fallen, and real wages had risen by only 5 per cent, industrial production per employed worker had risen fully 20 per cent.[148] Viewed in this light, family allowances were a way of perpetuating this system. They would raise the wages of married men just enough to shore up the principle of less eligibility, and the real issue of wages *vis-a-vis* profits would be neatly avoided.[149]

On the other hand, supporters of family allowances argued that overall wage rates were a separate issue. The situation in the late 1930s gave extra weight to their viewpoint, argued throughout the interwar years, that the three-child minimum wage would be both wasteful (in the case of families with fewer than three children) and inadequate (for families with more than three). The real problems of the UAB and UISC occurred only in very large families, and to try and solve the difficulty by basing a minimum wage on a family of great size was ridiculous, Duncan Sandys argued; the obvious solution was family allowances in wages.[150] Naturally, the Family Endowment Society leaders emphasized this argument in their late 1930s publications: Marjorie Green maintained that the level of wage increases industry could afford in the near future would be inadequate to solve the problem;[151] Mary Stocks deplored the situation where 'a man's economic environment should be so adjusted that the obviously remunerative course is a course which must in the end demoralise him as a worker and destroy his normal family status as a breadwinner — a course which involves him in the nerve-breaking tedium of enforced idleness', and likewise saw family allowances as the only way of raising the 'floor' of wages above the 'ceiling' of relief.[152]

By the end of the 1930s this latter view was being supported by many politically middle-of-the-road social investigators. There was a growing consensus that a complete reorganization of the social services was long overdue, and (especially interesting in the light of the Beveridge Report only a few years later) several writers suggested that some sort of statutory commission should be set up to do this, since these services had 'grown up in a very piecemeal way, without much regard either for consistency of principle or for the effect of one service on another'.[153] But, argued Political and Economic Planning (PEP), 'the failure of the wage-system to take any account of the disparities in family responsibilities is one of the greatest obstacles to further extensions of social provision'. Raising low wages might be one answer,

> but such a step would be quite impracticable, because it would dislocate the whole structure of differential rewards for skill, lay an impossible tax on many industries exposed to international

competition, and would, moreover, increase rather than diminish the contrasts in standards of living between workers in the same occupations with and without wives and children to maintain.

An attractive alternative would be a limited family allowance scheme of 5s 0d per week for each child after the third, which would cost £7 million per annum.[154] The Pilgrim Trust discussed the connection between large families and poverty, found that about two in five persons dependent solely upon unemployment assistance were being forced to live 'at a level that cannot be defended except on grounds of maintaining the wage incentive', and concluded that family-adjusted wages were the most appropriate answer.[155] If benefit and assistance rates were raised any higher, it was argued, then unemployment would increase;[156] an unemployed man could only be given full compensation for loss of employment if at the same time the state assumed new draconian powers of compulsion to ensure labour mobility and work-incentives.[157] The choice, maintained Gertrude Williams, was 'between the retention of a certain degree of personal freedom and a relatively inadequate subsistence for the unemployed on the one hand, and adequate maintenance and virtual slavery on the other'.[158]

To this section of opinion, therefore, family allowances in wages were the only way of ensuring adequate maintenance for the unemployed without destroying the work-incentives and labour mobility essential to the successful running of a free-market economy; in any reorganization of the social services family allowances would have to be introduced. To those on the political left, however, the real issue was capitalism's unwillingness or inability to pay decent wages; and family allowances were to be resisted at all costs, since they were simply a means of letting employers 'off the hook'. In its own way, this dilemma of the late 1930s was very similar to the dilemma faced by the 'Speenhamland' magistrates in 1795. They had managed to introduce a crude family allowance system as a means of avoiding having to introduce a statutory minimum wage. In the late 1930s it remained to be seen whether, given the opposition of the trade unions, the government could do the same.

Notes and References

1. *Report of the Unemployment Insurance Committee, 1927* (Blanesburgh Report) (1927), p. 9; Bentley B. Gilbert, *British Social Policy, 1914–1939* (1970), pp. 52–3.

2. In fact, there was widespread non-compliance among munitions workers.
3. Percy Cohen, *The British System of Social Insurance* (1931), p. 115.
4. ibid., pp. 115–48; Percy Cohen, *Unemployment Insurance and Assistance in Great Britain* (1938), pp. 19–37; Mary Barnett Gilson, *Unemployment Insurance in Great Britain* (1931), pp. 3–63; Eveline M. Burns, *British Unemployment Programs, 1920–38* (1941), pp. 35–110; Gilbert, op. cit., pp. 51–97.
5. Emphasized in Derek Fraser, *The Evolution of the British Welfare State* (1973), p. 170.
6. These were the rates from 12 December 1918. *Final Report of the Committee of Inquiry into the Scheme of Out-of-Work Donation*, Cmd 305 (1919), pp. 3–4.
7. Cabinet meeting of 6 November 1919, Cabinet 3(19), PRO CAB 23/18.
8. Blanesburgh Report, op. cit., p. 11.
9. Cabinet meeting of 1 June 1921, Cabinet 46(21), PRO CAB 23/26.
10. Cabinet meeting of 26 March 1930, Cabinet 17(30), PRO CAB 23/62.
11. Cabinet meetings of 5–7 November 1919, Cabinet 2–4(19), PRO CAB 23/18.
12. Cabinet meeting of 22 March 1920, Cabinet 15(20), PRO CAB 23/20.
13. Letters from these organizations in PRO T 161/41 (S.2585).
14. Cabinet memoranda by Minister of Labour, 'Out-of-Work Donation' (17 and 24 July 1920), ibid.
15. Cabinet meeting of 30 September 1920, Cabinet 53(20), PRO CAB 23/22.
16. Gilbert, op. cit., pp. 78–9.
17. R. C. Davison, *The Unemployed: Old Policies and New* (1929), pp. 97–9; Blanesburgh Report, op. cit., p. 12.
18. Several historians have noted the importance of this precedent. See, for example, C. L. Mowat, *Britain Between the Wars* (1966 edn), p. 128.
19. Minutes of the Committee in PRO CAB 27/114.
20. Cabinet Committee on Unemployment, 'Notes taken of a deputation of London Mayors, etc., on 16 September 1921', Lloyd George Papers, F/196/7/7.
21. For brief accounts, see B. Donoughue and G. W. Jones, *Herbert*

Morrison, Portrait of a Politician (1973), p. 49; Peter Rowland, *Lloyd George* (1975), p. 534; Lord Morrison, *Herbert Morrison, an Autobiography* (1960), pp. 84—5.

22. 'Report of a meeting between the Prime Minister and London Labour mayors at Gairloch, September 22nd, 1921', Lloyd George Papers, F/196/7/6.

23. Minutes of Cabinet Committee on Unemployment (6 October 1921), Lloyd George Papers, F/196/7/14.

24. 'The unemployment problem: memorandum by the Minister of Labour' (17 September 1921), PRO CAB 24/128.

25. Directorate of Intelligence (Home Office), 'Proposed date of monster unemployed demonstration' (26 September 1921); and 'Report on revolutionary organizations in the United Kingdom' (6 October 1921), ibid.

26. Cabinet Committee on Unemployment, 'Conclusions of meeting on 6 October 1921', PRO CAB 27/114.

27. Cabinet Committee on Unemployment, 'Memorandum by the Parliamentary Secretary to the Ministry of Labour' (13 October 1921), PRO CAB 27/120.

28. Relief of Distress Committee, 'Suggested distress fund' (note by the Ministry of Labour) (10 October 1921), PRO CAB 27/149.

29. ibid.

30. 'Report of Relief of Distress Committee' (11 October 1921), PRO CAB 24/128.

31. *Hansard*, vol. 147 (19 October 1921), col. 93.

32. The main objections raised were administrative. *Final Report of the Committee of Inquiry into the Scheme of Out-of-Work Donation*, Cmd 305 (1919), p. 9; *Minutes of Evidence Taken Before the Committee of Inquiry into the Scheme of Out-of-Work Donation*, Cmd 407 (1919), p. 83; memorandum by T. W. Phillips (4 April 1919) PRO PIN 7/14.

33. *Hansard*, vol. 138 (23 February 1921), col. 1001.

34. Memoranda in PRO PIN 1/3. This may have been what Sir Horace Wilson was referring to in 1939 when he stated that 'proposals for family allowances had been made at the beginning of the war of 1914—18, but had had to be abandoned because of Trade Union opposition'. Extract from minutes of 11th meeting of the ministerial Committee on Economic Policy (7 December 1939), PRO CAB 89/22.

35. Trades Union Congress and Labour Party, *Unemployment Insurance*, and *Resolutions to be Discussed at the Special Conference*

of the Trades Union Congress and the Labour Party, 27 January (both n.d., prob. January 1921).

36. *Hansard*, vol. 138 (17, 23 and 24 February 1921), cols. 336, 1001–2, 1239–40.

37. Defined as 40s 0d per week for the head of a household, 25s 0d for adults other than the head, and 5s 0d for children. ibid., cols. 1198–1203.

38. ibid., vol. 143 (15 June 1921), col. 464. This was during the debate on a Bill to reduce adult man's benefit from 20s 0d to 15s 0d per week.

39. ibid., vol. 147 (1 November 1921), cols. 1626–70.

40. ibid., vol. 152 (29 March 1922), col. 1376.

41. P. Cohen, op. cit. (1931), p. 119.

42. Cabinet meeting of 14 February 1923, Cabinet 9(23), PRO CAB 23/45.

43. Blanesburgh Report, p. 67, and *Royal Commission on Unemployment Insurance, Final Report* Cmd 4185 (1932), p. 20.

44. The only surviving Treasury file, for example, simply deals with the finance of the separate distress fund, PRO T 161/191 (S. 17960).

45. Blanesburgh Report, pp. 68–9.

46. Macnamara claimed that these were 'the main considerations' which led the Cabinet to continue dependants' allowances beyond their original six-month period. *Hansard*, vol. 152 (29 March 1922), col. 1376.

47. Ministry of Labour, *Report on National Unemployment Insurance to July 1923* (1923), p. 63.

48. Relief of Distress Committee, 'Conclusions of a meeting on 11 October 1921' PRO CAB 27/149.

49. Cabinet meetings of 8 and 22 March 1922, Cabinets 16 and 20 (22), PRO CAB 23/29.

50. J. L. Cohen, *Social Insurance Unified* (1924), p. 46.

51. Sir John Walley, *Social Security: Another British Failure?* (1972), pp. 47–50.

52. *Report on the Possibility of Developing Unemployment Insurance by Industries*, Cmd 1613 (1923).

53. *Interdepartmental Committee on Health and Unemployment Insurance: First and Second Interim Reports*, Cmd 1644 (1922), and *Third Interim Report*, Cmd 1821 (1923).

54. For a full account of the complex events surrounding the 'all-in' insurance activity, see J. Macnicol. 'The Movement for Family

Allowances in Great Britain, 1918–45', (University of Edinburgh
PhD thesis, 1978), pp. 262–6.

55. Memorandum by Sir Arthur Robinson and Horace Wilson (14
January 1924), PRO PIN 1/1.
56. Note of a discussion at the Ministry of Health on 29 November
1923 (8 December 1923), ibid; memorandum by Lord Eustace
Percy (n.d., prob. December 1923), PRO HLG 30/32.
57. Memorandum by Robinson and Wilson, op. cit.
58. Minutes of meeting of Anderson Committee (5 January 1924),
PRO PIN 1/2.
59. Memorandum by Robinson and Wilson, op. cit.
60. Memorandum by Percy, op. cit.
61. Note of a discussion at the Ministry of Health on 29 November
1923, op. cit.
62. Ministry of Labour memorandum (n.d., prob. December 1923),
PRO PIN 1/2.
63. Memorandum by H. W. Francis (n.d., prob. October 1923), PRO
HLG 30/32.
64. Ministry of Labour memorandum, op. cit.
65. Minutes of meeting of Anderson Committee (5 January 1924),
op. cit.
66. Memorandum by Robinson and Wilson, op. cit.
67. *Hansard*, vol. 163 (4 May 1923), cols. 1794–5.
68. ibid., vol. 147 (19 October 1921), col. 93.
69. ibid. (26 October 1921), cols. 934–42; and (1 November 1921),
col. 1671.
70. ibid., vol. 173 (20 May 1924), col. 2065.
71. Blanesburgh Report, pp. 31, 38.
72. Because this practice was not widespread, and because an account
of it would need to be complex, it has been left out of this study.
73. *Royal Commission on Unemployment Insurance, Final Report*,
op. cit., p. 20.
74. Bentley Gilbert, for example, dates its origins as 1932; Gilbert,
op. cit., p. 178. For a full account of the background to the 1934
Act, see Eric Briggs and Alan Deacon, 'The creation of the Unemployment Assistance Board', *Policy and Politics*, vol. 2, no. 1
(1973), pp. 43–62; John D. Millett, *The Unemployment Assistance Board* (1940), pp. 17–44; Burns, op. cit., pp. 162–79.
75. For example, government spokesmen were never able to explain
properly exactly what the Board's constitutional position was *vis-a-
vis* Parliament. *Hansard*, vol. 297 (12 February 1935), cols. 1803–7.

76. For their backgrounds, see Millett, op. cit., pp. 46–8.
77. See, for example, Violet Markham's recollections in *Return Passage* (1953), ch. 20.
78. *Hansard*, vol. 286 (26 February 1934), col. 786.
79. ibid., vol. 283 (30 November 1933), col. 1089.
80. *Annual Report of the Unemployment Assistance Board for 1935*, Cmd 5177, p. 6.
81. Children's Minimum Council pamphlet, *Observations on the Draft Unemployment Assistance Regulations* (21 July 1936); and Eleanor Rathbone in *Hansard*, vol. 289 (9 May 1934), cols. 1218–19.
82. *Hansard*, vol. 286 (26 February 1934), cols. 767, 771.
83. ibid., cols. 785–8.
84. For example, speech by Arthur Greenwood in *Hansard*, vol. 283 (30 November 1933), cols. 1108–10.
85. Unemployment Assistance Board memorandum no. 14 (30 August 1934), Violet Markham Papers, Box 29; Marjorie Green to Thomas Jones (17 September 1934) and (11 October 1934), PRO AST 7/32. Other letters from the Children's Minimum Council are contained in Violet Markham Papers, Box 47.
86. For example, letter by Eleanor Rathbone to *The Times* (31 October 1934).
87. 'I understand the Children's Minimum and Mrs Hubback are advancing yet again on the Unemployment Assistance Board with yet another memo', wrote Violet Markham to Sir George Newman. 'They keep saying you are such a nice man but somehow they don't seem to like your figures and are pained at your conclusions. How rare is the mentality that can face facts honestly when they don't square with the person's preconceived ideas'. Markham to Newman (18 October 1934), Violet Markham Papers, Box 43.
88. This was realized at the time by a few MPs. See Millett, op. cit., p. 51.
89. Minutes of the 4th meeting of the Unemployment Assistance Board (23, 24 and 25 July 1934), Violet Markham Papers, Box 27. The Ministry of Health maintained that general malnutrition *was* the Board's responsibility.
90. Minutes of 5th meeting (31 July 1934), ibid.
91. Unemployment Assistance Board memorandum no. 13: 'Suggested amendments of the basic scale' (30 August 1934), ibid., Box 29.
92. Statement by Professor Hallsworth, Minutes of 6th meeting (13 September 1934), ibid., Box 27.
93. Minutes of 6th meeting, ibid.

94. Unemployment Assistance Board memorandum no. 9: 'Memorandum on draft regulations' by W. Eady (19 July 1934), ibid., Box 29.
95. Unemployment Assistance Board memorandum no. 13, op. cit.
96. Unemployment Assistance Board memorandum no. 14: 'A "scientific basis" for the assessment of needs' (30 August 1934), ibid.
97. *Annual Report of the Unemployment Assistance Board for 1935*, Cmd 5177, p. 33.
98. Eleanor Rathbone seems to have realized all along that this would happen. She predicted that Betterton would be unable to keep his promises, and that less eligibility would be the deciding factor. *Hansard*, vol. 289 (9 May 1934), col. 1220.
99. 'A children's minimum', *British Medical Journal* (4 January 1936).
100. ibid.
101. Unemployment Assistance Board memorandum no. 13, op. cit. In 1936, however, this 'scaling down' policy was abandoned.
102. Unemployment Assistance Board memorandum: 'Note on the basis of the Board's scale' (May 1937), PRO AST 7/337.
103. Unemployment Assistance Board memorandum: 'Some observations by Miss Markham on the long-term policy and problems of the Board arising out of the annual report' (1937), Violet Markham Papers, Box 51.
104. ibid.
105. *Annual Report of the Unemployment Assistance Board for 1937*, Cmd 5752, pp. 6, 81—2.
106. ibid., *for 1935*, pp. 12—13.
107. ibid., *for 1937*, pp. 5—6.
108. *Annual Report of the Unemployment Assistance Board for 1936*, Cmd 5526, p. 5.
109. ibid. Violet Markham later recalled of the Board's applicants that 'the majority were elderly men who lacked either aptitude or adequate industrial experience to make them worth while to an employer', *Return Passage*, op. cit., p. 201. Critics of the Board strongly objected to this pessimistic view, and to the notion that men were 'too old' at the age of 45. Joan S. Clarke, *The Assistance Board* (1941), p. 8.
110. E. W. Bakke, *The Unemployed Man* (1933), pp. 137, 253—6, 263—70.
111. H. L. Beales and R. S. Lambert, *Memoirs of the Unemployed*

(1934), p. 26. The book contains (pp. 55—262) a series of auto-biographical case-studies illustrating this progression.

112. Max Cohen, *I was One of the Unemployed* (1945), p. 86.
113. *Hansard* (Lords), vol. 110 (7 July 1938), cols. 629—31.
114. ibid., vol. 113 (21 June 1939), col. 639.
115. *The Times* (22 March 1938), quoted in Theo Barker (ed.), *The Long March of Everyman* (1975), p. 215.
116. *Annual Report of the Unemployment Assistance Board for 1938*, Cmd 6021, pp. 48—50.
117. Memorandum by the Family Endowment Society to the Unemployment Insurance Statutory Committee, sent by Marjorie Green (Children's Minimum Council) to Violet Markham (6 May 1938), Violet Markham Papers, Box 43.
118. Markham to Green (12 May 1938), ibid.
119. Markham to Elsie Jones (12 October 1938), ibid.
120. Markham to Cadbury (11 July 1939), PRO AST 7/390.
121. 'The Board are obviously very interested in the question because of its reactions on their own work; but they have no legal power to take any practical action in regard to it'. Lord Rushcliffe to W. Elphinston (Church Assembly) (31 October 1938), ibid.
122. PRO AST 7/390: *Family Allowances, June 1938—December 1943*.
123. Correspondence in ibid.
124. *Report of the Unemployment Insurance Statutory Committee for 1934*, p. 2. The chairman was Sir William Beveridge, and the members were A. L. Ayre, A. Digby Besant, Captain C. C. Craig, Arthur Shaw, Miss K. J. Stephenson and Mary Stocks, with three civil servants. The debt was to be paid off by 1971.
125. Ronald C. Davison, *British Unemployment Policy, the Modern Phase Since 1930* (1938), pp. 53—4.
126. Beveridge always strenuously denied that the Committee was a mere rubber stamp for the Ministry of Labour. W. H. Beveridge, *The Unemployment Insurance Statutory Committee* (1937), pp. 34—5.
127. Minutes of the Unemployment Insurance Statutory Committee for 7 February 1935, Beveridge Papers, VII. 4 (all Unemployment Insurance Statutory Committee minutes contained herein).
128. For example, the Ministry of Labour maintained that criticism of the 2s 0d dependant's benefit in unemployment insurance on the grounds that it was not possible to maintain a child on that amount was 'largely due to misapprehension . . . the real position

is that 2s 0d has been thought to be the largest sum in respect of each dependent child which the finances of the insurance scheme enabled it to pay as a supplement to the basic rate of benefit'. H. C. Emmerson (Ministry of Labour) to Sir Clive Wigram (the King's Private Secretary) (6 June 1934), PRO AST 7/85. This, of course, protected the UISC from the full force of 'nutritional' criticism.

129. Minutes of the Unemployment Insurance Statutory Committee for 20 November 1936 and for 13 and 14 January 1938.

130. *Report of the Unemployment Insurance Statutory Committee for July 1935*, p. 18.

131. *Report of the Unemployment Insurance Statutory Committee for 1934*, p. 3.

132. ibid., pp. 15–16.

133. Minutes of the Unemployment Insurance Statutory Committee for 7 February 1935.

134. *Report of the Unemployment Insurance Statutory Committee for July 1935*, pp. 17–18.

135. *Hansard*, vol. 305 (24 October 1935), col. 471. The real reason may have been Treasury opposition to any change that might have raised the cost of assistance.

136. *Report of the Unemployment Insurance Statutory Committee for 1935*, pp. 28–9.

137. 'Note of a discussion on the unemployment insurance fund by the Ministry of Labour' (25 November 1936), PRO PIN 7/216.

138. Statement by J. L. Smyth (TUC), Minutes of the Unemployment Statutory Committee for 7 February 1935 and 9 January 1936.

139. ibid., for 20 November 1936.

140. ibid., for 14 and 15 January 1937.

141. Memoranda (1935 and 1936) in PRO PIN 7/214, and PIN 7/167.

142. *Report of the Unemployment Insurance Statutory Committee for 1935*, p. 38, and ibid. *for 1937* pp. 20–1, 25; Ministry of Labour memorandum, 'Claimants with families in which there are more than five dependent children' (1935), PRO PIN 7/214.

143. *Report of the Unemployment Insurance Statutory Committee for 1937*, p. 25.

144. *Report of the Unemployment Insurance Statutory Committee for 1938*, pp. 3, 8.

145. *Report of the Unemployment Insurance Statutory Committee for 1939*, p. 12.

146. Although this debate concerned the fate of 14 million insured

workers and their dependants, at one point a count had to be taken to see if the necessary quorum of 40 members was present. *Hansard*, vol. 333 (25 March 1938), col. 1553.

147. ibid., cols. 1552–3, 1537, 1568.

148. Juergen Kuczynski, *Hunger and Work* (1938), pp. 26, 107–9, 129.

149. For an expression of this view, see Socialist Party of Great Britain, *Family Allowances, a Socialist Analysis* (1943), pp. 9–12.

150. *Hansard*, vol. 333 (25 March 1938), col. 1544.

151. M. Green, 'Family allowances', *Labour Management* (November 1938), p. 206.

152. M. Stocks, *The Floor of Wages and the Ceiling of Relief* (Family Endowment Society pamphlet, 1937).

153. Political and Economic Planning, *Report on the British Social Services* (1937), p. 12. For a similar view, see B. Seebohm Rowntree, 'Family allowances', *Contemporary Review*, 154 (September 1938), p. 292; and P. Ford, *Incomes, Means Tests and Personal Responsibility* (1939), pp. 74–5.

154. Political and Economic Planning, op. cit., pp. 31, 166–7.

155. Pilgrim Trust, *Men Without Work* (1938), pp. 113, 209.

156. ibid., p. 113.

157. Ford, op. cit., pp. 69–70.

158. Gertrude Williams, *The State and the Standard of Living* (1936), p. 302.

6 Attitudes of Political Parties

In the interwar years, the movement for family allowances in Britain enjoyed the support of a wide spectrum of political opinion. As has been noted, Eleanor Rathbone and the Family Endowment Society campaigned essentially for the principle of family endowment to be applied wherever possible, and presented their case in a number of different ways so as to attract maximum support. Thus on the one hand family allowances could be seen by some sections of the Labour movement in the late 1920s as part of an exclusively socialist approach to the family that followed the maxim 'from each according to his ability to each according to his or her (family) needs' and redistributed wealth from rich to poor; yet at the other extreme some Conservative politicians in the late 1930s could see family allowances in imperialist, almost racialist, terms when they advocated them as a pro-natalist measure designed to ensure the continuation of the 'white races'. In short, the attitude of political parties towards family allowances in the interwar years provides a vivid illustration of how one particular social policy can be perceived in entirely different ways by different socio-political groups.

Since the general discussion of family allowances in Britain in the 1920s (as in other countries) took place within the context of a much wider discussion on minimum wages it is not surprising that the keenest interest in that decade should have been shown by the Labour movement. Within the Labour Party, a long-standing interest in the welfare of mothers and children was tending to manifest itself by the early 1920s in demands for widows' pensions — a logical outgrowth from which was that the principle of family endowment be applied to all families. The main impetus behind this latter movement was supplied by the Independent Labour Party (ILP), which had long been interested in the question of the minimum wage.

After the fall of the first Labour government in 1924, the ILP took upon itself the task of acting as an ideological ginger-group within the

Labour Party, in an attempt to push it towards a militantly socialist but constitutional position, and for the remainder of the 1920s it was very influential on party thinking.[1] Disillusioned with the performance of the 1924 Labour government, the ILP aimed at committing the party to a truly socialist programme which it would be obliged to implement when next in power. Thus from 1924 onwards the ILP gradually evolved such a programme, known as 'Socialism in Our Time', and officially endorsed it at its 1926 annual conference.[2] Socialism in Our Time was a wide-ranging strategy, involving the public ownership of banks and credit institutions, the nationalization of coal, electricity, transport and land, the reform of Parliament, the reorganization of agriculture, policies for unemployment — and, most important of all, the proposal for a 'Living Wage' augmented by family allowances.[3] The Living Wage policy was developed over the period 1924—6 by an ILP committee chaired by the economist J. A. Hobson, and including Arthur Creech Jones, Clifford Allen and H. N. Brailsford. Brailsford had been a member of Eleanor Rathbone's 1917—18 'Equal Pay and the Family' group,[4] and was responsible for forging links between the ILP and the FES (of which he was an active member);[5] most of all, he edited the ILP journal, the *New Leader*, from 1922 to 1926 and during that period it carried numerous articles warmly supporting family allowances by himself and others.[6]

The Living Wage policy was based on two justifications: first, the ethical case against the amount of inequality and suffering caused by the maldistribution of income; and second, the economic case (owing much to J. A. Hobson's earlier analyses of underconsumption) that higher wages would raise purchasing power, which in turn would stimulate industry and produce a fall in unemployment.[7] The precise monetary level of the Living Wage was never clearly defined, and there was some ambivalence over the question of whether industry would be able to afford it. Thus on the one hand, Brailsford could write that 'in fixing it [the Living Wage] we demand that the customary reference to "what industry can pay" shall be ruthlessly disregarded':[8] it was to be drawn up solely on the basis of the minimum nutritional needs of a man and wife (plus child allowances).[9] Yet on the other hand, some ILP members maintained that the Living Wage's exact level would have to be dictated by the amount that could be creamed off industrial profits without inflicting long-term damage (such as investment in new plant).[10] Such contradictions were gleefully seized upon by those on the right wing of the Labour Party, who bitterly resented the ILP, and of course there was a chorus of ridicule from orthodox economists who tended to see the solution to Britain's economic difficulties in wage reductions that would lower production costs and hence make exports more competitive on world markets; but essentially the concept of the Living Wage was more of a rallying-cry aimed at challenging the basic assumptions of capitalism than a precise cash level.

However, there was more substance to the ILP proposal for family allowances. The scheme was to be financed 'out of direct taxation of high incomes', and was initially to cover only the working class.[11] The cash figure quoted most often was 5s 0d per week for every working class child under or of school age, but sometimes higher figures were suggested — for example, 6s 0d or 7s 0d, 'if we can cut down armaments and the National Debt'.[12] Cost was to be no deterrent: when on one occasion there was a suggestion that allowances should cease after the fourth or fifth child, this was not for reasons of economy but in order to prevent 'undesirable multiplication of families'.[13] In order to allay trade union fears, family allowances would have to be clearly defined as '*an addition to wages* and not a method of redistributing existing wages'.[14] Thus there could be no countenancing of a scheme financed by an equalization fund (as in Europe) or by contributory insurance (as suggested by J. L. Cohen),[15] since both would merely redistribute income within the working class rather than from rich to poor, and would impose a crushing burden of weekly contributions on the low paid.[16]

For the ILP family allowances would serve many functions: they would recognize the rights of women and children, providing much-needed financial assistance to the working class mother ('the most sweated worker of today', as Dorothy Jewson put it);[17] they would pave the way to equal pay for equal work;[18] most important of all, they would raise working class purchasing power and create a demand in the home market which would revitalize industry by forcing it to turn away from the disrupted foreign markets and declining domestic sectors of coal, cotton, shipbuilding, iron and steel. The Living Wage—family allowances policy was thus 'the only fundamental method of tackling unemployment',[19] since it would 'create a vast new internal market. It would make a demand that would get every factory busily working to supply the needs of the home population'.[20] Finally, this new prosperity in industry would enable it to pay higher wages.[21]

Viewed in retrospect, the Living Wage programme stands out (along with Lloyd George's plan of 1928 and the 1930 Mosley memorandum) as one of the few examples of constructive and bold economic thinking in the interwar years. At the time, it was taken up with great enthusiasm by the ILP, and according to one reliable authority was vigorously pushed 'at thousands of public meetings' in the 1920s.[22] If this is true, then the cause of family endowment must have reached a wide audience.

The Family Endowment Society tried as best it could to capitalize on this wave of interest, severely handicapped though it was by lack of funds and small membership, and in 1926 launched a propaganda campaign aimed at persuading trade unionists in general, and miners in particular (in the aftermath of the Samuel Report), that family allowances were an integral part of socialist economics. Eleanor Rathbone arranged a scheme whereby a special cheap edition of *The Disinherited Family* was made available to trade union secretaries, those on low incomes and their wives;[23] the Society published a pamphlet aimed specifically at allaying Labour fears by quoting statements from foreign trade unionists denying that family allowances had lowered wages or weakened union solidarity;[24] and everything was done to lobby trade unionists personally: in the year 1929–30, for example, speakers toured the Midlands and the north of England, visiting sixty-four towns, arranging over a hundred meetings, and talking with over a thousand trade union officials, politicians and leaders of organizations.[25]

Similarly, the ILP worked hard in the period 1925–30 to whip up support for its plan. A Labour Family Allowances Committee was formed, and on 23 March 1929 held a large conference for representatives of trade unions, co-operative societies, trades councils, etc.[26] This campaigning aroused an enthusiastic response among Labour women. The Women's Co-operative Guild had been interested in the concept of 'a minimum for the family' since 1919,[27] and by the mid-1920s this had evolved into a solid support for family allowances.[28] A rather cautious interest was shown by the Women's Trade Union conference,[29] but the National Conference of Labour Women passed several resolutions in favour of a state-run scheme, and urged the Labour Party 'to proceed as quickly as possible' in formulating such a scheme.[30] As far as can be ascertained, grass-roots opinion within the Labour women's movement was strongly in favour of cash allowances.[31]

However, the Labour movement was run by men, and success for the ILP's scheme could only be achieved if the main Labour Party and the TUC annual conferences voted in its favour. It was here that the cause of family allowances became fatally entangled in the Labour movement's internal politics, providing an issue over which the right and left wings were to fight for control of the Labour Party.

In order to understand this political background, several factors must be borne in mind. The disappointment of the first Labour government

may have instilled in the ILP a desire to push the party further to
the left, but it also reinforced the belief of more cautious leaders like
Ramsay MacDonald that long and hard-won electoral support could
only be increased by presenting Labour as the party of moderation.
MacDonald viewed the ILP proposals as 'flashy futilities',[32] and feared
that Socialism in Our Time, if adopted, would become an electoral
millstone round the party's neck, alienating a large number of hitherto
undecided voters. He also realized full well that to give in to the ILP
would involve handing over to them the reins of power. Thus it was for
both ideological and tactical reasons that the Labour Party Executive
in 1927 quickly brought out *Labour and the Nation* — a policy document designed to steer the party away from Socialism in Our Time,
and one which made no mention of minimum wages or family allowances.[33]

For their part, rank-and-file trade unionists felt extremely vulnerable
in the aftermath of the General Strike and a situation of mass unemployment (total trade union membership fell from 8 348 000 in 1921
to 4 858 000 in 1930).[34] In particular, they were very sensitive on the
issue of wages: one trade unionist claimed in 1930 that the working
class had 'lost' £700 million in wage-cuts over the previous ten years,[35]
and there was a widespread belief that employers were trying to have
the value of social services taken into account in fixing wages.[36] Family
allowances appeared to offer employers a golden opportunity to cut
wages even further. The only practical instances of family allowances
in operation had been Speenhamland and European industrial schemes
— both of which seemed to provide irrefutable proof that wage reductions followed. Not surprisingly, many trade unionists viewed family
allowances with the greatest suspicion, and even those who were not so
hostile felt that a more immediate priority was to win back the money
lost in wage-cuts. In addition, family allowances tended to arouse in
male trade unionists the sort of gut-reaction expressed by Rhys Davies
(who, it must be remembered, campaigned for widows' pensions) when
he said that they were

> based on the assumption that the average working class father and
> husband was devoid of feelings of responsibility for his wife and
> children, and [were] a confession that the married man could
> not, either by personal qualities or Trade Union organization,
> secure an adequate income to maintain himself and his family.[37]

Trade union leaders tended to share these attitudes. The 1920s saw
British trade unionism turn away from the quasi-revolutionary approach

that had begun with the first successful formation of unskilled, militant unions in the 1880s and had culminated in the General Strike. For a number of reasons (the enervating effect of mass unemployment, the trauma of the General Strike, the more conservative shift in the General Council membership after 1925, the need to work for a majority Labour government), trade union leaders adopted a less political stance and concerned themselves more with improving conditions at work, hours and wage rates — an approach often termed 'Mondism'.[38] The leading exponents of this view were Ernest Bevin (general secretary of the Transport and General Workers' Union, 1921—40) and Walter Citrine (TUC general secretary, 1926—46) — the two most powerful figures in the trade union movement. For Bevin, the question of whether a factory had a canteen was more important than the nature of socialism. Both viewed the ILP as a dangerous clique of quasi-Marxist utopian intellectuals, the term 'intellectual' being used by Bevin as an expression of utter contempt. Bevin strongly resented what he considered was impudent and unwarranted interference in wage questions which should only be settled on the shop-floor by free collective bargaining;[39] Citrine called the ILP proposals 'one of the utterest jumbles of nonsense that was ever conceived'.[40]

It must also be remembered that many trade unionists were deeply suspicious of the real motives behind 'those gatherings of dear philanthropic ladies and gentlemen of the family endowment society and people of that kind, not all of whom are in the Labour Movement'.[41] The fact that the FES contained people of all political persuasions, including a Conservative Minister of Labour, and subtly altered its propaganda to suit each audience, did not go unnoticed. Many trade unionists believed that at heart the Society's leaders were deeply conservative, and could quote in justification such statements by Eleanor Rathbone as:

Are any of us quite satisfied that we are not moving towards a revolution of some kind, not perhaps a Russian revolution, but a revolution which, even if it takes constitutional forms, may be the outcome of the discontent so present in conditions of life today that when Labour gets into power with a sufficiently strong majority it will be forced by the pressure behind it into embarking on reforms, which, even if constitutional, may be dislocating to the whole basis and structure of industry? Is it not our duty as reasonable men and women to look to see whether there is no other method, and whether the family insurance is not the best method for insuring a higher standard of life among the workers (without dislocating industry and over-burdening the back of industry) by simply redistributing the available resources for the remuneration of the workers and so effecting a reasonable revolution?[42]

A final point to be borne in mind when considering trade union attitudes is that there was a very strong lobby of opinion within the Labour movement that regarded extensions of 'services in kind' as having greater priority — better maternal and child welfare services, the provision of free, tuberculosis-tested milk, and the expansion of health insurance to cover wives and children being the most important. Many who held this view also supported family allowances; but, like Mac-Donald, they believed that the Labour Party had to adopt only such proposals as were consistent with prevailing economic constraints, and faced with limited resources they chose services in kind as more urgently needed.[43] The ILP, of course, argued that to accept existing economic constraints was to accept limitations imposed by the capitalist class: Socialism in Our Time would make the economy more efficient and thus able to finance both alternatives. For all these reasons, therefore, the subject of family allowances became the centre of bitter controversy in the Labour movement in the late 1920s, raising all the issues which divided (and still divide) the left and right.

The inquiry into family allowances by the Labour movement was conducted by a TUC—Labour Party 'Joint Committee on the Living Wage', set up in July 1927. The Living Wage proposals had been considered by the TUC General Council on 22 March 1927; the discussion had been dominated by a hostile Bevin, who insisted that wage policies 'must spring from the unions themselves' and not become 'a party political issue'.[44] However, a demand for some sort of inquiry into family allowances had been introduced by the ILP at the 1926 Labour Party conference, and had been passed by a solid two-to-one majority.[45] Behind-the-scences activity by TUC leaders thus ensured that the Joint Committee, despite its title, ignored the main Living Wage proposals and merely conducted a limited, albeit very thorough, inquiry into family allowances alone.[46]

The Living Wage Committee consisted of six representatives from the TUC and six from the Labour Party, with W. Milne-Bailey of the TUC Research Department as secretary. In its three years of life, members dropped out and were replaced by others, so a full personnel list is misleading; but at any one time it contained several important figures in the Labour movement: George Lansbury, Hugh Dalton (initially the chairman), Herbert Morrison, Arthur Henderson, Oswald Mosley, Ellen Wilkinson and Mrs Ayrton Gould (Labour Party); Sir

Walter Citrine (who later became chairman), H. H. Elvin and Ben Turner (TUC).[47] Though constituted in July 1927, the Committee only began taking evidence in December — but thereafter there was conducted a wide-ranging examination of every aspect of family allowances.

First to give evidence were the ILP representatives, on 7, 8, 14 and 15 December 1927. The Committee's secretary, Milne-Bailey, had already made his attitude to the ILP quite clear in two rather caustic memoranda circulated to his colleagues,[48] and H. N. Brailsford, E. F. Wise and J. A. Hobson found themselves having to endure a very hostile cross-examination. Citrine was particularly irritated at the ILP's insistence that trade union action alone would not be able to achieve the Living Wage, and that political action through Parliament would also be necessary; this he evidently regarded as a deep insult to trade unionism. Herbert Morrison and Arthur Henderson challenged the practicality of the Living Wage proposals: would people tolerate the level of income tax necessary to finance them? By what stages would the proposals be passed through Parliament? How long would implementation take? What would happen if the House of Lords threw them out? To all these questions, and others of a similar nature, the ILP spokesmen gave reasonable replies, but the tidy, administrative minds of these two social democrats remained unconvinced that the Living Wage was anything but political pie-in-the-sky.[49]

Next it was the turn of the Family Endowment Society (represented by Eleanor Rathbone, Olga Vlasto, Mrs Freeth and Mrs E. M. L. Douglas) on 26 January 1928. True to form, the Society had bombarded the Committee with memoranda, pamphlets, invitations to meetings, letters and so on, over the preceding months, and in their oral evidence the leaders took great pains to allay trade union fears. Mrs Freeth, for example, spoke of her tours round mining districts, and the enthusiasm of ordinary miners for family allowances. But Citrine was still very suspicious of their likely effect on wages, and eventually managed to force Eleanor Rathbone to admit that ultimately family allowances could only be introduced at the expense of wage rises — though, of course, she maintained that such a redistribution would be far more beneficial for workers' families.[50]

Finally, the Committee took evidence from a variety of witnesses: J. L. Cohen outlined his insurance-based scheme; Mary Stocks gave the point of view of the National Union of Societies for Equal Citizenship; Hugh Dalton voiced his personal support for family allowances and a group of witnesses made out the case for extensions of services in kind as a better alternative.[51]

In September 1928 the Committee published an interim report in which it summarized, from the point of view of the Labour movement, all the arguments for and against family allowances.[52] Essentially, it argued, the question was whether cash allowances or extensions of services in kind had greater priority: there was general agreement in the Labour movement that *some* sort of special provision was needed for children. The ILP scheme, if applied to the insured population alone, would cost about £125 million per annum — whereas only about £70—80 million would be needed to make the public health and educational services 'almost complete' in terms of the Labour Party's existing plans.[53]

Once this interim report was published, the TUC General Council circulated it to member unions, together with a questionnaire, and the results were published in the 1929 TUC annual report. To the question 'are you in favour of further financial provision being made for children?', fifty-three unions (aggregate membership 2 127 965) replied in the affirmative, and two unions (membership 366 514) in the negative; of these fifty-three unions, nineteen (membership 1 146 774) favoured this being achieved by cash allowances, and thirty-three (membership 980 786) preferred extensions of social services.[54] In view of this somewhat inconclusive result, the Joint Committee was asked to investigate the matter further and come to a definite decision.

Meanwhile, ILP members were continuing to raise the subject of family allowances at Labour Party conferences. At the 1927 conference the Living Wage was debated, and out of the seven speakers who participated five were strongly in favour of family allowances.[55] At the following year's conference Dorothy Jewson of the ILP moved that the Joint Committee's interim report be referred back to the Party Executive so that the latter might make a decision on whether family allowances should be included in the next election programme, but Arthur Henderson, the chairman, fended off this challenge by promising that the Joint Committee would be reporting soon.[56] In 1929, however, Dorothy Jewson forced the conference to debate the issue on a motion: she put forward the ILP case that apart from greatly relieving family poverty, especially in the depressed areas, family allowances would raise purchasing power (thus boosting the economy) and would actually strengthen trade union solidarity during industrial disputes 'because children would be paid whether the man was in work or not'.[57] The ensuing debate vividly illustrated the conflict of views within the Labour movement. Ernest Bevin wanted no discussion until the Joint Committee had finally reported, and was very hostile to the whole Living Wage programme. Other speakers wanted child welfare services developed first, and felt that the enormous cost of family allowances made them a political impossibility. (It must be remembered that by then a Labour government was in power.) Yet an equal number of speakers (notably Herbert Smith of the Miners' Federation, and ILP representatives) supported the motion enthusiastically.[58] Clearly, Labour Party leaders were well aware of the hostility felt by certain influential TUC leaders towards family allowances, for in winding up the debate Arthur Henderson (who had been in favour of family allowances at the 1927 conference) made a very lukewarm speech suggesting that the matter be looked into further, with no decisions being made in the meantime, and somewhat unconvincingly maintained that the party had 'done magnificent educational work' and made 'splendid progress' on the subject over the previous two years.[59]

Eventually, in February 1930, the Joint Committee decided to issue majority and minority reports: nine members had come out in favour of cash family allowances, three in favour of services in kind.[60] Faced with this impasse, the Committee's secretary, Milne-Bailey, circulated the two reports to the TUC General Council, and sought the advice of a number of prominent economists. Interestingly, one of these was J. M. Keynes, who in 1939–40 was to play such an important role in the attempts to have family allowances introduced as part of wartime economic policy. On this occasion, however, the great economist was unenthusiastic: he said he was engrossed with other aspects of economics and could give no opinion; if anything, he favoured the minority report.[61]

The TUC General Council held several inconclusive meetings, and eventually, on 28 May 1930, decided to adopt the minority report by sixteen votes to eight.[62] Clearly, Bevin and Citrine had been working behind the scenes; but with a Labour government in power, facing rising unemployment and an impending economic crisis, they would have had little difficulty in persuading fellow Council members to squash the idea of family allowances completely. Meanwhile, Eleanor Rathbone was doing everything she could to whip up support among trade unionists for the still unpublished majority report, the contents of which had been leaked to the Press. In June 1930 she collected the signatures of some of her more influential supporters (including Beveridge, Hobson, J. L. Cohen, E. D. Simon and Gilbert Murray) on a letter which requested that the Joint Committee's reports be published immediately; copies of this were sent to all trade unions, General Council members and the Labour Party Executive, and subsequently the Family Endowment Society organized a conference on the issue.[63] As on previous occasions, the Society's somewhat over-enthusiastic lobbying caused considerable resentment among TUC leaders.[64]

The Joint Committee's Final Report was published in June 1930. The majority favoured cash allowances as 'the most valuable step that can now be taken to further the welfare of the nation's children', and recommended an Exchequer-financed scheme confined to those not covered by income tax, paying 5s 0d per week for the first child and 3s 0d per week for subsequent children.[65] The minority maintained that the cost of this (£70 million) would greatly hinder expansions of services in kind. 'It is merely blinking at the facts', they stated, 'to imagine that any Government in the near future is going to be able to raise this sum in addition to all other commitments, including extensions of the social services'. Before any decision on family allowances could be taken, there would have to be introduced a complete medical service for all children from birth to school-leaving age; a pre- and post-natal maternity service with cash payments for each child for the first year or two after birth; the raising of the school-leaving age, with adequate maintenance allowances during the additional year; the provision of nursery schools for children up to school age; the provision of 'adequate, healthy homes'; the elimination of tuberculosis; and the supply of pure milk.[66]

Finally, at the TUC annual conference in September 1930 the last act was played out. C. T. Cramp opened the debate by explaining the General Council's thinking. They had decided to reject family allowances, he said, primarily on grounds of practicability, since 'anything we do as a Trade Union Movement ought to be capable of achievement within a reasonable time and not merely held up as an ideal to be achieved some time or other'; the enormous cost of family allowances made them an impossibility in the existing economic situation — for example, the Treasury had just had to pay out £60 million in order to shore up the unemployment insurance scheme; in addition, the Council considered services in kind more important and feared the possible effect of family allowances on union solidarity.[67] A long debate ensued, in which all the familiar arguments were repeated and no agreement reached: for example, on the question of union solidarity the opponents of family allowances insisted that European schemes had been successfully used by employers as a means of enforcing industrial discipline, while supporters could point to the example of the General Strike which, they claimed, had remained solid in Durham because the strikers' children were maintained by the Boards of Guardians, whereas in Nottingham there was no such maintenance and the strike collapsed.[68] The two women who spoke in the debate were both strongly in favour of family allowances, and criticized the majority of speakers who had judged the issue solely in terms of whether the trade union movement would benefit rather than in terms of the children's needs; the Miners' Federation were also supporters.[69] Eventually, however, the assembled delegates voted against a reference back (that is, in favour of the minority report) by 2 154 000 votes to 1 347 000.[70] Much the same happened at the Labour Party conference in October. A brief debate was yet again initiated by Dorothy Jewson, but in view of the TUC's decision the conference voted against a reference back by 1 740 000 votes to 495 000, and all the ILP was left with was a vague promise by Arthur Henderson that the Party Executive would 'keep the matter open' and continue discussions with the TUC.[71] It was 'kept open' for another decade.

The year 1930 was thus crucial to the movement for family allowances, because it marked the end of the Labour movement's interest which had seemed so promising five years earlier. TUC leaders had successfully fended off the ILP's challenge by turning the Living Wage controversy into a very limited discussion of family allowances; and thereafter, despite considerable grass-roots support for cash allowances among trade unionists, they decided to award extensions of child welfare services greater priority. Family allowances — or, more accurately, the ILP's presentation of them — raised fundamental issues about wage bargaining and the political ideology of the Labour Party, and thus aroused determined opposition from more conservative leaders like Bevin and Citrine. In any case, even if family allowances had become part of the Labour Party's programme it is highly unlikely that they would have been introduced by the 1929—31 Labour government, dependent as it was on traditional Gladstonian finance. One can hardly imagine a Chancellor like Philip Snowden agreeing to such a costly social policy.

For their part, the Family Endowment Society leaders felt bitterly disappointed at this lost opportunity. To them, the TUC's opposition was a blatant example of the 'Turk complex' at work: the unions' much greater interest in the cause of old age pensions, Eva Hubback later wrote caustically, 'may well have been because at any one time only about 10 per cent of Trade Union members had more than two dependent children, while nearly all the old age pensioners themselves had votes'.[72] For the whole of the 1930s, relations between the Family Endowment Society and the trade union movement remained rather strained.

In the 1920s family allowances aroused some interest within the Liberal Party. Although seriously weakened by the Lloyd George–Asquith split for much of the decade, and the victim of long-term changes in electoral loyalties, the Liberal Party of the 1920s still considered itself a force to be reckoned with. The ideological soul-searching undertaken by the party at this time, in an attempt to create a Liberal revival, caused it to investigate a number of new ideas. Family endowment was one of these.

In the early 1920s Liberals had been sympathetic towards the idea of widows' pensions. When the Labour MP Rhys Davies introduced a motion in the House of Commons on 6 March 1923 proposing pensions for widows or for those whose family breadwinner had become incapacitated, fifty Liberals voted for and only eight against.[73] Family allowances made their first official appearance in Liberal circles in 1924 when (mainly thanks to Beveridge) they were discussed at a Liberal Summer School at Oxford and at a conference of Liberal Summer School movement at Cambridge.[74] Evidently, however, there was still much suspicion over the idea because of its association with the ILP: the *Liberal Magazine* of September 1924 called it 'a piece of pure Socialism'.[75] During 1925, however, family allowances began to attract more attention. Once again they were discussed at the Summer School,[76] and within the Royal Commission on the Coal Industry Beveridge was persuading Sir Herbert Samuel (a prominent Liberal) to include them in the Commission's report. But the most significant event was the appointment, in July 1925, of a Women's National Liberal Federation Committee to investigate family allowances.[77]

Interest within the Women's National Liberal Federation (WNLF) had been growing in 1925,[78] and in June of that year its Council passed a resolution, introduced by Lady Violet Bonham Carter, to the effect that 'the question of Family Endowment raises an issue of great national importance' and that the Council should appoint a committee of inquiry into the subject.[79] In the following month, therefore, a Family Endowment Committee was appointed, with Mrs Dorothea Layton (wife of the economist, Walter Layton) as chairwoman, and a membership of Lady Violet Bonham Carter, Mrs Margaret Wintringham, Lady Emmott, Mrs Isabella Herbert and Mrs Corbett Ashby.[80] This committee met practically every fortnight from the beginning of October 1925 to the end of March 1926, and took evidence from 'economists, teachers, manufacturers, mothers, and representatives of different sections of the community', among whom were experts like Beveridge, J. L. Cohen, Eva Hubback, and Professors D. H. Robertson and D. H. Macgregor.[81]

In April 1926 the Committee published an interim report,[82] and at the next annual Council meeting, on 22 and 23 June 1926, Mrs Layton introduced a long motion, in the light of the interim report, which supported the principle of family allowances 'as the most practical means of making provision for the minimum needs of the children of the nation', welcomed the Samuel Commission's recommendations on the subject, expressed the hope that private industry would begin to initiate schemes, adding that 'such schemes need not prejudice in any way the introduction of a National Scheme which the Committee prefer', and finally requested that the Family Endowment Committee continue its labours for another year so that it could come up with more precise recommendations which the Council could then firmly accept or reject.[83] Mrs Layton's motion was carried by the relatively healthy majority of 231 to 178, and thereafter the Committee continued taking evidence. Eventually their final report was published in April 1927; it emphasized that the need for family allowances was the product of long-term historical trends (such as children changing from producers of income to consumers), pointed out that family endowment existed in many areas of social services, and concluded that industrial equalization fund schemes would be the best form of development, with insurance-based schemes second best.[84]

In May the report was discussed at the annual Council meeting, and Mrs Layton must have had high hopes of it being accepted. She introduced a motion (seconded by Lady Emmott) calling on the Council to take up the cause of family allowances for state and municipal employees, to recommend to the Liberal Industrial Inquiry (which was being conducted at the time) that family allowances be introduced in their proposals, and to urge industry to initiate equalization fund schemes. This time, however, there was strong opposition from some Council members: one speaker, for example, said the motion 'would be helping on the movement towards the nationalization of children' and asked 'if allowances were paid to the mother do you think she could keep the money away from a dissolute or drunken husband?' Feelings such as these were in a majority on the Council, and Mrs Layton's motion was defeated.[85]

So ended the WNLF's official interest in family allowances. Some, like Mrs Layton, continued campaigning: she spoke to the July 1927 Liberal Summer School at Cambridge,[86] and later that year, in October, attended the Family Endowment Society's conference at the London School of Economics as a WNLF representative.[87] On occasions, the topic would briefly resurface within the WNLF: in its 1929 pamphlet

Liberal Policy for Women, for example, there was a discussion of the need for equal pay and provision for family responsibilities which concluded, albeit somewhat lamely, that 'whether this should be achieved through a system of family allowances or otherwise is a matter for consideration'.[88] But by the end of the 1920s the subject had been quietly dropped.

Had the WNLF been wholeheartedly in favour of family allowances it is possible that it might have influenced the main Liberal Party. The Family Endowment Society evidently considered there was sufficient interest in the party for them to publish in 1929 a pamphlet appealing to Liberals.[89] In addition, there were some prominent Liberals in the Family Endowment Society – Ramsay Muir, E. D. Simon, John Murray and Professor Gilbert Murray – who stood as parliamentary candidates in the 1920s and presumably would have liked the party to include family allowances in its official programme.[90] However, evidently there was in the party much suspicion and hostility towards the idea. For example, when the subject was debated at the 1928 annual conference of the Union of University Liberal Societies – a body that might have been more favourably disposed towards social reform than the rest of the party – a motion was carried (after a sharp division of views, and by a small majority) 'that under present conditions, social, economic and political, there can be no room on the Liberal Programme for any Scheme of Family Endowment'.[91] And when the party published a pamphlet on its policies for children there was no mention of family allowances, merely a vague statement that 'the wealth produced by the nation must be more justly shared, so that any industrious working man may have in his own pocket enough money to bring up his children in health, happiness and independence'.[92]

The only positive legacy seems to have emerged out of the Summer School discussions and research activities. These were directed at designing a new Liberal policy for revitalizing industry that would, it was hoped, appeal to the electorate and help bring about a Liberal revival. Out of the Summer School activities Lloyd George organized a Liberal Industrial Inquiry, the Executive Committee of which contained two members of the Family Endowment Society's Council, E. D. Simon and Ramsay Muir.[93] In addition, membership of the Special Committees included another two family allowance campaigners, Eva Hubback and Mrs Corbett Ashby.[94] Not surprisingly, therefore, the Industrial Inquiry's report contained a discussion of family allowances: they were seen as the most feasible way of providing for family needs, while still leaving a margin for the reward of special ability and effort. From another angle the proposal means that the loss of wages which the employee without dependents [*sic*] suffers is a compulsory saving or postponement of wages[95] against the time when he has a family and needs a supplement to his standard wages

and the report suggested that schemes could be introduced run either on a contributory insurance basis or by industrial pools.[96]

Compared with the Labour and Liberal Parties, the interest shown by the Conservative Party in family allowances in the 1920s was virtually non-existent. Although only 7 Conservative MPs voted for Rhys Davies's 1923 mothers' pensions motion in the Commons (with 239 voting against),[97] the Conservative government of 1924–9 did introduce the 1925 Widows', Orphans' and Old Age Contributory Pensions Act which by June 1928 was paying pensions of 10s 0d per week to 251 000 widows (with allowances of 3s 0d or 5s 0d per week going to their 344 800 children) and allowances of 7s 6d per week to 15 000 orphans.[98] But beyond that, the idea of supplementing working class wages to bring them more in line with family needs evidently held little appeal in official Conservative circles. Although widows' pensions were discussed at the 1923 Conservative Party annual conference (one speaker admitting that women's wages were insufficient to support a family of four of five) and a motion was passed approving of the idea,[99] family allowances were never discussed at any of the conferences in the 1920s.[100]

The Family Endowment Society had on its Council one prominent Conservative politician – Sir Arthur Steel-Maitland, who was Minister of Labour from 1924 to 1929. Steel-Maitland (1876–1935) had served as a Special Commissioner to the 1905–9 Royal Commission on the Poor Laws and was interested in social problems; he was, for example, probably the only Conservative minister ever to have slept in common lodging houses and gained a knowledge of the inside of a workhouse, and was generally liked by the Labour movement.[101] As Minister of Labour at the time when family allowances were enjoying much discussion *vis-a-vis* wages questions it is to be expected that he might have exerted his influence within the government. Yet the Steel-Maitland Papers contain no record of his ever having done so, even at the time of the Samuel Report (which, of course, recommended family allowances); nor do they contain any letters from Eleanor Rathbone asking for his help.[102] Indeed, but for his name on the Council list there is no evidence that Sir Arthur Steel-Maitland took any active interest in the Family Endowment Society.[103] All in all, therefore, family allowances were almost completely ignored by the Conservative Party in the 1920s.

Family allowances thus enjoyed a limited amount of discussion within political parties in the 1920s,[104] but in no way did they ever become an issue of great importance. Apart from the ILP leaders, politicians were cautious: at a time when fiscal retrenchment was the economic orthodoxy most generally accepted, the sheer cost of a state-run family allowance scheme made it appear a practical impossibility for the foreseeable future. Striking proof of this can be seen in what happened after 1931. In the new climate of extreme financial austerity family allowances disappeared from political discussion, and for most of the 1930s were rarely mentioned within the three main political parties.

However, from about 1935 onwards Eleanor Rathbone began to gather together in the House of Commons an all-party group of MPs which grew in numbers until, in the Second World War, it made up a considerable pro-family allowance lobby. The development of this group was closely connected with the emergence of a 'middle opinion' that has been noticed by two recent historians.[105] With the Labour Party greatly weakened after the 1931 split, the Liberal Party in decline, the Conservative Party effectively leading a National Government whose policy on social reform was to do as little as possible, conventional party politics within Parliament appeared to be in the doldrums; and by contrast, outside Parliament violent clashes took place between communists and fascists. In this situation, there emerged a group of politicians of liberal views who accepted the need for collectivist measures within a capitalist economy and aimed at forming a middle-way consensus between the extremes of left and right that would evolve a programme of liberal reforms based on long-term planning and empirical social research.[106]

Typical of the way this middle opinion strand of thought evolved was the case of Harold Macmillan. As a young Conservative MP in the 1920s, representing the predominantly working class constituency of Stockton-on-Tees, Macmillan allied himself with other young liberal Tories like Robert Boothby, Oliver Stanley, R. S. Hudson and Anthony Eden. He became increasingly disillusioned with Baldwin's leadership and, while out of Parliament in 1929—31, contemplated joining Oswald Mosley's New Party. After re-entering Parliament in 1933 he set about gathering support for the ideas he had been developing since the 1920s for greater planning in industry, social reform and international relations.[107] In the 1930s Macmillan was active in organizing the Next Five Years Group (whose membership also included Eleanor Rathbone, Eva Hubback, Seebohm Rowntree, J. A. Hobson and Professor Gilbert Murray)[108] and took an active interest in social problems, including family poverty and the need for family allowances.[109]

The exact size of this pro-family allowance Commons group of the late 1930s is very difficult to estimate. Certainly, it had reached 152 by the middle of 1941,[110] but no firm evidence of its strength before then is available.[111] Exactly how many MPs in the late 1930s would have supported a family allowances Bill is impossible to say. The campaign conducted in the Commons was led by a very small group consisting (apart from Eleanor Rathbone) of Leo Amery, Duncan Sandys, Robert Boothby, Harold Macmillan, John C. Wright and Robert Cary (Conservative), David Adams (Labour) and Graham White (Liberal). They tended to raise the topic every time the problems of the UISC or UAB were discussed: if benefit and assistance rates could not be brought up to nutritionally-adequate levels without touching on wages and destroying work-incentives, they argued, then the problem had to be tackled at the wages end through family allowances.

The all-party group of Eleanor Rathbone supporters was thus spearheaded by a number of Conservatives who felt alienated by their party's negative attitude to social reform. The most important of these was Leo Amery,[112] who had served in Baldwin's 1924–9 government but now found himself rather in the political wilderness. Leo Amery first heard about family allowances just after the First World War, when he met the wife of a Lille manufacturer who told him of the equalization fund system run by her husband and a number of other French employers in the area; 'she was enthusiastic on the merits of the scheme as a contribution to social welfare, but also hopeful that it might, in the long run, contribute to the restoration of France's sadly depleted population'. Amery observed with interest the growth of the European schemes, and during the mining dispute of 1926 'urged on Baldwin its adoption, at any rate for the mining industry'. Only in 1936, however, did he study family allowances seriously, at which time he was beginning to realize the extent of family poverty in Britain – added to which were the 'overlap' arguments *vis-a-vis* the UISC and UAB. Realizing the issue was 'the most urgent aspect of social policy' he became an active propagandist for family allowances: he wrote numerous articles on the subject, made speeches in Parliament and in public, was an active leader of the all-party Commons group, investigated existing private industrial schemes, and even persuaded the board of Maclean's Ltd, the chemical manufacturers (on which he served), to introduce a family allowance system for their employees.[113]

Since Leo Amery was the most important figure among the pro-family allowance Commons group of the late 1930s it is illustrative of this section of opinion to analyse his motives clearly. His first concern, he maintained, was over the health and nutrition of the nation's children. As he saw it, 'children are both the creators and sufferers of poverty in large families',[114] and it was deplorable that 25 per cent of the child population were growing up under-nourished.[115] He had read a large number of the recent poverty surveys – he showed knowledge of the investigations in Sheffield, Merseyside, Miles Platting, Southampton, and the work of Boyd Orr, Rowntree, the BMA, the Pilgrim Trust and the Children's Minimum Council – and quoted extensively from these surveys when advocating family allowances in Parliament[116] or at public meetings such as the BMA's April 1939 conference on nutrition (where family allowances were discussed at length).[117]

Amery also advocated family allowances in pro-natalist, 'national security' terms. For example, in the House of Commons in November 1938 he maintained that social reform and rearmament went hand in hand, since both were 'part of a wider effort for national regeneration'. 'How can we', he asked, 'confronted by dangers not of today and tomorrow but of the generations which lie ahead, contemplate with equanimity the prospect of our population, already small compared with some of our competitors, steadily dwindling, above all in the younger spheres of life?'[118] Again, when writing on 'Family allowances in industry' in the magazine *Co-Partnership* in June 1938, he expressed an industrialist's concern that the threatening decline in the population would mean a decrease in demand for goods, a fall in purchasing power, high taxation to support an increasingly aged and non-productive population, and a growing expenditure on national defence 'against great who are concentrating all their abilities upon the maintenance of their numbers as well as upon the expansion of their armaments'.[119]

Thirdly, Amery strongly supported the less eligibility argument for family allowances. If unemployment benefit and assistance levels were too low, but could not be raised without overlapping onto wage rates, then family allowances were the obvious answer. As an employer, Amery was insistent that the solution did not lie in overall wage increases; industry simply could not afford this, he maintained. 'If we could, by a wave of the wand, bring the wage level of this country all round up to what is required for a large family, that would be the most obvious and most desirable thing to do, but frankly that is not possible today', he said, basing his case on Eleanor Rathbone's argument that the three-child minimum wage would be both wasteful and inadequate in families with less or more than three children respectively.[120] To talk of all-round wage rises was 'merely evading the issue'; the only solution was a system of family allowances, which, Amery suggested, should be an insurance-based scheme providing 5s 0d per week for all children after the second, based on contributions of 4d per week from adult male employees and 2d per week from adult female employees and juveniles, with equivalent amounts from employers and the state. Such an arrangement would, he believed, overcome the overriding objection of cost.[121]

Leo Amery clearly saw family allowances as a conservative social reform. 'This is essentially a conservative measure and will reflect credit on our party', he wrote to Kingsley Wood in 1942,[122] when, as Secretary of State for India, he was attempting to convert his Cabinet colleagues; and in another letter at that time he emphasized to Churchill that family allowances were 'a reform which the nation as a whole will keenly welcome and which our Party in particular will feel is a Conservative reform building up the family and not merely a concession to socialism or trade unionism'.[123] At the start of the Second World War (when family allowances were being discussed both inside and outside the government as a possible means of controlling wages) Amery wrote in a letter to *The Times* that an immediate introduction of family allowances 'would not only relieve the existing hard cases, but would afford a logical basis upon which a stand could be made against all further wage increases, except to the extent they are directly justified by a rise in the cost of living'.[124]

Statements like these only served to heighten the suspicions of trade unionists. Ellen Wilkinson (who had actively supported family allowances in the 1920s) bitterly commented in 1938 that 'what the Amery type want is to feed the existing and potential cannon-fodder with the greatest economy and lack of waste. Pay the money for the upkeep of each child; don't give it to the individual workman who may have few or no children. In short, apply the means test to wages'.[125] In the late 1930s, Labour leaders viewed such Conservative support for family allowances as designed to obscure the real issue of low wages: the Labour MP George Buchanan, for instance, pointed out that

Amery was a railway company director, yet wages of railwaymen were very low, some being 'not far above starvation level'.[126]

Not surprisingly, the Labour movement remained very suspicious of this all-party support for family allowances. Thus when Marjorie Green wrote to the TUC on behalf of the Family Endowment Society suggesting an informal meeting, she was sent a discouraging reply.[127] In February 1939 the TUC was invited to participate in the British Medical Association's conference on nutrition: its Economic Committee re-considered family allowances briefly but decided to abide by the 1930 decision.[128] Thus at the BMA conference George Gibson, the TUC representative, repeated all the familiar arguments in favour of services in kind as having the greater priority: Gibson even claimed that a cash allowance would be mis-spent by parents, since 'even with the best will in the world, it is questionable whether the average parent of the middle class, let alone the working classes is competent to decide the best method of allotting an increased income in respect of the absolute welfare and future outlook of a child'.[129]

However, there was by now a glimmer of interest in the Conservative and Liberal Parties. At the 1937 Conservative Party conference Duncan Sandys introduced a motion expressing great concern over the decline of the British birth-rate, the most serious result of which would be to endanger the security of the British Empire, he maintained. Among possible remedies proposed by Sandys, marriage loans and family allowances figured prominently.[130] Eugenic fears were frequently mentioned, and the conference passed Sandys's motion without, however, calling on the government to consider family allowances.[131] Clearly the pro-natalist arguments for family allowances were beginning to arouse some interest among Conservatives for 'national defence' reasons,[132] but only political outsiders like Amery, Boothby, Wright and Sandys were wholeheartedly in favour.

Within the Liberal Party, on the other hand, the very end of the 1930s saw a growing interest in family allowances, spearheaded by Graham White.[133] In common with other 'middle opinion' politicians, White believed a middle way could be found between extremes of left and right,[134] and was very interested in a reform of the social services, the abolition of the means test, the problem of poverty and a nutritionally-adequate minimum wage, the need to stimulate demand in the economy, and so on.[135] White made no mention of family allowances in his 1935 General Election manifestos and speeches,[136] but by 1939 he had decided that in his next appeal to his electors he would stress that the three most needed measures were old age pensions, the extension of medical benefit to the dependants of insured people, and 'a scheme of family allowances or some similar step to improve nutrition'.[137]

In the House of Commons, Graham White was a strong advocate of family allowances on child poverty grounds, rarely if ever mentioning the birth-rate arguments. Like other Eleanor Rathbone supporters, he took the opportunity of suggesting family allowances whenever the problems of the UAB and UISC were discussed,[138] and wanted a complete overhaul of the social services, in order to remove the many administrative anomalies and overlaps, including an official investigation of family allowances.[139]

The need for a reorganization of the social services was, of course, widely acknowledged by social administrators in the late 1930s: indeed, the House of Commons discussed a motion on this very subject on 22 February 1939, rejecting it by the comparatively narrow margin of 172 votes to 149.[140] In May 1939, no doubt partly due to Graham White,[141] the Liberal Party decided to take up the cause of a social services reorganization plus family allowances[142] and make improved child nutrition one of its main aims.[143] Family allowances were discussed at the Liberal Summer School on 9 August 1939,[144] where Lawrence Cadbury made a speech presenting them primarily as a pro-natalist measure, emphasizing the serious industrial consequences of a declining population,[145] and Richard Titmuss delivered a paper on maternal mortality.[146] At the Summer School Lord Samuel announced that the party was going to make family allowances a major issue at the next General Election: 'We shall make this item a speciality of Liberalism', he said, 'and bring it as prominently as we can before the nation. Neither the Labour nor the Conservative Party is taking up the matter effectively'.[147] Quite what would have been the response of the electorate to this appeal is impossible to say, since one month later war broke out and changed everything.

Thus in the interwar years family allowances had at one time or other aroused the interest of all sections of political opinion, even if (with the exception of the Liberals in 1939) they never became an official policy of any of the three main parties. In the 1920s they had been seen by the Labour movement very much as a necessary part of the minimum wage concept, with pro-natalist arguments hardly ever mentioned; but eventually had been abandoned because of their high cost, because they had been presented by the ILP, and because of trade union opposition. Liberals (mainly women) had also shown interest, and had tended to favour the gradual spread of family allowances through industrial or contributory insurance schemes. The 1931 economic crisis acted as an enormous setback, but by the late 1930s interest in political circles was resurfacing, mainly among Conservatives disenchanted with the Baldwin—Chamberlain hegemony. In this period, anti-poverty arguments were still mentioned, but so also were pronatalist, imperialist 'national defence' ones; and, most important of all, family allowances were now being presented as an *alternative* to a statutory minimum wage. Overshadowing all of this, however, was the hostility and suspicion of the trade union movement. In the late 1930s trade union leaders still felt very vulnerable to wage reductions, and tended to regard family allowances as a means of concealing the fundamental issue of low pay. Until they could be persuaded to change their minds, family allowances would remain a political impossibility.

Notes and References

1. Arthur Marwick, 'The Labour Party and the welfare state in Britain, 1900—1948', *American Historical Review*, 73 (December 1967), p. 393.
2. *ILP Annual Conference Report for 1926*, pp. 76—87.
3. ibid., pp. 76—8; G. D. H. Cole, *A History of the Labour Party from 1914* (1948), pp. 197—8; Ralph Miliband, *Parliamentary Socialism* (1973), p. 152.
4. For an early expression of his ideas, see Brailsford, 'Equal pay and the family wage', in *A Share in Your Motherland* (1918), pp. 9—17.
5. For example, Eleanor Rathbone spoke at the 1924 ILP Summer School. *New Leader* (22 August 1924).
6. See articles in the *New Leader* by Brailsford (9 October 1925); Hugh Dalton (15 January 1925); Ernest Hunter (30 January 1924); and Mary Stocks (17 April 1925).
7. H. N. Brailsford *et al.*, *The Living Wage* (1926), pp. 8—12.
8. H. N. Brailsford, *Socialism for Today* (1926), p. 77.
9. *The Living Wage*, op. cit., p. 31.
10. ILP pamphlet, *The Living Income* (n.d., prob. 1929), p. 4. To confuse matters further, Brailsford on one occasion maintained that in demanding the Living Wage he was 'asking for the impossible'. Robert E. Dowse, *Left in the Centre* (1966), p. 130.
11. Speech by P. J. Dollan, *Labour Party Annual Conference Report for 1926*, p. 274; H. N. Brailsford, *Families and Incomes: the*

Case for Children's Allowances (1926), pp. 11—12.

12. ILP pamphlet, *Labour's Road to Power* (n.d., prob. 1926), p. 7.
13. *The Living Wage*, op. cit., pp. 22—3.
14. Ernest E. Hunter, *Wages and Families* (1928), p. 7.
15. J. L. Cohen, *Family Income Insurance* (1926).
16. Brailsford in W. H. Beveridge (ed.), *Six Aspects of Family Allowances* (1927), p. 19.
17. Dorothy Jewson, *Socialists and the Family* (1926), p. 4. See also Minnie Pallister, 'The justice of family allowances', *Socialist Review* (June 1926), pp. 40—2.
18. *Labour's Road to Power*, op. cit., p. 8.
19. Hunter, op. cit., p. 5.
20. *New Leader* (22 May 1925).
21. Hunter, op. cit., p. 5. In addition, the cost of food imports would be cut by the introduction of a new agricultural policy which would result in a better-fed population. *Socialism for Today*, op. cit., pp. 113—16.
22. Dowse, op. cit., p. 225.
23. Correspondence between Eleanor Rathbone and Stanley Unwin (October 1926), Allen & Unwin Eleanor Rathbone File.
24. Family Endowment Society pamphlet, *Trade Union and Labour Opinion Favourable to Family Allowances* (1928).
25. *Family Endowment Society Annual Report for 1930*, p. 2.
26. *Invitation to Labour Family Allowances Committee Conference 23 May 1929*. The Committee included J. L. Cohen, G. D. H. Cole, Hugh Dalton, Mrs Agnes Dollan, Ernest Hunter, Arthur Creech Jones, George Lansbury and Ellen Wilkinson.
27. In 1919 this concept had tended to consist of three elements — widows' pensions, motherhood endowment and the State Bonus scheme. A motion in favour of all three was passed at the Guild's Annual Congress in June 1919. *Women's Co-operative Guild Annual Report for 1919—20*, pp. 2, 5, 12, 28.
28. ibid., *for 1925—6*, p. 18, and *for 1926—7*, p. 17. See also Women's Co-operative Guild, *Notes for the Study of Family Allowances* (n.d., prob. 1925).
29. *Notice of First Annual Women's Trade Union Conference for 1926*, pp. 4—10.
30. *National Conference of Labour Women: Report for 1927*, pp. 42—3; *for 1929*, pp. 64—5; and *for 1930*, pp. 42—54.
31. See letters in *The Labour Woman* (1 September 1930), pp. 137—8.
32. Quoted in Cole, op. cit., p. 198.

33. There was merely a promise 'to abolish the grosser scandals of underpayment', op. cit., p. 22.
34. David Butler and Anne Sloman, *British Political Facts, 1900—1975* (1975), p. 229.
35. Speech by Arthur Hayday, *Labour Party Annual Conference Report for 1930*, p. 178.
36. In February 1930, for example, there was published the Macmillan Report on a textile-industry wage dispute which suggested that, when comparing the pre- and postwar standard of living of the worker, the value of recent expansions in social services should be taken into account. *Report by a Court of Inquiry, Concerning the Matters in Dispute Regarding Wages in the Northern Counties Wool Textile Industry*, Cmd 3505 (1930), p. 26.
37. *Labour Party Annual Conference Report for 1930*, p. 176.
38. So named after the Mond-Turner talks of 1928—9 between representatives of the TUC and large employers, aimed at arriving at a better understanding between the two sides of industry. These talks were seen as a 'sell out' by the trade union left, notably A. J. Cook.
39. Alan Bullock, *The Life and Times of Ernest Bevin*, vol. I (1960), pp. 389—90; Dowse, op. cit., pp. 134—5.
40. Living Wage Committee, Report of meeting on 9 February 1928. TUC Records, File 117 (all Living Wage Committee minutes contained herein).
41. Speech by C. T. Cramp, *Trades Union Congress Annual Report for 1930*, p. 407.
42. Speech to the Faculty of Insurance, 1927, quoted in Socialist Party of Great Britain pamphlet, *Family Allowances, a Socialist Analysis* (n.d., prob. 1943), pp. 14—15.
43. For example, Dr Alfred Salter, a Labour Party expert on public health, argued that family allowances could only accompany extensions of services in kind if the nation had something in the region of £500 million to spare — which he considered impossible. Living Wage Committee minutes (15 March 1928).
44. Extract from General Council minutes (22 March 1927), TUC Records, File 117.
45. *Labour Party Annual Conference Report for 1926*, pp. 274—5.
46. Sylvia Mann, 'Trade Unionism, the Labour Party and the Issue of Family Allowances 1925—30' (University of Warwick MA thesis, 1978), p. 38.
47. Full membership list in TUC Records, File 117.

48. Memoranda by Milne-Bailey, 'ILP Evidence' (3 December 1927), and 'The ILP Living Wage Scheme' (6 December 1927), ibid.
49. Living Wage Committee minutes (7, 8, 14 and 15 December 1927).
50. Living Wage Committee minutes (26 January 1928).
51. Living Wage Committee minutes (9, 16 and 23 February and 1, 7, 15 and 22 March 1928).
52. As far as can be ascertained, the interim report seems to have been published just prior to the 1928 TUC annual conference. In the preceding months, Bevin had rather petulantly tried to delay its publication, complaining that there was insufficient information in it. Bevin to Citrine (30 July 1928), TUC Records, File 117.
53. Trades Union Congress General Council and Labour Party Executive: Joint Committee on the Living Wage, *Interim Report on Family Allowances and Child Welfare* (Parts I–III) (1928), esp. pp. 11, 16, 17–27, 31, 37.
54. *Trades Union Congress Annual Report for 1929*, p. 258. A table giving individual unions' voting figures is contained in TUC Records, File 117. The chief opponents of family allowance were Bevin's Transport and General Workers' Union (membership 300 000) and the National Union of Railwaymen (327 000); however, the Miners' Federation threw its massive support (membership 725 000) behind family allowances.
55. *Labour Party Annual Conference Report for 1927*, pp. 216–21.
56. ibid., *for 1928*, pp. 167–8.
57. ibid., *for 1929*, pp. 159–60.
58. ibid., pp. 161–8.
59. ibid., pp. 168–9.
60. Living Wage Committee minutes (5 February 1930).
61. Keynes to Milne-Bailey (4 March 1930), TUC Records, File 118.
62. Trades Union Congress General Council minutes (28 May 1930).
63. Circular letter of 10 June 1930 and invitation to conference on 9 July 1930, TUC Records, File 118.
64. Memorandum by E. P. Harries on meeting of Trade Union Group of MPs (17 July 1930), ibid.
65. *Trades Union Congress Annual Report for 1930*, pp. 220–1 (the report is contained herein, but was also published separately). The majority were J. L. Beard, J. Hill, R. T. Jones, Miss A. Loughlin (TUC), J. L. Adamson, Ethel Bentham, Mrs Ayrton Gould, Joseph Jones and F. W. Jowett (Labour Party).
66. ibid., pp. 218–9. The minority were H. H. Elvin, F. Wolstencraft (TUC) and W. H. Hutchinson (Labour Party). Citrine and Harry

Snell, MP disagreed with both reports and signed neither.

67. ibid., pp. 381—3.
68. ibid., pp. 388—91.
69. ibid., pp. 395—7, 383—5.
70. ibid., p. 409.
71. *Labour Party Annual Conference Report for 1930*, pp. 174—9, 212—13.
72. Hubback in E. Rathbone, *Family Allowances* (1949), p. 279.
73. Voting figures from the *Liberal Magazine* (April 1923), pp. 246—7.
74. *Family Endowment Society Annual Report for 1925*, p. 2.
75. *Liberal Magazine* (September 1924), p. 548.
76. *Liberal Woman's News* (June 1925), p. 73.
77. ibid. (July 1925), p. 92.
78. In the April 1925 issue of the *Liberal Woman's News*, pp. 44—5, Eleanor Rathbone had written a short article on family allowances. As always, she presented her case in the form most acceptable to her audience: in this instance, she made no mention of a state-financed scheme but suggested organization through industrial pools or contributory insurance.
79. *Report of the Council Meeting of the Women's National Liberal Federation for 1925*, ibid. (June 1925), p. 69.
80. There were some minor changes of personnel later. One addition was Miss Lucy Mair as honorary secretary, who was secretary to Professor Gilbert Murray (a member of the FES) and the daughter of Mrs Janet Mair, Beveridge's secretary. Dorothea Layton and Margaret Corbett Ashby were FES members.
81. *Women's National Liberal Federation Annual Report for 1926—7*, pp. 19—20. The records of the Liberal Party are now housed in the University of Bristol Library, but are as yet unindexed, and so it was impossible to discover whether any papers of this committee have survived.
82. *Interim Report of the Family Endowment Enquiry Committee set up by the Women's National Liberal Federation* (1926). The report considered a state scheme to be 'the most logical and just' although 'at the moment outside the scope of practical politics' (p. 3), went on to discuss organization by contributory insurance or industrial pools (pp. 4—6) and concluded with some comments on possible effect on the birth-rate and wage levels (pp. 7—8).
83. *Report of the Council Meeting of the Women's National Liberal Federation for 1926*, pp. 2—3; *Liberal Magazine* (August 1926), p. 467.
84. Women's National Liberal Federation, *Final Report of the Family*

Endowment Enquiry Committee: Children's Allowances (1927). There was also a suggestion (pp. 18—19) that the state could set an example by paying family allowances to its employees and encouraging local authorities to do the same.

85. *Report of the Council Meeting of the Women's National Liberal Federation for 1927*, pp. 5—6.
86. *Liberal Woman's News* (September 1927), p. 127.
87. ibid. (November 1927), p. 148.
88. Women's National Liberal Federation pamphlet, *Liberal Policy for Women* (1929), p. 27.
89. Paul Western, *Family Allowances — a Policy for Liberals* (Family Endowment Society pamphlet, 1929).
90. According to the *Family Endowment Society Annual Report for 1930*, p. 2, during the 1929 General Election 'the subject of family allowances was raised in many constituencies. A number of candidates were approached, and many of all parties expressed interest in and sympathy with our aims, and it was not uncommon to find the cause of family allowances advocated in election addresses.' However, in the collection of 1929 Liberal election addresses (in the University of Bristol Library) neither Simon's nor Muir's mentions family allowances.
91. *Liberal Magazine* (February 1928), p. 102.
92. Liberal Party pamphlet, *Give the Children a Chance* (1927), p. 19.
93. *Britain's Industrial Future, being the Report of the Liberal Industrial Inquiry* (1928), pp. v, viii. The Executive Committee also contained H. D. Henderson, Rowntree and Keynes — all of whom were sympathetic to family allowances.
94. ibid., p. viii.
95. This idea was remarkably similar to that applied, in a different context, to wartime wages policy (including family allowances) in Keynes's *How to Pay for the War* (1940).
96. *Britain's Industrial Future*, op. cit., pp. 190—2. A state scheme was considered too expensive.
97. Voting figures in *Liberal Magazine* (April 1923), pp. 246—7.
98. Conservative Party pamphlet, *What the Conservative Government Has Done for Women and Children, 1925—1928* (1928), p. 6.
99. *Conservative Party Annual Conference Report for 1923*. Reports for the 1920s are partly in the form of press cuttings, and contain no page numbers.
100. ibid., *for 1920 to 1930*.

101. Press cuttings in Steel-Maitland Papers, Scottish Record Office GD 193/107/1.
102. See, for examples, ibid. GD 193/81/1, and GD 193/109/5 (on the 1926 coal dispute) and GD 193/244 (miscellaneous articles and letters, 1922–30).
103. Apart, of course, from his introduction of family allowances for staff of the London School of Economics.
104. They also enjoyed investigation by bodies like the International Association for Social Progress, which set up a subcommittee to look into family needs and the social services (the committee included J. L. Cohen, Professor A. M. Carr-Saunders and Professor D. H. Macgregor) and published a *Report on Family Endowment* (1927), which merely summarized the arguments for and against, and a *Report on Family Provision through Social Insurance and Other Services* (1928) which concluded (p. 17) with a brief discussion of possible family allowance schemes.
105. Arthur Marwick, 'Middle opinion in the thirties: planning, progress, and political "agreement" ', *English Historical Review*, 79 (April 1964), pp. 285–97; Paul Addison, *The Road to 1945* (1975), pp. 18, 38–40, 43–4.
106. ibid. For an interesting personal account, see Lord Salter, *Memoirs of a Public Servant* (1961), pp. 241–7.
107. Anthony Sampson, *Macmillan* (1967), pp. 21–36.
108. Harold Macmillan, *Winds of Change, 1914–39* (1966), pp. 373–4, 485–8. For list of the Group's members, see ibid., pp. 634–6.
109. See, for example, speech in *Hansard*, vol. 337 (24 June 1928), col. 1440. In *The Middle Way* (1938), pp. 38–65, Macmillan discussed in depth the problem of low wages *vis-a-vis* Rowntree's and Boyd Orr's researches on minimum needs; and then (pp. 301–11) went on to discuss the necessity of a government-established minimum wage, including family allowances.
110. Note of deputation of MPs to Kingsley Wood (16 June 1941), PRO PIN 8/163.
111. A very interesting source of information would be the Leo Amery Papers, but access to these was not granted. The Graham White Papers (in the House of Lords Record Office) consist of 21 large boxes of uncatalogued papers, which, while containing much interesting primary material on the Liberal Party and other matters (including a very large file on the administration of the Eleanor Rathbone Memorial Trust, of which White was a director),

include next to nothing on the pro-family allowance group of MPs. The only item is an exchange of correspondence between White and Amery in April 1940, which is of no significance. In an interview with the author, Air Commodore John Cecil-Wright (who, as Wing Commander J. A. C. Wright, was also a member of the all-party group) said that he doubted whether much material would have survived, since communication between members of the group was usually by word of mouth, telephone, messages in the House of Commons, etc.

112. Amery, Leopold Stennett; b. 1873, educated at Harrow and Oxford; barrister, and Conservative MP for Birmingham Sparkbrook, 1911–45; a number of Cabinet posts, 1919–24, then Secretary of State for Colonies, 1924–9; Secretary of State for India and Burma, 1940–5; died 1955.
113. Leo Amery, *My Political Life, Vol. III. The Unforgiving Years, 1920–1940* (1955), pp. 205–6.
114. *Hansard*, vol. 337 (24 June 1938), col. 1426.
115. ibid., vol. 341 (14 November 1938), col. 574.
116. ibid., cols. 576–7.
117. British Medical Association, *Nutrition and the Public Health* (1939), pp. 91–104.
118. *Hansard*, vol. 341 (14 November 1938), col. 574.
119. Leo Amery, 'Family allowances in industry', *Co-Partnership* (June 1938), p. 3.
120. *Hansard*, vol. 341 (14 November 1938), cols. 578–9.
121. British Medical Association, op. cit., pp. 96, 102–3.
122. Amery to Wood (30 May 1942), PRO T 161/116 (S. 43697/3).
123. Amery to Churchill (30 May 1942), PRO PREM 4 (97/5).
124. *The Times* (14 December 1939).
125. Ellen Wilkinson, in *Tribune* (8 July 1938), quoted in Amery, op. cit., p. 207.
126. *Hansard*, vol. 338 (18 July 1938), col. 1863. Buchanan was, however, generally a supporter of family allowances.
127. Green to secretary, TUC Social Insurance Department (24 August 1938), and reply (25 August 1938), TUC Records, File 118.
128. Trades Union Congress Economic Committee memorandum, 'Family allowances' (7 March 1939), ibid.
129. British Medical Association, op. cit., pp. 112–14.
130. *Conservative Party Annual Conference Report for 1937*, pp. 37–9.

131. ibid., pp. 39—43.
132. The next motion discussed at the conference was on the 'integrity and unity of the Empire', ibid., pp. 43—5.
133. White, Henry Graham (1880—1965); educated at Birkenhead School and University of Liverpool; Liberal MP for Birkenhead East, 1922—4 and 1929—45; President of the Liberal Party 1954—5 and Vice-President 1958—9.
134. 'In this Election the sterile arguments about Socialism and Capitalism are obsolete'. 1935 General Election Manifesto by Graham White, in Graham White Papers (uncatalogued).
135. ibid. In the Graham White Papers there is a large file dealing with his interest in unemployment.
136. ibid.
137. White to W. R. Davies (23 January 1939), ibid.
138. See, for example, *Hansard*, vol. 337 (24 June 1938), cols. 1431—8; and ibid., vol. 345 (23 March 1939), cols. 1496—9.
139. ibid., vol. 349 (30 June 1939), cols. 828—31. 1935 General Election manifestos, op. cit.
140. *Hansard*, vol. 344 (22 February 1939), cols. 395—460.
141. In October 1937, the Council of the Women's Liberal Federation had overwhelmingly passed a motion in favour of family allowances. *Report of Council Meeting of the Women's Liberal Federation for 1937*, p. 4.
142. *Liberal Policy: Resolutions Adopted by Meeting of the Assembly of the Liberal Party Organisation* (11 and 12 May 1939), pp. 5—6.
143. *Liberal Policy: A Speech Delivered to the Council of the Liberal Party Organisation on the 15th March 1939 by Sir Archibald Sinclair.*
144. *Liberal Magazine* (September 1939), p. 432.
145. L. J. Cadbury, *A Population Policy and Family Allowances* (1939), esp. pp. 1—3.
146. Press cutting from *Birmingham Post* (10 August 1939), contained in PRO AST 7/390.
147. ibid.

7 The Second World War

Not True Plurality - fierce resistance

By 1939 the movement for family allowances was just over twenty years old, and at this point it is useful to make a quick resume of what had been achieved in these years. The principle of family endowment was a very old one, and had been incorporated into a number of social policies; but on the vital question of family allowances in wages little progress had been made. Family allowances had been supported for many different reasons by a wide spectrum of opinion, but this had tended to confuse issues, and often arguments seemed to contradict each other. Generally, these arguments fell into two categories, the family poverty and the demographic, but although a vast amount of evidence had been produced in support of both, this evidence had been rejected by the government. By the late 1930s Eleanor Rathbone had managed to gather together an all-party pro-family allowances group in the House of Commons, but it mostly consisted of political outsiders like Amery and Macmillan who had little influence over their respective parties. The interest shown by the Labour movement in the 1920s had quickly died away, and throughout the 1930s the trade unions remained implacably opposed. In contrast to Europe, Britain had developed very few private industrial schemes. The only area of promise was in unemployment policy, where by the late 1930s family allowances were being tentatively considered as an effective means of preserving less eligibility. Moreover, such evidence as has survived indicates that the version of family allowances contemplated was the industrial equalization fund one; a universal, state-financed system (the Family Endowment Society's ultimate objective) was never considered. All in all, the situation in 1939 was that the government had successfully resisted the campaign for family allowances for twenty years, and all the signs were that it could hold out for at least another twenty.

Yet within four years the government had committed itself to the introduction of a universal, tax-financed family allowance system, and

in 1945 the Act was passed. This chapter will examine how this change
came about, and since the events of 1939—45 were extremely complex
it is convenient to divide them up into four periods. The first ran from
the outbreak of war in September 1939 to the end of 1940; in this
period family allowances were intensively examined by the Treasury
as a means of controlling inflation. The second period began in early
1941 with renewed activity on the part of Eleanor Rathbone and her
supporters, culminating in their deputation to the Treasury on 16
June 1941, and ended with the publication of a White Paper on family
allowances in May 1942. The third period covered the work of the
Beveridge Committee (actually begun in mid-1941), its recommendation of family allowances in the Beveridge Report, and the government's
reaction. Finally, the fourth period began in mid-1943 and ended with
the passage of the 1945 Act; in this, it was mainly administrative details
that were settled.

The Treasury had opened a file on family allowances in 1938[1] (the same
year as the UAB) in response to the growing parliamentary pressure
from Eleanor Rathbone's supporters, who were demanding some sort
of official inquiry on the lines of a Royal Commission.[2] The Treasury
decided on a policy of cautious hostility, and advised the Chancellor,
Sir John Simon, to be very careful of what he said: he should not
appear implacably opposed to such an inquiry, but at the same time
he should avoid making any rash promises that might lead to the introduction of a scheme which, however limited in scope, would cost the
Treasury a considerable amount.[3]
   This policy of wary opposition suddenly changed with the outbreak
of the Second World War in September 1939. For at least two years
before the outbreak of war pressure had been exerted on the government by businessmen,[4] industrialists[5] and economists (including J. M.
Keynes)[6] to formulate a cohesive wartime economic policy covering
price controls, wage regulation, levels of taxation, profits, the adjustment of industry to war needs, the financing of the war effort, and so
on. Above all, such dangers as rapidly-spiralling inflation, widespread
strikes or flagrant profiteering had to be avoided. In June 1939, therefore, a small committee called the 'Survey of Financial and Economic
Plans' was set up under the leadership of Lord (Sir Josiah) Stamp, with
its other two members being the economists H. D. Henderson and
Sir Henry Clay.[7]
   The Stamp Survey worked throughout the second half of 1939
on the many likely problems presented by a war economy. One of the

most crucial of these was the relationship between wages and the cost of living. Above all else, the greatest danger in a war economy would be runaway inflation; economists had the financial chaos of post-1918 Europe firmly in mind, and realized that rampant inflation would disastrously undermine the war effort.[8] A war economy would open up a whole new range of employment opportunities for the working class, with high wages; this would result in increased consumption (particularly of non-essentials), which would be met by short supplies (owing to disrupted trade), and prices would rise; in response to this, employees (who would be in a relatively strong bargaining position) would seek large wage rises. When added to the abnormally high level of public expenditure, this would soon produce high inflation — and in a time of high inflation the public would tend not to save, thus withdrawing capital from the war effort.[9]

The Stamp Survey's solution to this problem was to suggest that in wartime the adjustment of wages should be proportional to the rise in the cost of living — beyond a certain minimum figure — only for the first £2 per week of the income of an adult male wage-earner, with a lower figure for women and juveniles, and less than proportional for larger incomes.[10] However, the great drawback of this, Stamp realized, was that a uniform figure of £2 per week would take no account of differing family sizes, and hence varying financial need. To be effective and acceptable, a wages policy would have to be related to family needs, and thus the controversial question of family allowances would have to be tackled. Once introduced, a temporary wartime family allowance scheme would undoubtedly become permanent, Stamp warned — but this might be a small price to pay, given its vital importance in any fight against inflation. The best policy, he suggested, would be for the government to take the initiative and introduce a system of family allowances that would cost the Treasury as little as possible — either one run by employers, or a contributory scheme linked to health or unemployment insurance.[11]

Within the Stamp Survey, H. D. Henderson appears to have been the keenest advocate of family allowances,[12] but in fact the strongest influence was exerted by an outsider who was a close friend of Stamp, Henderson and Clay — J. M. Keynes. Soon after the outbreak of war, Keynes began to clarify the ideas he had been considering since 1937 and then launched a one-man crusade to have those ideas incorporated into official policy. On 20 October 1939 he lectured the Marshall Society at Cambridge on 'War Potential and War Finance'; four days later he sent copies of his proposals to the Chancellor of the Exchequer,

Clement Attlee, R. H. Brand, Stamp, Henderson and the editor of *The Times*; on 27 October he outlined his ideas to a dinner attended by civil servants, ministers and MPs; and on 14 and 15 November he published two articles in *The Times* entitled 'Paying for the War'.[13]

Keynes's ideas, which were finally published in February 1940 in the short book *How to Pay for the War*, were somewhat more detailed than those of the Stamp Survey. As he saw it, voluntary savings by the general public would never be sufficient to fill the gap between tax revenue and expenditure on the war effort, and thus the government would have to introduce some form of compulsory borrowing via deductions from wage packets. This 'deferred pay' would be paid back once peace had returned, and thus the ordinary wage-earner would emerge from the War richer — unlike the situation during the First World War, when it was the profiteers and rich investors who had made a financial killing by lending money to the government. Consumption would be reduced overall for the duration of the War, but the lower income groups would have their living standards protected by the establishment of an agreed minimum, below which deferred pay would not be levied, plus a system of family allowances amounting to 5s 0d per week per child up to the age of 15 years. The overall effect of this, Keynes believed, would be to increase the consumption of families with incomes less than £3 15s 0d per week, to leave unchanged the consumption of those with incomes of about £5 per week, and to reduce the consumption of those with incomes greater than £5 per week by an average of one-third.[14]

By 1939 Keynes was one of the most respected economists in Britain, and his ideas on wartime finance seem to have met with enthusiastic approval from fellow economists.[15] However, two factors prevented him from exerting official influence on the Treasury at the start of the War: first, as a past critic of the National Government he was something of a *persona non grata* with ministers, and only after the fall of the Chamberlain government in May 1940 was he given an official position;[16] secondly, a more practical reason was that he was recovering from a serious illness and could not undertake work that was too demanding.[17] Nevertheless, he pulled all available strings to get his ideas publicized,[18] and clearly expected that through the Stamp Survey these ideas would find acceptance in Whitehall.[19]

Throughout November and December 1939 the Stamp Survey discussed the wartime case for family allowances as a device for controlling inflation and protecting the living standards of the low paid.[20] Stamp argued that since trade union demands for higher wages proportional to the cost of living would depend for their justification on the hardship suffered by the lowest income groups (especially those with large families to support), 'the Government could cut away this support for the trade union claim completely by extending the system of national insurance to cover family allowances'.[21] Rapid price rises were causing great hardship at the start of the War: taking September 1939 as an index of 100 for both wages and prices, by December prices were 112 and wages 103, and by March 1940 prices were 115 and wages 108.[22] In many industries, trade unions were pressing strongly for wage increases equal to the rise in the cost of living,[23] and inevitably family allowances were being suggested by Eleanor Rathbone and her supporters as a remedy for this.[24] Several large industries had decided to meet trade union demands by granting cost-of-living wage increases in relation to family needs, and Stamp thought that this should be encouraged.[25] Ultimately, he believed, the aim should be to introduce a Keynes-type wartime economic policy which would include a family allowance scheme run by contributory insurance; the UISC had been making a profit for some time, and with low unemployment in wartime this would increase: this profit could go towards financing family allowances.[26]

So great was the need to damp down wage demands and control inflation that the Treasury immediately began collecting information on family allowances and seeking out the opinions of interested parties.[27]

The first to be consulted were other government departments. The most important of these was, of course, the Ministry of Labour, since it had prime responsibility for wages policy, and here the Treasury encountered strong opposition. The Minister of Labour, Ernest Brown, said that he was personally sympathetic to the idea of family allowances but was convinced that the trade unions would never accept them.[28] Civil servants at the ministry were generally opposed: wages could only be based on the skill of the worker and not on family needs, they maintained; neither arguments about alleged child malnutrition in a small number of families nor considerations of war finance could justify the launching of a massive new social policy that would be bound to continue in peacetime.[29] Stamp's proposal, a ministry official pointed out, viewed family allowances 'not so much as a general social improvement but as a means of buying off pressure for wage rises', and since the unions would be opposed, some other method of wage control would have to be devised.[30]

The members of the Stamp Survey needed no reminding of the strength of trade union opposition to their plans. At the start of the

War, trade union leaders (especially Ernest Bevin and Sir Walter Citrine) were deeply distrustful of the Chamberlain government's willingness to distribute the economic sacrifices of wartime equally among all classes. When the TUC General Council met the Prime Minister immediately after the outbreak of war Bevin insisted that the government would have to introduce strict price controls, and when these were not forthcoming he adopted the attitude that the working class henceforth had the right to claim higher wages in exactly the same way that industrialists were being allowed high profits after tax. In the eyes of trade union leaders, Chamberlain and his ministers were the 'guilty men' of Munich and mass unemployment, and not to be trusted.[31]

Realising the depth of trade union hostility, Stamp decided to use Seebohm Rowntree as a mediator. Rowntree had taken a keen interest in the problems of a wartime economy,[32] and on 5 December had sent a memorandum to Stamp suggesting that price controls be accompanied by a cost-of-living bonus on wages and family allowances of 5s 0d per week for every dependent child after the second.[33] Stamp clearly hoped that as an employer with a deep interest in social policy, Rowntree could persuade both employers and unions to accept a 'wage-control plus family allowances' package. Accordingly, he met Rowntree and persuaded him to send his memorandum to employers' organizations and trade union leaders.[34]

Employers reacted very favourably. They were being pressed by their respective unions to grant wage rises equal to cost-of-living rises, and were unsure of what to do in the absence of government guidelines; evidently they approved of the contents of Rowntree's memorandum, because having sent copies of it to two hundred employers' organizations in England and Wales he received requests for a further thousand copies.[35] But trade union leaders reacted angrily. Bevin wrote a letter to Rowntree which is worth quoting extensively as a vivid illustration of trade union suspicion; after apologizing for his delay in replying, Bevin went on:

> My time has been taken up in trying to get wages commensurate with the cost of living. I am determined to keep them up to a proper level. The powers that be have won the first round but that is only a temporary victory for them. As our people sicken of this business they will revolt against the depression of their standards. I disagree entirely with your thesis and the answer to it is in the last paragraph. No employer will make a sacrifice unless he is compelled to.[36] All the prices I have seen fixed, and the charges being made, indicate that taxation and everything

else is included and the Employers rake off on the top, and in this farcical state of Society for one class to be trying to measure another upon a fodder basis is intolerable.[37]

Bevin's letter was passed round several ministers and officials, and caused great dismay. Ernest Brown insisted that no co-operation would come from the unions until price controls were introduced; Keynes found Bevin's letter 'truly shocking', but said that he would try to see Bevin personally and get him to change his mind, since, as he put it, 'his bark is often worse than his bite'; and throughout late January and February 1940 there were rather half-hearted suggestions about a joint conference of all sides to produce some sort of agreement.[38] Clearly, though, all concerned realized that the trade unions' opposition to the Stamp proposals was caused by factors much more fundamental than a mere dislike of family allowances; only a change in the government, removing the Chamberlainites and bringing in the Labour Party, could have won their co-operation.

However, by early 1940 another source of opposition to family allowances was developing. Treasury officials were realizing that a national family allowance scheme, even if contributory, would end up as a very expensive social reform – and, in addition, since price rises were flattening off the Stamp proposals appeared to hold less and less validity. The 'real question', argued Edward Hale (Treasury), was 'whether the grant of family allowances in any form will in practice make it possible to avoid increases in wages which would otherwise be unavoidable and which would cost more than the family allowances',[39] and by the spring of 1940 this was becoming less and less likely. By mid-1940 many wartime social policies were being introduced – food subsidies, rationing, extensions of school milk and meals provision[40] – and the Treasury maintained that these were far more effective in meeting urgent need than family allowances would be.[41] Thus by almost the middle of 1940 the Treasury's attitude had hardened into what it was to remain throughout the rest of the War: a determination to resist any wartime scheme, in the hope that once peace returned the case for family allowances would be greatly weakened.

Ironically, it was just around this time that there occurred important political changes which, had they taken place earlier, might have resulted in the implementation of the Stamp proposals. In May 1940 the Chamberlain government was replaced by Churchill's Coalition, and the entry into ministerial office of the Labour leaders Attlee, Bevin, Morrison, Dalton and Greenwood meant that the trade unions were henceforth much less suspicious of government proposals for family allowances, since they knew that their interests would be protected.[42] The change of government also brought Keynes and other liberal economists into positions of official power.[43] And the anti-inflation arguments for family allowances publicized by Keynes, Rowntree, Amery and others at the start of the War[44] had breathed new life into Eleanor Rathbone's campaign, so that by mid-1940 it was gathering momentum once again: Family Endowment Society publications began to appear in rapid succession (repeating the familiar arguments, but with a noticeably greater air of confidence),[45] government departments were lobbied[46] and the all-party group of supporters in the House of Commons grew in strength. This renewed activity reached a peak in early 1941, at which point began the second phase in the development of family allowances in the Second World War.

The most significant feature of this period was the change in attitude that took place within the Labour movement. Rank-and-file opinion within the trade union movement and the Labour Party had always been quite favourable to family allowances, and in the first two years of the War this grass-roots support increased. In particular, numerous organizations of Labour women passed resolutions in support of family allowances and made the TUC General Council aware of their feelings.[47] However, TUC leaders were generally unenthusiastic, and some, like Sir Walter Citrine (the TUC general secretary), Charles Dukes (National Union of General and Municipal Workers), and Arthur Deakin (Transport and General Workers' Union), were bitterly opposed for the traditional wage-bargaining reasons.[48] Thus when Eva Hubback and Leo Amery attempted to win the General Council over by sending them numerous letters, pamphlets and invitations to Family Endowment Society meetings in the early months of 1940, they encountered a somewhat frosty reaction;[49] union leaders took more notice of Amery's letter to *The Times* of 14 December 1939, in which he advocated family allowances as a basis upon which the government could make a stand against large wage claims in wartime.[50]

By early 1941, however, these suspicions were beginning to melt away, for several reasons. The presence in Churchill's Cabinet of several Labour Party leaders (particularly, of course, Ernest Bevin as Minister of Labour) radically altered union leaders' attitudes to government wage policies: by July 1940 Bevin had been given the power to direct labour anywhere he saw fit, to fix wages and hours of work and, within a framework of free collective bargaining, refer industrial disputes to a new National Arbitration Tribunal.[51] Increasing pressure was being applied by the Labour Party: in August 1940 the Labour Party Policy Committee came out in favour of a state-financed family allowance scheme of 5s 0d per child per week (to be accompanied by the abolition of child tax allowances) and asked the TUC to reconsider its position.[52] By mid-1941 fifty-two Labour and three National Labour MPs had declared themselves in favour of family allowances, and a 'Family Allowances Labour Group' had been formed (with John Parker MP, as chairman, Edith Summerskill MP, as secretary and the same headquarters as the Family Endowment Society) to put pressure on the TUC.[53] Another important factor was that by early 1941 the anti-inflation, wage-control arguments for family allowances which had so antagonized trade union leaders at the start of the War had disappeared and had been replaced by more acceptable ones relating to family poverty: in particular, by mid-1941 family allowance supporters could argue that there were now so many forms of family endowment in wartime social policy − billeting allowances, war pensions, separation allowances, income tax child rebates, disablement pensions, and so on − that virtually the only people not enjoying family benefits were those below the tax threshold in civilian employment.[54] Thus although TUC leaders were still rather cool towards the leaders of the Family Endowment Society[55] they were now prepared to listen to Seebohm Rowntree when he attended a meeting of the TUC Economic Committee on 8 April 1941 and outlined the child poverty case for family allowances, quoting the evidence from his 1936 York Survey.[56]

After several delays and inconclusive discussions, the TUC General Council reluctantly decided on 23 March 1941 to refer the matter to the next Labour Party annual conference.[57] At the conference, in June, there was still opposition from trade unionists on the wages question (led by Charles Dukes), but more speakers were for family allowances than against, and although no decision was taken, the debate clearly showed how opinion was changing.[58] Later in the year, in September, an even more significant event occurred when the TUC annual conference re-opened the question of family allowances for the first time since 1930. By this time, the TUC General Council's Economic Committee had recommended family allowances in principle, subject to the proviso that any scheme should be tax-financed and state-run; thus at the conference there was only a brief discussion, mainly of the child poverty case, and then with little comment the matter was referred to the General Council for further investigation.

Most remarkable of all, very little concern was expressed on the wages question.[59] By late 1941, therefore, supporters of family allowances were confident that it would only be a matter of time before the General Council gave its approval.

Riding on this new wave of interest, the Family Endowment Society leaders decided to concentrate on lobbying the Chancellor, Kingsley Wood. In February, March and April 1941, questions on family allowances were put to Wood in the House of Commons, and on each occasion he gave a reply that was discouragingly vague.[60] However, this only seems to have goaded Eleanor Rathbone into even greater activity, and on 29 April a motion was put down in the Commons welcoming a national scheme of family allowances, signed by 152 MPs.[61] Three days later she wrote to the Chancellor, asking him to receive a deputation.[62]

By this time the Treasury seems to have realized that public and political pressure was growing at such a rate as would make it very hard to resist demands for family allowances in the long run; to be too discouraging to Eleanor Rathbone's deputation might only provoke them into demanding a full Commons debate, which would greatly assist their cause. The best policy, the Treasury decided, would be to delay as much as possible in order to ensure that any scheme would be a postwar one, limited in scope and low in cost. A wartime scheme would be expensive and inflationary, and might therefore upset the delicately-balanced war economy.[63] Besides, argued Kingsley Wood, the growing shortage of labour was resulting in greater opportunities for well-paid work and increased household income without any supplementation by the state.[64] However, Eleanor Rathbone's tactic at this juncture was to pester the Chancellor with technical questions on the financial implications of a system of family allowances, and eventually he admitted in the Commons that a universal 5s 0d allowance for each child under 15 years of age would cost £130 million – but if existing child allowances in income tax and the social services were abolished, then the cost would be nearer £35 million.[65] This, Treasury officials realized only too well, was a particularly difficult argument for them to oppose.

However, in pursuing these delaying tactics the Treasury was suddenly blessed with a great stroke of luck. Just as its officials were preparing to meet Eleanor Rathbone's deputation, the government announced the appointment of an inter-departmental committee under Sir William Beveridge to look into the reorganization of the social services.[66] The appointment of this committee, whose chairman was a long-standing supporter of Eleanor Rathbone, ensured that henceforth pressure would be taken off the Treasury. More importantly, since the Beveridge Committee's terms of reference related specifically to *postwar* reconstruction its appointment guaranteed that family allowances would never be introduced in wartime.

Eleanor Rathbone's deputation met Kingsley Wood (and representatives of other departments) on 16 June 1941. It was nominally led by John Cecil Wright (Conservative), and besides Eleanor Rathbone it consisted of six MPs — Clement Davies (National Liberal), Sir Francis Fremantle (Conservative), Kenneth Lindsay (National Liberal), John Parker (Labour), Wilfred Roberts (Liberal) and Edith Summerskill (Labour). Each speaker outlined different aspects of the wartime case for family allowances: the growing support from all sections of political opinion, the evidence from recent poverty surveys and from evacuation, the increased economic dependence of children if the school-leaving age was raised, the growing number of other child allowances, and (particularly in Eleanor Rathbone's case) the pro-natalist arguments. In the course of a somewhat vague reply, Kingsley Wood agreed to launch an official inquiry, but warned that the government might decide that extensions of services in kind would be more beneficial.[67]

The inquiry was conducted by Edward Hale, a senior Treasury official, and was made as limited as possible. Hale was instructed simply to summarize the main arguments for and against, and investigate such questions as administration and cost, without making any pronouncements on the desirability of family allowances[68] — which task he evidently found very difficult, because 'while there has been a good deal of propaganda by Miss Rathbone and her friends there has been no public controversy, so that if it is a question of extracting arguments from pamphlets and reported speeches the result would be quite one-sided'.[69] The most important thing, however, was to seek the advice of other government departments on these practical questions, and throughout the period June to August 1941 Hale did this.

First of all, there was the problem of whether the scheme should be contributory or non-contributory. This was a question that aroused strong reactions — employers would want the former, trade unions the latter — but in reality, the Treasury realized, the distinction had always been largely illusory, and would be even more so in the future if income tax liability was extended downwards to cover most of the working class.[70] Given this situation, Hale was inclined to favour a contributory scheme 'since the idea that the burden of the cost of any scheme of this kind could be prevented by any method of finance from falling on the working population is an illusion which it would be wrong to encourage', though he did recognize that 'labour opposition to family allowances could be bought off by a non-contributory scheme'.[71] However, any decision on this would have to take into account a second problem – the question of whether child tax rebates should be abolished. Merging the two systems (that is, allowing parents to keep either the family allowance or the child tax allowance, but not both) would be administratively very complex and might involve the use of an unpopular means test.[72]

Then there was a third related problem – the scope of the scheme. Income tax rebates covered the first child, so family allowances should too. But if the first child were excluded, the cost of providing 5s 0d allowances would fall from about £132 million to about £58 million per annum; and starting with the third child would lower it to only about £23 million.[73] Strong opposition to a universal scheme came from Sir George Reid of the Assistance Board. Reid insisted that most wages were sufficient to meet the needs of two or three children: 'The suggestion that family allowances should include all children', he wrote, 'is due, I feel, to a muddled pre-occupation with very low rates of wages, for which family allowances are not the appropriate remedy at all.'[74]

Even stronger opposition came from the Board of Education over the question of whether the money to finance a scheme of cash allowances might not be better allocated to services in kind. Jealously protective of their traditional role as overseers of the health of schoolchildren, Board officials insisted that an extension of free milk and meals schemes was the only way of ensuring that the money reached the children.[75] 'I feel sure', minuted the Board's new president, R. A. Butler, 'that if we are out to improve the conditions of childhood the most effective way of doing so would be to provide *free* meals, *free* milk and *free* boots and clothing for all children who satisfy an income test.'[76] The Board pressed this view strongly, and finally succeeded in having the 1942 White Paper remind the reader five times that the same amount of money might be better spent on child welfare services.[77]

Finally, there were problems of administration and staffing (greatly exacerbated by wartime labour shortages, particularly in clerical labour)[78] and the question of whether, in view of the Beveridge Committee's work, any scheme would have to be a postwar one.[79]

By October 1941 Kingsley Wood realized that the results of Hale's inquiry would have to be published as a government White Paper, and accordingly circulated drafts of it to the Cabinet. Clement Attlee (Lord Privy Seal), Ernest Brown (Minister of Health), R. A. Butler (President of the Board of Education) and — not surprisingly — Ernest Bevin (Minister of Labour) were all against its publication,[80] but Wood realized that he had no choice.[81] Accordingly, after fully six months of further consultation and re-drafting (much to the irritation of Eleanor Rathbone's supporters in the House of Commons)[82] the White Paper was published in May 1942.

It could hardly have been a less encouraging document, reflecting Treasury hostility in general, and Hale's dry, administrative viewpoint in particular. After summarizing briefly the case for (child poverty in large families, increasing wages without causing inflation, counter-acting the decline in the birth-rate, the anomaly of child tax allow-ances) and the case against (the possible effect on wage bargaining, the greater need for services in kind), it went on to consider the rela-tive merits of a contributory or non-contributory scheme, and was distinctly lukewarm towards both, emphasizing at every stage the administrative problems. Even on a question like payment to the mother or father, which was a highly emotive issue with the Family Endowment Society leaders, the White Paper merely pronounced the gloomy verdict that 'to whichever parent payment were made there would be no possibility of ensuring that the additional income was properly spent'. Finally, there was an outline of the respective costs of different schemes, such as one linked to the income tax sys-tem.[83]

The discouraging tone of the White Paper greatly disappointed Eleanor Rathbone's supporters. Its emphasis on an income limit and, therefore, means-testing, seemed to John Cecil Wright to smack of a 'soup kitchen' approach to the problem of family poverty; also, a means test would act as an unjust deterrent.[84] Eleanor Rathbone expressed apprehension that the Treasury was trying to delay matters until after the War, when Parliament might be less concerned with social reform.[85] Thus when the Commons debated family allowances on 23 June 1942 she and her supporters made sure that a motion was passed by the House urging the government to give 'immediate consideration' to the question of a national scheme.[86] Bowing to the inevitable, Kingsley Wood agreed to this, subject to three conditions which, he said, would probably be clarified by the autumn: a recom-mendation of family allowances in the Beveridge Report, a favourable decision by the TUC annual conference, and the nation's economic position.[87]

Soon after the White Paper was published, Kingsley Wood recommended to his ministerial colleagues that any decision on family allowances be delayed until the Beveridge Committee had reported,[88] and this was the Treasury's official view for the next seven months. Within Whitehall, there was continued hostility towards family allowances from civil servants of other departments. The Ministry of Food, for example, argued strongly in favour of more provision in kind as a better alternative,[89] and discussions on the 'cash versus kind' issue went on inside the Treasury over the summer of 1942. Civil servants were evidently irritated that family allowance supporters had not given much thought to practical questions like these:

> So far as I can unravel the confusion of thought in the minds of the Family Endowment Society [wrote Hale caustically], they tend rather to the second point of view [that is, cash] and trust that by labelling the payment 'family allowance' and giving it to the mother, they can cause it to have a different effect on the family budget from that of an increase of the same amount in the wage earner's income — which I don't believe.[90]

In fact, Treasury officials were wondering if this point could be used as an argument against family allowances: the government was already committed to an expansion of services in kind for children, and (providing this cost less than a family allowance scheme) it might be possible to expand these services even further, thus fending off pressure for cash allowances.[91]

The summer of 1942 is a convenient point at which to end this survey of the second phase in the development of family allowances in the Second World War. In this period, political support for Eleanor Rathbone's cause grew rapidly, and in a rather reluctant reponse to this there appeared a government White Paper. At the same time, however, the Treasury's determination to delay family allowances until after the War was greatly assisted by the appointment of the Beveridge Committee. Accordingly, this second period possessed a certain air of unreality, since for much of it all concerned were waiting for the Beveridge Report to be published. The third phase of development, therefore, covered the work of the Beveridge Committee.

The origins of the Beveridge Report have been well described by a number of writers.[92] As early as December 1940, at a very uncertain period in the War, Churchill had decided to launch a study of postwar problems, putting Arthur Greenwood (Minister Without Portfolio) in charge of this, and on 24 February 1941 Greenwood appointed a Ministerial Committee on Reconstruction Problems.[93] One of the subjects briefly considered by this committee was family allowances, Greenwood being very keen that they should be included in any post-war reorganized social security scheme.[94] By April 1941 discussions were being held within Whitehall on the need for an inter-departmental committee to investigate the reorganization of health insurance and workmen's compensation (Ernest Bevin being particularly keen to see completed the work of a suspended Royal Commission on Workmen's Compensation, appointed in 1938),[95] and by June a chairman had been appointed (Sir William Beveridge), the scope of investigation had been widened, and the terms of reference enlarged so that the Committee was required 'to undertake, with special reference to the inter-relation of the schemes, a survey of the existing national schemes of social insurance and allied services, including workmen's compensation, and to make recommendations'.[96]

By his interpretation of these last four words, Beveridge transformed what might have been a drily factual survey of existing services into the most famous single document in the history of British social policy. Initially resentful at being shunted off into what appeared to be an administrative backwater,[97] he gradually realized the magnitude of the opportunity he had been presented with and by June 1942 had decided that his forthcoming report was going to be 'quite revolutionary'.[98]

Beveridge evidently ran his Committee with a firm hand, and on several important matters he relegated it to something of a rubber stamp on his fixed ideas.[99] One of these was family allowances: from his experience with the UISC Beveridge had become convinced that family allowances in wages would have to be incorporated into any reorganized social security scheme in order to ensure work-incentives and labour mobility. Beveridge believed that there was 'no need to argue the general case for family allowances', the only points at issue being administrative questions (whether allowances should vary with the age of the child, what the upper age limit should be, what to do in the case of broken homes, and so on).[100] On 11 December 1941 Beveridge circulated to his colleagues the memorandum 'Basic problems of social security with heads of a scheme', in which he firmly outlined the 'less eligibility case' for family allowances:

> It is unreasonable to provide against want during interruption of earnings — namely, the responsibility for the maintenance of dependent children without resources specially allocated for that

purpose. Allowances designed as a guarantee against want during interruption of earnings must take account of the family responsibilities of the recipient. If they do so, they are bound in an appreciable number of cases to be equal to or greater than the earnings of the recipient, thus producing an indefensible position of penalising children if, and because, their father returns to work or good health. No satisfactory social security scheme can be framed except on the basis of universal children's allowances.

In the face of these firmly-held convictions the Committee members could hardly have raised a note of dissent even if they had wanted to, and thus they confined themselves to discussing only the administrative questions.[101]

This created rather an awkward situation when, on behalf of the Family Endowment Society, Eleanor Rathbone and Eva Hubback gave written and (on 2 June 1942) oral evidence to the Committee, for, having spent over twenty years campaigning for the principle of family endowment, they suddenly found themselves being cross-examined on intricate administrative problems (such as whether the allowance level should vary according to the amount of rent paid by the household) to which they had no thought-out answers.[102]

However, there was one administrative detail on which Eleanor Rathbone and Eva Hubback disagreed, and this was the question of whether child tax rebates should be abolished. Eva Hubback supported this, arguing that to have the two systems existing side-by-side would unfairly favour the rich: a man earning £15 per week, she pointed out, already received the generous amount of 9s 7d per week per child in tax relief. Eleanor Rathbone strongly disagreed, maintaining that there was a need to stimulate the birth-rate of the professional classes and that abolishing child tax allowances would be administratively complex.[103] It was an important issue – much more than a mere administrative detail – but Beveridge merely shelved it by declaring that the question of tax rebates was outwith the Committee's terms of reference.[104]

The most important question to be settled was the level of the allowance, and in deciding this Beveridge sought the advice of the special subcommittee (consisting of Seebohm Rowntree, R. F. George, Professor A. L. Bowley and Dr H. E. Magee) which had been set up to calculate minimum subsistence. According to Beveridge the 'subsistence principle' was one of the most important features of the report, and was based on the evidence of the poverty surveys of the previous two decades:[105] repeatedly, Beveridge acknowledged the influence of the 'impartial scientific authorities' who had 'made social surveys of the conditions of life in a number of principal towns in Britain' before the War, and who had 'determined the proportions of the people in each town whose means were below the standard assumed to be necessary for subsistence'.[106] Ostensibly, therefore, all benefits, including family allowances, were calculated according to an objective standard of scientific minimum subsistence.

However, matters were a little more complex than this. The ideal to be aimed at was a standard fixed 'by reference to reasoned estimates of the cost of providing housing, food, clothing, fuel and other necessities'. But there were three factors which, according to Beveridge, might cause benefits to be fixed at a level below subsistence: the financial resources of the nation; the possible effect on voluntary insurance through friendly societies and the like; and, most important of all,

> the possible effect on the readiness of recipients to take employment in preference to benefit . . . While most men can be trusted to prefer work to idleness even when there is little financial difference between wages and benefit, there is a danger that benefits up to subsistence level will weaken the incentive of men to take employment and their readiness to take unfamiliar employment or employment at a distance.[107]

There is no doubt that the minimum subsistence subcommittee worked long and hard at calculating a scientific basis for minimum needs.[108] But there is equally no doubt that at the back of their minds was the decidedly *un*scientific consideration that benefits would have to be kept below wage levels. Early on, the Committee's secretary, D. N. Chester, warned that to fix benefits too high would reduce incentives to voluntary saving and would result in an overlap onto wages; however, if on the other hand the standard arrived at was too low, this 'would raise the much wider question of minimum wages and the raising of the standard of living of the working classes'.[109] The members of the subcommittee were well aware of this dilemma, Rowntree on one occasion declaring that 'in arriving at the amount of benefit to be paid to unemployed persons it would in our opinion be unjustifiable to allow for a dietary more costly than can be afforded by a large proportion of working-class families when the chief wage-earner is in work'.[110] The way out of this difficulty was through the provision of family allowances:

a system of universal family allowances would allow benefits for adults to be increased considerably above subsistence level without seriously conflicting with wages. But if there is no universal system of family allowances even the payment of benefits on subsistence level would be above the lowest level of wages.[111]

Beveridge undoubtedly did see family allowances as a valuable means of combating poverty and removing some of the economic obstacles to parenthood: for example, he agreed with Eleanor Rathbone that the family-of-five minimum wage would be an expensive, clumsy and inefficient way of tackling the problem of family poverty. Ostensibly, therefore, he arrived at the level of the allowance by reference to the cost of maintaining a child: this, at 1938 prices, amounted to 7s 0d per week on average[112] which, with additions for rises in the cost of living since 1939, resulted in a figure of 9s 0d per week; from this, he deducted 1s 0d in respect of services in kind for children to be provided by the state.[113] However, this could easily be criticized as nothing like a realistic figure: on the Boyd Orr standard, for example, the sum would have had to be about 14s 0d.[114] The suspicion must remain that it was the less eligibility function of family allowances that appealed most to Beveridge, and it was more on these grounds that the figure of 8s 0d was chosen.

Proof of this can be found in the discussions that took place in the summer of 1942 with the Treasury over the cost of the Beveridge scheme, discussions which culminated in the 'deal' of August 1942 between Keynes and Beveridge whereby Keynes promised to obtain Treasury support for the forthcoming report, in return for which Beveridge agreed to keep the additional burden of cost to the Treasury down to £100 million per annum for the first five years.[115] As these discussions progressed, the exclusion of the first child from the scope of the family allowance scheme was more and more frequently suggested.[116] In spite of the fact that this made a mockery of the notion of meeting subsistence needs, Beveridge was quite amenable, on the grounds that exclusion of the first child would still leave a sufficient gap between benefit and wages.[117] Thus when paring down the cost of his scheme in response to Keynes's request, one of the measures he took was the exclusion of the first child – which reduced the total cost of the scheme from £163 million to £110 million.[118] The interesting point to note, however, is that Beveridge refused to reduce the amount and scope of family allowances any more than this, on the grounds that such a reduction would destroy their effectiveness as an agent of less eligibility. For example, he pointed out to his Committee that it might be possible to limit the 8s 0d allowance to children of parents who were on benefit and give, say, 6s 0d to the second and subsequent children of parents who were earning; but he warned that 'the main objection is that [this] narrows the gap between earnings and benefit income'.[119]

In the published version of the report, Beveridge was characteristically frank about his reasons for recommending family allowances. The anti-poverty and demographic arguments were mentioned, but more importantly, children's allowances were 'Assumption A' without which the integration of social security, full employment and economic growth could not be accomplished:

> The maintenance of employment — last and most important of the three assumptions of social security — will be impossible without greater fluidity of labour and other resources in the aftermath of war than has been achieved in the past. To secure this, the gap between income during earning and during interruption of earning should be as large as possible for every man.[120]

It was a classic restatement of the dilemma experienced by the UISC and UAB in the late 1930s, and Beveridge's solution to it was that proposed by most social investigators of the time: family allowances were an alternative to much more radical and expensive wage rises;[121] they would push up the wages of married workers with children just enough to ensure the labour mobility and work-incentives necessary to the successful working of the postwar economy.

While the Beveridge Committee was conducting its work, the Labour movement was finally coming round to a wholehearted approval of family allowances. On 18 March 1942 the TUC General Council devoted a special meeting to the subject. By now, Sir Walter Citrine was in favour; he believed that the trade union movement had two main aims, 'firstly, to improve capitalist society so that they could get the highest standard of living for the workers, and, secondly, to amend the uneven distribution of wealth', and he believed that family allowances would further these aims. Discussion ranged over the wages question and the anti-poverty case, with most speakers in favour. Those long-standing opponents of family allowances, Charles Dukes and Arthur Deakin, were now reduced to rather incongruous arguments: Dukes was against family allowances because 'we definitely had a surplus population . . . an increase in the population would not be good for this country', and Deakin complained that 'they were being asked to provide cannon fodder in order to prevent race suicide'. Eventually the General Council approved, by seventeen votes to eight, a state-financed, non-contributory, non-means-tested scheme.[122] The last real obstacle had been removed, and in May and September 1942 the Labour Party and TUC annual conferences respectively passed motions in favour of family allowances.[123] By now, both the Liberal and Conservative Parties were also showing considerable interest.[124]

The Beveridge Report was published on 1 December 1942, and for the next five months the subject of family allowances became rather overshadowed by the furore surrounding the report's acceptance with enthusiasm by the public and muted hostility by the government.[125] The period between the report's publication and the acrimonious House of Commons debate on its proposals (on 16, 17 and 18 Feburary 1943) saw a determined rear-guard action by several ministers, led by the Chancellor, Sir Kingsley Wood, aimed at postponing any decision on the report's implementation until after the War.[126] Similar moves took place within the Conservative Party, where a committee set up to examine the Beveridge Plan (under Ralph Assheton) gave grudging approval on condition that many of the proposals were watered down and a decision on them delayed until after the War, when Britain's economic position would be clearer.[127]

Within Whitehall, the opposition was, not surprisingly, led by the Treasury, which took the line that while the Beveridge Report could be regarded as an ultimate objective, no commitments should be made on how long it would take to reach that ultimate objective, since much would have to depend on the strength of the postwar economy. Realizing that public opinion would make it impossible for the government not to introduce family allowances, the Treasury now aimed at reducing their cost as much as possible by basing them on a contributory scheme of finance, or by attaching an income limit to the conditions of eligibility.[128]

Other government departments voiced opposition, too. On 10 December 1942 a committee of departmental representatives was set up, under Sir Thomas Phillips of the Ministry of Labour, and (working in conjunction with a Cabinet Committee on Reconstruction Problems) was given a month in which to pronounce a verdict on various administrative problems contained in the Beveridge proposals, such as whether benefits and contributions should be flat-rate. At the fifth meeting of the Committee, on 29 December, discussion turned to the question of whether family allowances should be introduced, and the reactions of civil servants were quite hostile. Several of them wondered if the prewar arguments still held any validity, and there was general agreement that no scheme should start until after the War had ended. The work-incentive arguments were appreciated, but on the other hand the pro-natalist ones attracted no support whatsoever, and several suggestions were made for reducing the scope of the scheme (such as starting only with the third child). Most important of all, the Phillips Committee decided to recommend a figure of 5s 0d instead of the 8s 0d proposed by Beveridge. This was partly because of anticipated expansions of services in kind, but also because a 5s 0d allowance

> had the virtue of *not* pretending to be a subsistence rate. If an attempt at a subsistence rate were made (especially in a non-contributory scheme) it would be very unstable and there would be pressure for its increase if the cost of living rose or if the medical experts revised their views on the minimum adequate diet. It was therefore advisable to start low.[129]

This hostile view was shared by other government departments, whose opinions the Phillips Committee sounded out. The Board of Education reiterated its preference for services in kind;[130] the Ministry of Labour feared that wage bargaining would be affected, and that family allowances would lead on to demands for a government-enforced minimum wage;[131] and the Treasury continued its running battle by questioning Beveridge's pro-natalist arguments, recommending an income-limit qualification for eligibility, and calling for 'an examination whether the small minority of cases where wages are below subsistence minimum should not be attacked in some other way rather than by a remedy whose main cost arises in the many cases where from this angle help is unnecessary'.[132] Thus in its report the Phillips Committee gave a very grudging approval to family allowances, subject to the proviso that an income limit be applied and the level reduced from the Beveridge-recommended 8s 0d.[133] This was referred to the Committee on Reconstruction Priorities, and it in turn recommended to the Cabinet that the government should accept in principle family allowances of 5s 0d per week for each child after the first, the 5s 0d being justified by proposed increases of services in kind.[134]

In the midst of this unfavourable atmosphere the Family Endowment Society requested permission to send a deputation to the Chancellor to press on him the need for the immediate introduction of family allowances. The TUC was now in favour and the Beveridge Committee had reported, they pointed out, and thus had been fulfilled two of the three conditions which Wood had stipulated in the

Commons in June 1942.[135] Wood agreed, and received the deputation on 14 January 1943. The Society was represented by nineteen MPs, plus other public figures like Seebohm Rowntree, Lawrence Cadbury and Professor Gilbert Murray. The points made were much the same as before except that — possibly in a desperate search for new arguments — the pro-natalist case was given far more emphasis than in the past: in its written evidence the Society went so far as to suggest that, in order to raise the birth-rate of the professional classes, the Beveridge scheme should be supplemented by an additional family allowance scheme for higher income groups operated through contributory insurance or the tax system.[136] In her oral evidence, Eleanor Rathbone was quite obsessed by the demographic aspect. It was, from a national long-term point of view, by far the most important question, she maintained, and went on to make the sweeping claim that 'the State has a means of either stimulating the birth-rate or checking it through the system of family allowances, so giving the community some power over its future destinies'.[137]

As on previous occasions, civil servants regarded the Society's deputation as little more than a time-wasting nuisance: 'Only Rowntree had anything new to say', was the acerbic comment of Bernard Gilbert, the Treasury's Under-Secretary.[138] To a lesser or greater extent, this had been their attitude towards the Society all along, but now that they were concerned primarily with solving the administrative problems they found the Society's general statements of principle (particularly as regards the highly speculative demographic arguments) very irritating. In June 1943, for example, Eleanor Rathbone and Eva Hubback were allowed to meet and talk with Thomas Sheepshanks, the civil servant who was by then working out how and when family allowances should be implemented; Sheepshanks found the meeting very unhelpful, and wrote of the two ladies:

> In point of fact, I discovered that although they have no doubt studied the question for a number of years, they had not really applied their minds to all the difficulties and had only the most nebulous ideas about such difficult questions as whether the family should be the family by blood or the economic family. Indeed, I do not think that the point had occurred to them.[139]

The spring of 1943 marked the end of the third 'Beveridge' stage in the development of family allowances in the period 1939–45. The fourth and final stage ran from April 1943 to the passage of the Family Allowances Act in June 1945. By this time elements in Whitehall and the Cabinet (in particular, Churchill and Wood) who had hoped that the Beveridge proposals could be drastically watered down had had to give way, in the face of a rebellious House of Commons, the evident strength of public feeling, and strong opposition from ministers like Herbert Morrison. During this period, therefore, it was mainly the administrative problems of implementation that were worked out, by a 'Central Staff' of departmental representatives under Thomas (later Sir Thomas) Sheepshanks, Controller of Insurance at the Ministry of Health.[140]

Evidently the message of the February 1943 House of Commons debate on the Beveridge Report had been firmly implanted in the minds of ministers and civil servants, for when the Central Staff came to discuss family allowances on 12 and 14 April 1943 there was immediate agreement that a scheme would have to be introduced, possibly within a matter of months — though it was recognized that this would be an administrative nightmare, and might be inflationary.[141] Thus from April 1943 onwards, the Central Staff ironed out the major administrative problems — payment to mother or father, whether the family unit should be the 'economic' or the 'blood' family, the upper age limit, how to treat children of aliens, and so on.[142]

That these questions took fully two and a half years to settle must raise in the historian's mind the possibility that delaying tactics were being used. After all, many of these administrative problems had been solved in the First World War through the administration of separation allowances.[143] Again, had the Stamp Survey won general approval for its family allowance scheme, there is no doubt that the administrative problems would have been solved in a matter of days. For example, was it really necessary for the residence qualifications for eligibility to take one and a half years to solve, with many repetitious memoranda being circulated?[144]

There can be no doubt that the Treasury was still employing delaying tactics, even at this late stage hoping that a postwar scheme could be reduced in scope and cost. Treasury officials circulated numerous memoranda in 1943—5, all gloomily outlining the arguments against a wartime family allowance scheme — it would be inflationary, it would exacerbate problems of supply and demand, wartime wages were adequate for family needs, and so on[145] — and even after the passage of the 1945 Act Treasury officials tried to postpone a decision on when payments should commence until after hostilities had ceased.[146] Evidently these tactics exasperated the new Labour Chancellor, Hugh Dalton, for on the final memorandum he angrily dismissed his officials' caution, insisting that family allowances were 'much the best of our social service advances'.[147]

Yet on the other hand, there equally can be no doubt that the implementation problems were enormous, being greatly exacerbated by wartime shortages and by the fact that other aspects of postwar reconstruction were being worked on simultaneously. The question of how to pay allowances in respect of children in institutions, for example, was complicated by the reorganization of children's services then being undertaken.[148] Civil servants clearly felt aggrieved that the public in general, and Eleanor Rathbone's supporters in particular, were quick to criticize the government for taking so long without appreciating the magnitude of the administrative problems.[149] Ministers likewise felt very sensitive about the delays. Sir William Jowitt, the Minister for Reconstruction,[150] frequently impressed on civil servants the need to work quickly, in view of public opinion, and urged Sheepshanks to complete the final draft of the Family Allowances Bill as soon as possible.[151] Thus it is probable that even without the Treasury's delaying tactics, the difficulties of launching a scheme in wartime would have been considered overwhelming.

In this final phase, two controversies arose. The first was over the question of whether the allowance should be paid to the mother or the father. This had long been an emotive issue with the Family Endowment Society leaders, and was one of the few administrative details they insisted on. Payment to the mother was seen by them as a way of recognizing the economic rights of women, guaranteeing that the money would be spent wisely, and keeping the allowance separate from the father's wages — an important point, if trade union opinion was to be appeased.[152]

In their initial discussions, Central Staff officials appear to have had no strong preferences either way: they recognized on the one hand that the issue was deeply important to women's organizations,[153] but on the other hand payment to the father as guardian raised fewer legal difficulties[154] — a point strongly emphasized by the Home Office, which warned that payment to the mother could be contrary to existing family law.[155] The War Cabinet Committee on Reconstruction (which worked with the Central Staff, pronouncing on the latter's recommendations) was made aware of public opinion on the issue by a Ministry of Information poll (taken on 19 December 1943), which showed 59 per cent of the sample favouring payment to the mother, 16 per cent to the father, and 25 per cent to either parent,[156] but eventually — after some indecision — it decided to favour payment to the father as the normal economic head of the household.[157] Accordingly when the White Paper on Social Insurance was published in September 1944, this was the provision made, although the mother was also entitled to cash the allowance.[158]

Naturally, the wrath of the Family Endowment Society was aroused, and it sent a deputation to Sir William Jowitt on 10 October 1944. Both in its written and oral evidence,[159] it repeated the familiar arguments for payment to the mother; but, as with all previous deputations, civil servants remained distinctly unimpressed by the Society's arguments on matters of principle: on the point that payment to the mother would raise the status of women, they found it 'curious to rely on the payment of a few shillings each week to achieve this desirable aim'.[160]

The controversy continued right up to the debates on the Family Allowance Bill in the House of Commons.[161] However, at the last minute, on 6 March 1945, the Cabinet decided that in view of the strength of public and political feeling on the matter, a free vote on that part of the Bill should be allowed,[162] and in the face of almost unanimous opposition (Eleanor Rathbone having announced that she would vote against the Bill unless it granted payment to the mother) Jowitt gave way.[163]

In deciding initially for payment to the father, the government had had more than mere legal difficulties in mind. Though Jowitt had favoured payment to the mother at first, he had changed his mind in the face of warnings from ministers and civil servants that payment to the mother might lead on to demands that the allowance be raised to cover the full cost of maintaining a child.[164] The decision was even made to change the name from 'children's allowances' (the term used by government spokesmen in the Commons debates on the Beveridge Report) to 'family allowances' 'in order to emphasise that these allowances do not purport to provide maintenance for each child but represent a general subvention to the family needs'.[165] Just before the Commons debates on the Bill, the Chancellor, Sir John Anderson, issued a stern warning to Jowitt not to give the impression that the allowance had any relation to the needs of the individual child in case this led on to demands that it should be raised to a level representing full maintenance;[166] and thus in the debates Jowitt was very careful to emphasize that the measure was primarily designed to benefit the family as a whole.[167]

This leads on to the second area of controversy in the 1943—45 period — the decision to lower the level of the allowance from the Beveridge-recommended 8s 0d down to 5s 0d. As has been shown, both the Treasury and the Phillips Committee wanted a 5s 0d figure because this would obviously be below subsistence and would thus release the government from the obligation of increasing the level of the allowance as the cost of living rose.[168] However, in public government spokesmen tended to give a different justification: full maintenance (which Beveridge calculated at 9s 0d per week per child) was not being provided because the government intended developing services in kind to children beyond the 1s 0d equivalent which Beveridge envisaged[169] – indeed, a high cash allowance might even hinder the 'fullest development' of such services, said Anderson;[170] in addition, full maintenance should not be provided because 'nothing should be done to remove from parents the responsibility of maintaining their children'.[171]

The discrepancy between the private and public reasons for cutting family allowances from 8s 0d to 5s 0d was thus quite striking, and it is likely that the real reason was related to the general decision to abandon the Beveridge principle of providing subsistence benefits. Ostensibly, this was done because of the problems envisaged in altering benefits in line with changes in the cost of living while keeping contributions unchanged,[172] and because the principle of flat-rate benefits and contributions necessitated fixing the latter at a level that low-wage earners could afford, thus automatically placing an upper limit on what could be paid out in benefits.[173] But clearly this was a partial victory for the Treasury in its long campaign to keep the cost of the Beveridge proposals in general, and family allowances in particular, as low as possible.

Both these controversies surfaced in the Commons debates on the Family Allowances Bill between March and June 1945. But apart from them, and a small rumpus over whether there should be duplication with servicemen's family allowances, the general tone of the debates was one of satisfaction that an important precedent had been established. Left-wing speakers like Aneurin Bevan still made the point that the introduction of family allowances was a tribute to the fact that the existing industrial system was unable or unwilling to pay adequate wages, but in spite of that Bevan approved of the measure.[174] Most speakers believed that a new era of state legislation for children was being ushered in – 'the country has become child conscious', said Lady Astor[175] – and that this would automatically result in more measures: at one point, Sir William Jowitt said that he felt 'this is probably the first of a series of Family Allowance Bills'.[176] In view of this, most MPs were willing to overlook the Bill's defects, and concentrated instead on paying tribute to Eleanor Rathbone's remarkable persistence in campaigning over the past twenty-five years. On 15 June 1945 the Bill received the Royal Assent, and on 6 August 1946 the first family allowances were paid.

This final chapter is obviously crucial to the story of how and why family allowances were introduced. As has been shown, by 1939 the government was still flatly rejecting the arguments for family allowances, yet six years later the Act was passed. Did this come about through a sudden acceptance by ministers and civil servants of these arguments, in which process the conditions of war played a vital role?

The theory that there is a strong causal connection between the intensity of a war and the degree of social change and reform which accompanies it has enjoyed some popularity among historians and sociologists over the last thirty years. First outlined by Aristotle, then Spinoza and Herbert Spencer, the theory was further developed by Stanislav Andreski,[177] and received perhaps its most interesting historical application as regards social policy in the Second World War in Richard Titmuss's *Problems of Social Policy* (1950) and his essay 'War and social policy' (1955). Titmuss argued that the imminence of invasion in mid-1940 in Britain brought about a new attitude on the part of government and citizens alike towards equality and the need for social policies, particularly social policies benefiting women and children.[178] 'The mood of the people changed and, in sympathetic response, values changed as well', he wrote, going on to suggest that the traumatic events of Dunkirk 'summoned forth a note of self-criticism, of national introspection, and . . . set in motion ideas and talk of principles and plans'.[179]

However, the 'war and social change' theory has been strongly criticized as being too general (Abrams, for example, has questioned whether it can be applied to the First World War, which ushered in few permanent social reforms),[180] and too often based on very superficial evidence. Titmuss, for example, made much of an editorial in *The Times* on 1 July 1940, which called for social justice, the abolition of class differences, a fairer distribution of wealth, and so on, and included the declaration that 'the new order cannot be based on the preservation of privilege, whether the privilege be that of a country, of a class or of an individual'. This he took as evidence of the fundamental change of attitude towards social reform that had been brought about by the War, and subsequent historians have often followed suit.[181] Yet in that particular issue of *The Times*, five times the amount of space is devoted to the 'Court Circular and Society News', chronicling the activities of the British aristocracy. Clearly, the change of attitude was in reality rather less fundamental than Titmuss believed it to be.

It is hardly likely that the events described in this chapter fit a 'war and social change' explanation. Certainly, the Second World War brought about a change-over in the technique of government, from the *laissez-faire* approach that had dominated in the interwar years to the liberal—reformist 'middle way' interventionism that had been slowly developing in the 1930s — a change-over that took place most rapidly in May 1940 with the entry into the government of Labour Party leaders and previous political heretics like Churchill, Macmillan and Amery. In addition, there undoubtedly was great public interest throughout the War in what sort of Britain the people were fighting for, as the events surrounding the Beveridge Report showed. The movement for family allowances benefited enormously from this, and ministers and civil servants realized that they had to concede to popular pressure to some extent. However, this is not the same thing as saying that they necessarily accepted the *arguments* of social reformers. In the case of family allowances, ministers (Amery, Greenwood, Dalton and Morrison excepted) and civil servants generally did not. As this chapter has shown, the two crucial stages in the development of family allowances occurred during the Stamp Survey and the Beveridge Committee's work. In the former, family allowances were seen primarily as a means of holding down wages and combating inflation; in the latter, as a means of ensuring less eligibility, work-incentives and labour mobility. In both cases, it was the needs of the economy rather than the children that dominated discussion. To re-emphasize this point finally, it is useful to conclude with a summary of how the family poverty and the demographic arguments fared in wartime.

The former can be dealt with quickly. In the 1939—41 period, much of the activity centred on the Treasury, and there is no evidence that relieving poverty was ever its aim. 'At the present moment', Edward Hale summed up in April 1940, 'any proposal must be judged by one criterion alone, namely, whether it will help to win the war',[182] and thus Treasury discussions of family allowances centred on factors like wage control, inflation, problems of supply and demand, and so on; besides, by mid-1940 the Treasury's attitude was one of resolute opposition. Nor were other departments enthusiastic about the family poverty arguments: as has been shown, departments like the Assistance Board maintained that if acute child poverty still existed (and this was thought unlikely), then the remedy lay elsewhere — possibly in an expansion of services in kind, as the Board of Education wanted. Indeed, departmental opposition was so strong that Kingsley Wood only just managed to publish the 1942 White Paper. Beveridge undoubtedly saw family allowances as helping to alleviate family poverty, but equally undoubtedly regarded this function as secondary: for him, their less eligibility function was paramount. It was on this basis that family allowances were accepted by the government, and thereafter, in the 1943—5 discussions on administrative problems, arguments about family poverty were rarely mentioned.

A lengthier discussion must be given to the demographic case, however, for the Second World War saw concern over the falling birth-rate reach its zenith, and in the 1939—45 period the Family Endowment Society stressed the pro-natalist arguments more strongly than ever before. This was particularly true of Eleanor Rathbone, whose language on this point often became crudely racialist and imperialist. In the Society's deputation to Kingsley Wood in June 1941, she warned that the 'Anglo-Saxon race' was diminishing in proportion to the 'yellow and coloured races';[183] when giving evidence to the Beveridge Committee, she said she wanted child tax allowances enlarged in order to stimulate the birth-rate of the professional classes while at the same time suggesting that economies could be made by omitting the first child from the scope of family allowances;[184] and this plea was repeated in another deputation to Wood in January 1943.[185] Yet when directly challenged on the question of whether family allowances really would influence the birth-rate, she would make extremely vague statements such as:

> The argument that Family Allowances abroad have not increased the birth rate is partly irrelevant and partly untrue; irrelevant, because everywhere the amounts were too small to meet more than part, usually a small part, of the minimum cost of child maintenance — untrue because in fact there is evidence that everywhere the system did help both to slow down the falling birth rate and to increase the survival rate.[186]

What she appeared to be saying was that a 5s 0d allowance would not be enough to affect the birth-rate, and that a higher figure was therefore needed,[187] but this simple point was often submerged beneath a jumble of contradictory statements — as in the evidence she and Eva Hubback gave to the Royal Commission on Population, where they said that family allowances could provide more than just an economic inducement to parenthood but could also change general attitudes to the family; they should be introduced immediately because of the gravity of the birth-rate decline; they would be an effective and flexible pro-natalist policy, because they could be 'raised or lowered as the population position improves or deteriorates'; yet at the rate of 8s 0d per week they would only affect the birth-rate of those living at sub-sistence level; but they would have little effect on the 'less responsible' parents belonging to the 'social problem group'.[188]

In fairness, it must be remembered that by this time the leaders of the Family Endowment Society had been campaigning for over twenty-five years and were nearing the end of their lives. Seeing their goal so tantalizingly within reach, they tended to seize upon any argument, however implausible, to aid their cause. Also, in stressing the demo-graphic aspects they were only following a trend of opinion within the socio-political elite, which was becoming increasingly concerned about the population problem. As has been shown, this trend (which reached a peak during and just after the Second World War) had its origins in the post-1870s fall in fertility and Britain's relative economic decline, and by the 1940s was manifesting itself in several ways, one of which was a tendency to envisage woman's role primarily as that of depend-ent housewife and mother, rather than as equal competitor in the labour market. Perhaps the crudest and most explicit expression of this came in the Beveridge Report's assertion that 'in the next thirty years house-wives as mothers have vital work to do in ensuring the adequate con-tinuance of the British race and of British ideals in the world',[189] but numerous other more subtle examples can be found in the statements of the political intelligentsia of the time, such as the evidence, given in her private capacity, of Eva Hubback to the Royal Commission on Population, where she argued that, in view of the need for a higher birth-rate, women's 'justifiable demand for a measure of economic independence' should be answered not by greater job opportunities but '(a) by a really adequate system of family allowances (paid to *her*), and (b) by introducing some arrangement as is common in Scandinavia by which each spouse has a right to half the joint income'; in addition, she argued, education in schools (particularly for girls) should place great emphasis on the importance of family life.[190] Although eugenic ideas attracted less popularity than they had done in the 1920s and 1930s, there was still great disquiet over differential fertility: Roy Harrod, for example, stressed the need to raise the birth-rate of the higher income groups because 'they are a repository of a large part of our knowledge, ideas, culture, and the art of right behaviour in the more complex affairs of life, and if they do not replace themselves . . . the total stock of wisdom in the nation suffers constant loss'.[191]

Eloquent testimony to this growing concern over the birth-rate can be found in the House of Commons debate of 16 July 1943 on the trend of population, which resulted in the Minister of Health, Ernest

Brown, promising to set up a Royal Commission on the subject.[192] In this atmosphere, it is hardly surprising that family allowances were seen as a possible remedy – a misconception which may have been further perpetuated by Churchill's radio broadcast on the Beveridge Report in March 1943, in which he discussed family allowances in pro-natalist terms, warning that

> if this country is to keep its high place in the leadership of the world and to survive as a great power, our people must be encouraged by every means to have larger families. For this reason, well thought out plans for helping parents to contribute this lifeblood to the community are of prime importance.[193]

But to what extent were discussions on family allowances within Whitehall influenced by all this? The Stamp Survey and Treasury investigation of 1939–41 certainly were not. In his report, Beveridge dispelled the notion that children's allowances alone would influence the birth-rate, but said that their introduction might induce a climate of opinion favourable to more pro-natalist measures.[194] In none of the Committee's surviving papers is there any evidence that allowances were seriously seen as pro-natalist. Certainly, Beveridge was very concerned about the population problem, and wrote many articles on it at this time.[195] But, while wanting income tax rebates for the professional classes and skilled wage-earners enlarged in order to remove the economic obstacles to their infertility,[196] he maintained that only if economic inducements were combined with a change in public opinion would the birth-rate be raised.[197] The 1942 White Paper gave the demographic arguments the very briefest of mentions,[198] and the 1944 White Paper on social insurance ignored them completely. In the Commons debates on the Family Allowances Bill, Sir William Jowitt firmly maintained that pro-natalist arguments had little validity at that stage; only when the Report of the Royal Commission on Population was published could the question be answered.[199] Even more striking is the complete absence of any evidence that demographic considerations influenced the policy-decisions of civil servants: a typical example of one of the very few occasions on which the topic was even mentioned was a Ministry of Labour memorandum of December 1942, which very briefly referred to the failure of French and Belgian family allowance schemes to raise their birth-rates, and commented 'there is no reason for expecting a different result in this country'.[200]

If one examines the government's reaction to the population question in general in the period 1939—45, one finds little faith being placed in family allowances as a remedy on their own. The 1942 White Paper on the *Current Trend of Population in Great Britain* made no mention of them, and merely summarized the available evidence on demographic change, ending with a fairly optimistic prediction that the British population would number almost 46 million in 1971.[201] The government, of course, responded to the public concern by announcing, on 16 July 1943, the appointment of the Royal Commission on Population. In the preliminary discussions about the appointment of the Royal Commission a number of outstanding issues were discussed, but family allowances were not included.[202] Evidently the prevailing view within Whitehall was much as it had been in the 1930s: until more exact information was available on specific fertility-rates, no claims could be made for family allowances.[203] The Registrar-General, S. P. Vivian, seems to have felt that family allowances could be a stimulus to fertility — though he was not sure how powerful a stimulus — but he correctly believed that an upward trend in the birth-rate was already operating.[204] The Royal Commission received a large amount of evidence, both written and oral, and throughout it there were periodic and rather nebulous discussions of the pro-natalist effect of family allowances.[205] Its report made a plea that the level of the allowance be increased, particularly in the case of older children, and that the first child be included.[206] But, of course, the Royal Commission was appointed in mid-1943, by which time the government had decided that they would have to introduce family allowances; in any case, by the time it reported in 1949 the birth-rate had risen sufficiently to damp down concern — indeed, the report was never even discussed in Parliament.

If the demographic argument can be said to have achieved anything, it was probably to implant in the minds of ordinary people the misconception that family allowances were designed to induce them to produce more children. The attitudes of ordinary people tend to remain tantalizingly hidden from history, particularly in the case of social policy, but two wartime surveys provide interesting evidence. Slater and Woodside, in their survey of two hundred lower-middle and working class families, discovered a widespread feeling that family allowances were a pro-natalist bribe — which people deeply resented, though they did approve of them as an alleviation of hardship in large families; however, couples felt that at 5s 0d they would have little effect on the birth-rate.[207] Likewise, Mass-Observation encountered many objections to what was seen as the 'bribery' element, and found that a large majority of couples felt that cash allowances would have no influence on the complex web of factors that caused them to have children.[208] Apart from these two sources, one is left with little scraps of evidence — such as the letter from a representative of Harrow Trades Council declaring that 'our impression is that these allowances are given to encourage the birth rate'[209] — all of which suggest that while the demographic arguments made little impression on those in the government, they certainly influenced the perceptions of ordinary people.

Therefore, both the family poverty and the demographic arguments played little part in causing the government to accept family allowances in the period 1939—45. Although there undoubtedly was an increased concern over the health and life-chances of children in the early years of the War, there is no evidence that the War induced a fundamentally different attitude on the part of those in government such as caused them to agree with the Family Endowment Society's arguments. Family allowances came about for two reasons. First, there was the anti-inflation, wage-control Treasury plan of 1939—40 which, by arousing interest in family allowances as an immediate wartime policy, gave a tremendous boost to the campaign and created a wave of public and political pressure that forced the government to take an interest — even if this interest was very half-hearted. There is no doubt, however, that the government (and the Treasury in particular) could have successfully resisted this pressure almost indefinitely had it not been for a second and much more important factor — the recommendation by Beveridge of this interest was very half-hearted. There is no doubt, however, that the government (and the Treasury in particular) could have successfully resisted this pressure almost indefinitely had it not been for a second have validity: the Second World War undoubtedly speeded up trends that were in evidence in the late 1930s, when there was a growing consensus among social policy experts that (a) the social services needed a drastic reorganization, and (b) in any such reorganization the problem of men with large families being better off financially when unemployed than when employed needed to be tackled by the introduction of family allowances. The fact that Beveridge, an Eleanor Rathbone supporter, was selected to lead this reorganization made little difference: family allowances would probably have been recommended anyway. At the end of the 1930s the government was presented with two possible solutions to the benefit—wage overlap problem: either it could launch a large-scale state intervention into many industries in order to ensure that wages were raised to nutritionally-adequate levels, or it could introduce a system of family allowances which would push up the wages of married men just high enough for less eligibility to be enforced. The opposition of the trade unions was an immense obstacle to the latter course until the Second World War, which brought about certain conditions conducive to trade union co-operation – the entry of the Labour Party into government, virtual full employment, and higher wages.

Thus despite all the arguments of the Family Endowment Society on family poverty, encouraging the birth-rate and raising the economic status of women and children, family allowances were attractive to the government only in so far as they were an alternative to, and a way of avoiding, the whole question of minimum wages, and also as a way of ensuring the work-incentives and labour mobility essential to the successful working of a free-market economy.

Notes and References

1. PRO T 161/1116 (S 43697/1), *Family Allowances 1938—40*.
2. *Hansard*, vol. 337 (29 and 30 June 1938), cols. 1899—1900, 2102—3; ibid., vol. 338 (11 July 1938), col. 917.
3. Treasury memorandum (n.d., prob. June 1938), PRO T 161/1116 (S 43697/1).
4. Sir John Anderson to Neville Chamberlain (17 May 1939), PRO T 160 (885/F 17545).
5. Memorandum, 'Economic defence', signed by W. H. Coates, Oswald Falk, Oliver Lyttleton, Arthur Salter, George Schuster, Israel Sieff, R. L. Wedgwood (21 April 1939), ibid.
6. D. E. Moggridge, 'Economic policy in the Second World War', in Milo Keynes (ed.), *Essays on John Maynard Keynes* (1975), p. 179.
7. Correspondence in PRO T 160, op. cit.; D. N. Chester (ed.), *Lessons of the British War Economy* (1951), pp. 3—4; W. K. Hancock and M. M. Gowing, *British War Economy* (1949), p. 47.
8. R. S. Sayers, *Financial Policy, 1939—45* (1956), p. 23.
9. ibid., pp. 3—4. On pp. 1—22 Sayers gives an excellent summary of the general problems of wartime finance.
10. Memorandum by Stamp, 'Control of prices' (26 October 1939), PRO CAB 89/22.
11. Memorandum by Stamp, 'Wages and the cost of living' (30 November 1939), PRO T 161/1116 (S 43697/1). Stamp calculated that

contributions of 8d per week each from employers, employees and the state would yield 3s 0d to 4s 0d per week per child.

12. Stamp's memorandum (ibid.) was based on one written by Henderson on 20 November 1939. PRO CAB 89/22.

13. Moggridge, op. cit., pp. 179–80; Roy Harrod, *The Life of John Maynard Keynes* (1951), pp. 488–9.

14. J. M. Keynes, *How to Pay for the War* (1940), pp. iii, 1–11, 32, 43. Interestingly, Keynes advocated the abolition of income tax allowances (p. 39).

15. For example, F. A. Hayek's review of *How to Pay for the War* in the *Economic Journal*, 50 (June–September 1940), p. 322.

16. Paul Addison, *The Road to 1945* (1975), p. 117.

17. Roy Harrod in D. E. Moggridge (ed.), *Keynes: Aspects of the Man and His Work* (1974), p. 14.

18. For example, he arranged for a House of Lords debate on wartime finance to coincide with publication of *How to Pay for the war*.

19. Correspondence between Keynes and Stamp in PRO CAB 89/22.

20. For example, 'Conclusions of 50th informal meeting' (8 November 1939), ibid.

21. Memorandum by Stamp, 'Differential allowances for increases in the cost of living' (28 November 1939), ibid.

22. United Kingdom Statistical Office, *Annual Abstract of Statistics, No. 84, 1935–46* (1948), pp. 118, 252.

23. For example, memorandum from the Directors of ICI to the Chancellor (27 November 1939), PRO CAB 89/22.

24. In early 1940 there were repeated requests that the Chancellor receive a deputation. For example, Rathbone to T. Crookshank (Treasury) (25 January 1940), PRO T 161, op. cit.

25. Extract from minutes of 11th meeting of Ministerial Committee on Economic Policy (7 December 1939), PRO CAB 89/22.

26. Memorandum by Stamp (28 November 1939), op. cit.

27. The file PRO T 161, op. cit., contains many press cuttings, reports of speeches, articles etc. and is very large.

28. Extract from minutes of 11th meeting, op. cit.; Brown to Stamp (15 February 1940), PRO CAB 89/26.

29. Ministry of Labour memorandum (19 February 1940), PRO T 161, op. cit.

30. F. Tribe to B. Gilbert (Treasury) (21 December 1939), ibid.

31. Alan Bullock, *The Life and Times of Ernest Bevin*, Vol. I (1960), pp. 644–5.

32. For example, letter by Rowntree in *The Times* (16 October 1939).
33. Rowntree to Stamp (5 December 1939), PRO CAB 89/26.
34. Correspondence in PRO CAB 89/26.
35. Rowntree to Stamp (8 and 10 January 1940), ibid.
36. Rowntree had suggested that employers should try to keep selling prices down and should take the initiative in introducing wage and price controls. Rowntree to Bevin (12 December 1939), ibid.
37. Bevin to Rowntree (29 December 1939), ibid.
38. Brown to Stamp (20 January 1940); Keynes to Stamp (12 January 1940); and other correspondence in PRO CAB 89/26.
39. Memorandum by Hale (29 April 1940), PRO T 161, op. cit.
40. For details, see R. M. Titmuss, *Problems of Social Policy* (1950), p. 509.
41. Memorandum by F. Hemming, 'Family allowances' (3 September 1940), PRO CAB 89/24.
42. A point stressed by Hilary Land, 'The introduction of family allowances', in P. Hall, R. Parker, H. Land and A. Webb, *Change, Choice and Conflict in Social Policy* (1975), pp. 178—80.
43. Sayers, op. cit., p. 45.
44. See, for example, letters to *The Times* by Rowntree (20 November 1939), Amery (14 December 1939), L. J. Cadbury (6 January 1940), Beveridge (12 January 1940) and J. H. Richardson (18 January 1940).
45. For example, E. Rathbone, *The Case for Family Allowances* (1940).
46. Letters from Rathbone and Amery in PRO T 161, op. cit.
47. Letters and pamphlets of 1940—3 in TUC Records, File 118. See, for example, Standing Joint Committee of Industrial Women's Organisations, *Memorandum on Family Allowances* by Susan Lawrence (January 1940).
48. Deakin was Bevin's protégé, and shared many of the latter's attitudes.
49. Hubback to TUC General Council (29 February 1940); Amery to Citrine (19 and 21 February 1940), TUC Records, File 118.
50. G. Woodcock to H. Elvin (2 May 1940), ibid.
51. Angus Calder, *The People's War* (1971 edn), pp. 123—4, 133—4.
52. Labour Party Policy Committee memorandum, 'Family allowances' (August 1940), TUC Records, File 118; Trades Union Congress General Council minutes (23 October 1940).
53. The Group published two pamphlets in July 1941, *Family Allowances and the Labour Movement* and *The War Time Case for*

Family Allowances.
54. ibid.
55. For example, G. Woodcock to Eva Hubback (24 April 1941), TUC Records, File 118.
56. Memorandum by Rowntree (9 April 1941), ibid. Rowntree expended considerable effort lobbying the TUC. For example, he sent a copy of his memorandum to every delegate attending the September 1941 TUC Annual Conference. Rowntree to Citrine (14 September 1941), ibid.
57. Trades Union Congress General Council minutes (23 April 1941).
58. *Labour Party Annual Conference Report for 1941*, pp. 166–9.
59. *Trades Union Congress Annual Report for 1941*, pp. 372–6.
60. *Hansard*, vol. 369 (26 February 1941), col. 527; ibid., vol. 370 (27 March 1941), col. 702; ibid., vol. 371 (29 April 1941), col. 348.
61. 88 Conservatives, National Labour or National Liberals; 52 Labour; 7 Liberals; 5 Independents.
62. Rathbone to Wood (2 May 1941), PRO T 161/1116 (S 43697/2).
63. Memorandum by B. Gilbert (14 May 1941), ibid. On 7 April there had been introduced the Keynes-inspired budget which formed the basis of wartime economic policy.
64. Memorandum by Wood (7 June 1941), ibid. The number of insured unemployed fell from an average of 1 871 387 in 1938 to 233 508 in 1941. United Kingdom Statistical Office, op. cit., p. 114.
65. *Hansard*, vol. 372 (12 June 1941), cols. 363–4; and (3 July 1941), col. 1525; ibid., vol. 373 (15 July 1941), col. 454.
66. The Committee's appointment was publicly announced on 10 June 1941 by Arthur Greenwood, Minister Without Portfolio.
67. Note of deputation (16 June 1941), PRO PIN 8/163.
68. Memorandum by B. Gilbert (17 June 1941), PRO T 161/1116 (S 43697/2).
69. Hale to Gilbert (29 October 1941), PRO T 161/1073 (S 43697/02/2).
70. E. Lester (Treasury) to Hale (4 July 1941), PRO T 161/1073 (S 43697/02/1); memorandum by Gilbert (17 June 1941), op. cit.
71. Memorandum by Hale, 'Family allowances' (19 August 1941), PRO T 161/1073 (S 43697/02/1).
72. ibid; Hale to S. P. Chambers (Inland Revenue) (8 July 1941), ibid.
73. *Family Allowances: Memorandum by the Chancellor of the Ex-*

chequer, Cmd 6354 (May 1942), p. 7.

74. Reid to Hale (12 August 1941), PRO T 161/1073 (S 43697/02/1).
75. D. Davidson (Board of Education) to Hale (19 August 1941), PRO T 161/1073 (S 43697/02/1).
76. Butler to Wood (21 October 1941), ibid.
77. Cmd 6354, op. cit., paras, 2, 4, 5, 9 and 26.
78. Memorandum by Hale (19 August 1941), op. cit.
79. Gilbert to Sir Horace Wilson (20 August 1941), PRO T 161/1073 S 43697/02/1).
80. Memorandum by Sir Horace Wilson (24 October 1941), PRO T 161/1073 (S 43697/02/2).
81. Hale to Gilbert (29 October 1941), ibid.
82. For example, *Hansard*, vol. 378 (26 March 1942), col. 2149.
83. Cmd 6354, op. cit., pp. 2, 4–6, 7–11.
84. *Hansard*, vol. 380 (23 June 1942), col. 1859.
85. ibid., col. 1863.
86. ibid., col. 1944.
87. ibid., col. 1941.
88. 'Memorandum by the Chancellor to the Lord President's Committee' (29 May 1942), PRO T 161/1116 (S 43697/3).
89. Lord Woolton to Wood (4 May 1942), ibid.; C. H. Blagburn (Ministry of Food) to G. S. Dunnett (Treasury) (15 May 1942), ibid.
90. Hale to Gilbert (5 June 1942), ibid.
91. E. C. Lester (Treasury) to Hale (18 August 1942), ibid.
92. For example, Jose Harris, *William Beveridge, a Biography* (1977), pp. 378–83; Paul Addison, op. cit., Ch. 8.
93. Material in PRO PREM 4 (88/1), esp. memorandum by Churchill, 'Study of post-war problems' (30 December 1940).
94. Greenwood to Sir George Chrystal (23 January 1941), PRO PIN 8/163.
95. Memorandum of 16 May 1941, and other correspondence in PRO PIN 8/85.
96. *Social Insurance and Allied Services* (Beveridge Report), Cmd 6404 (1942), p. 2.
97. Beveridge was not a modest man, and could be very difficult to work with. Hugh Dalton, for example, found him 'full of egoism and petulance . . . a most tiresome man' (Dalton Diaries, vol. 26, 8 May 1942), and Ernest Bevin disliked him intensely.
98. ibid. (5 June 1942).
99. Civil servants resented this greatly. The Report was to have contained a statement that the various government departments 'have

given their views within the Committee frankly', but at the Treasury's insistence this was removed, and the final published version (Beveridge Report, p. 20) gave a very subdued version. Hale complained that 'Departments all felt — this was certainly the case with the Treasury — that the time available was insufficient for an adequate Departmental examination of issues involving the whole structure of the social services'. Hale to Beveridge (2 October 1942), PRO PIN 8/87.

100. Memorandum by Beveridge, 'Family Endowment Society: notes for examination' (1 June 1942), Beveridge Papers, VIII. 39.
101. Memorandum by Beveridge, 'Basic problems of social security with heads of a scheme' (11 December 1941), and minutes of Beveridge Committee, PRO CAB 87/76.
102. The Society's written evidence and a note of the deputation are contained in PRO PIN 17/1.
103. Memorandum of meeting between the Beveridge Committee and the Family Endowment Society (2 June 1942), ibid.; memorandum by E. Rathbone, 'Notes on the cost of alternative schemes of state-paid allowances' (19 May 1942), Beveridge Papers, VIII. 39.
104. Memorandum of meeting, op. cit.
105. Beveridge Report, pp. 76–90, 165–6; Janet Beveridge, *Beveridge and His Plan* (1954), pp. 107–8.
106. Beveridge Report, p. 7.
107. SIC (42) 3, 'The scale of social insurance benefits and the problem of poverty. Memorandum by the chairman' (16 January 1942), pp. 1, 16–17, Beveridge Papers, VIII. 28.
108. See large amount of material in Beveridge Papers, VIII. 28.
109. Memorandum by Chester, 'Fixing rates of benefit' (5 January 1942), ibid., VIII. 27.
110. Memorandum by Rowntree, 'Calculation of the poverty line — food requirements' (n.d., prob. early 1942), ibid., VIII. 28.
111. 'Fixing rates of benefit', op. cit.
112. Memorandum by Beveridge, 'Subsistence needs and benefit rates' (14 September 1942), Beveridge Papers, VIII. 28.
113. Beveridge Report, p. 90.
114. Speech by Hugh Lawson, *Hansard*, vol. 408 (8 March 1945), col. 2339.
115. Lord Beveridge, *Power and Influence* (1953), p. 309.
116. For example, memorandum on meeting at the Treasury (22 July 1942), PRO PIN 8/87. In her evidence to the Beveridge

Committee, Eleanor Rathbone had suggested this as a possible economy, while still insisting that income tax child allowances should be retained. 'Notes on the cost of alternative schemes', op. cit.

117. SIC (42) 21st Meeting (24 June 1942), PRO CAB 87/78.
118. Memorandum by Beveridge, 'Revision of SIC (42) 100 to 24/8/42' (28 August 1942), Beveridge Papers, VIII. 27.
119. ibid. See also W. H. Beveridge, *The Pillars of Security* (1943), p. 125.
120. Beveridge Report, p. 154.
121. 'Raising of wages has proved to be no cure for poverty', Beveridge informed his Committee, going on to declare that family allowances were an alternative way of effecting a 'moderate redistribution of income' from the childless to parents. 'The scale of social insurance benefits', op. cit., p. 8.
122. Trades Union Congress General Council, minutes of special meeting (18 March 1942).
123. *Labour Party Annual Conference Report for 1942*, pp. 132—7; *Annual Report of the Trades Union Congress for 1942*, pp. 129, 301.
124. *Family Allowances: Report of the Special Committee of the Liberal Party Organisation* (June 1941); memorandum from Joseph Ball (Conservative Research Department) to Kingsley Wood (25 April 1940), PRO T 161/1116 (S 43697/1).
125. Harris, op. cit., pp. 419—26.
126. War Cabinet meeting of 14 January 1943, WM 8 (43); and memorandum by the Chancellor (11 January 1943), PRO CAB 65/33.
127. Hartmut Kopsch, 'The approach of the Conservative Party to social policy during World War II' (University of London PhD thesis, 1970), pp. 109—24. Though many liberal Conservatives supported the report, the overall aim of the party seemed to Harold Nicolson to be to approve of it in principle and then 'whittle it away by detailed criticism', H. Nicolson, *Diaries and Letters, 1939—45* (1970), p. 264.
128. Memoranda by Gilbert (7 December 1942), PRO T 161/1129 (S 48497/02), (11 December 1942) and (26 January 1943), PRO T 161/1116 (S 43697/3).
129. Minutes of 5th meeting of Phillips Committee (29 December 1942), PRO PIN 8/115. The 1942 White Paper had mentioned the figure of 5s 0d 'for illustration because this is the rate that has been proposed by advocates of family allowances'. Cmd

6354. op. cit., p. 3. What was significant about the Phillips Committee decision was that it specifically abandoned the Beveridge principle that the value of the cash allowance plus services in kind should ostensibly amount to subsistence.

130. Board of Education memorandum, 'Children's allowances — cash or kind?' (11 December 1942), PRO PIN 8/116.

131. Ministry of Labour memorandum, 'The effect of children's allowances on wages' (18 December 1942), ibid.

132. Treasury memorandum, 'Family allowances' (Appendix C to 'Report of the Phillips Committee' (January 1943), PRO PIN 8/115.

133. Report of the Phillips Committee, ibid.

134. Interim Report of the Committee on Reconstruction Priorities (11 February 1943), WP (43) 58, PRO CAB 66/34. War Cabinet meeting of 12 February 1943, WM 28 (43), PRO CAB 65/33.

135. Hubback to Wood (8 December 1942), PRO PIN 8/16.

136. 'Memorandum by the Family Endowment Society in relation to the deputation on 14/1/43', ibid.

137. Note of proceedings of deputation (14 January 1943), ibid.

138. Handwritten comment by Gilbert on duplicate of letter from P. D. Proctor (Treasury) to Hubback (15 January 1943), PRO T 161/1116 (S 43697/3).

139. Sheepshanks to T. Daish (8 June 1943), PRO PIN 8/16.

140. Memorandum, 'Progress of the examination of the Beveridge Report' (2 November 1943), PRO PIN 8/123. Churchill had suggested in February 1943 that such a committee should be formed to draw up the Beveridge legislation so that it could be introduced by the first postwar government — which he clearly thought would be a Conservative one. 'Beveridge Report — note by the Prime Minister' (15 February 1943), WP (43) 65, PRO CAB 66/34.

141. Central Staff minutes (12 and 14 April 1943), PRO PIN 8/1; memorandum on children's allowances (n.d., prob. April 1943), PRO PIN 8/2.

142. See material in PRO PIN 17/1—16; and, in particular, PRO PIN 17/2.

143. For example, for discussions in 1938—40 on the anticipated administrative problems of separation allowances, under the Prevention and Relief of Distress scheme, see PRO T 162/563 (E 19143/06).

144. Material in PRO PIN 17/5.

145. 'Memorandum on finance of Beveridge Plan for discussion on 20/10/43', PRO T 161/1193 (S 48497/017).

146. Gilbert to Sir Edward Bridges (Treasury) (25 June 1945); Bridges to Sir Thomas Phillips (27 June 1945); memoranda by Gilbert (16 July and 2 October 1945), PRO T 161/1199 (S 52494/01).

147. Handwritten comment by Dalton on memorandum by Gilbert (2 October 1945), ibid. Labour had taken office on 27 July.

148. Material in PRO PIN 17/3.

149. For example, Sheepshanks expressed irritation that the policy of no duplication with service pay allowances, which the Central Staff had considered very carefully, was seen by critics in terms of 'doing down the soldier serving in the Burmese jungle'. Sheepshanks to Jowitt (2 June 1945), PRO PIN 3/65.

150. Jowitt was Minister Without Portfolio with responsibility for the reconstruction programme, 1942—4, and Minister of National Insurance, 1944—5.

151. Sheepshanks to E. Bean (15 September 1943), PRO PIN 8/123; Sheepshanks to H. George (6 October 1943), PRO PIN 17/2.

152. In two deputations to Jowitt in March and August 1943, the TUC supported payment to the mother. See material in PRO PIN 8/7. However, the Ministry of Labour, normally very sensitive to TUC opinion, favoured the father as legal guardian. Memorandum on attitude of departments to administrative questions (n.d., prob. June 1943), PRO PIN 17/2.

153. Several women's organizations (for example, the Married Women's Association) sent deputations to Jowitt on this. PRO PIN 8/65—6.

154. Memorandum on children's allowances (n.d., prob. April 1943), PRO PIN 8/2.

155. Memorandum by Home Office (4 February 1944), PRO PIN 8/132.

156. S. Taylor (Ministry of Information) to M. A. Hamilton (Reconstruction Secretariat) (28 December 1943), PRO PIN 17/4.

157. 'Extract from minutes of 19th meeting of Reconstruction Committee' (6 March 1944), ibid.

158. *Social Insurance, Part 1*, Cmd 6550 (1944), p. 15, para. 53.

159. Contained in PRO PIN 8/65.

160. Memorandum of deputation (10 October 1944), ibid.

161. Eleanor Rathbone was, of course, marshalling support on this issue. See letters to Beveridge (2 March and 13 April 1945), Beveridge Papers, VI. 10.

162. War Cabinet meeting of 6 March 1945, WM 26 (45) 7, PRO

CAB 65/49.
163. *Hansard*, vol. 408 (8 March 1945), col. 2285; ibid, vol. 410 (10 May 1945), cols. 2056—76.
164. Memorandum, 'Family allowances' (4 February 1944), PRO PIN 17/4; War Cabinet meeting of 6 March 1945, op. cit.
165. R. Hamilton Farrell (Central Staff) to J. Rowlatt (Parliamentary Draftsman) (12 April 1944), ibid. When the Central Staff sent a memorandum to the TUC summarizing the arguments for and against payment to the mother, this point was not mentioned. T. Daish to H. V. Tewson (TUC) (6 August 1943), PRO PIN 8/7.
166. Anderson to Jowitt (7 March 1945), PRO PIN 17/4.
167. *Hansard*, vol. 410 (10 May 1945), col. 2031.
168. Minutes of 5th meeting of the Phillips Committee, op. cit.
169. Statement by Anderson, *Hansard*, vol. 386 (16 February 1943), col. 1667; statement by Jowitt, ibid., vol. 408 (8 March 1945), col. 2262.
170. ibid., vol. 386 (16 February 1943), col. 1666.
171. *Social Insurance, Part 1*, op. cit., p. 14, para. 50.
172. Statement by Anderson, *Hansard*, vol. 386 (16 February 1943), col. 1669.
173. *Social Insurance, Part 1*, op. cit., p. 7, paras. 12, 13.
174. *Hansard*, vol. 408 (8 March 1945), cols. 2345—6. Bevan had been one of those who signed the 1941 Commons motion.
175. ibid., col. 2333.
176. ibid., vol. 410 (10 May 1945), col. 2045.
177. S. Andrzejewski (Andreski), *Military Organisation and Society* (1954).
178. 'The more, in fact, that the waging of war has come to require a total effort by the nation the more have the dependent needs of the family been recognised and accepted as a social responsibility'. R. Titmuss, 'War and social policy', in *Essays on 'The Welfare State'* (1976 edn), p. 84).
179. R. M. Titmuss, *Problems of Social Policy* (1950), p. 508.
180. P. Abrams, 'The failure of social reform, 1918—20', *Past and Present*, 24 (April 1963), pp. 43—64.
181. For example, Derek Fraser, *The Evolution of the British Welfare State* (1973), p. 194. Fraser even reprints the editorial as an appendix (p. 265).
182. Memorandum by Hale (29 April 1940), PRO T 161/1116 (S 43697/1).

183. Note of deputation (16 June 1941), op. cit.
184. Memorandum of meeting (2 June 1942), op. cit.
185. 'Memorandum by Family Endowment Society in relation to the deputation on 14/1/43', op. cit.
186. ibid.
187. See, for example, her statement in *Hansard*, vol. 391 (16 July 1943), cols. 555—8.
188. Royal Commission on Population, 'Summary of evidence by Mrs Eva Hubback and Miss Eleanor Rathbone on behalf of the Family Endowment Society' (October 1944), PRO RG 24/10; report of oral evidence by Rathbone and Hubback (27 October 1944), PRO RG 24/9.
189. Beveridge Report, p. 53.
190. 'Memorandum of evidence by Eva M. Hubback' (n.d., c. 1944), PRO RG 24/11.
191. R. F. Harrod, *Britain's Future Population* (Oxford Pamphlets on Home Affairs, 1943), p. 29.
192. *Hansard*, vol. 391 (16 July 1943), cols. 544—653.
193. Quoted in Sir John Walley, *Social Security: Another British Failure?* (1972), p. 80.
194. Beveridge Report, pp. 8, 154.
195. See Beveridge Papers, IXa. 78—9.
196. W. H. Beveridge, 'Children's allowances and the race', in *The Pillars of Security* (1943), pp. 159—60.
197. Typescript articles by Beveridge in *The Star* (October 1945), and *Political Quarterly* (March 1946), Beveridge Papers, IXa. 81 (pt. II).
198. *Family Allowances*, Cmd 6354, op. cit., p. 2.
199. *Hansard*, vol. 408 (8 March 1945), col. 2260.
200. Ministry of Labour memorandum, 'The effect of children's allowances on wages' (18 December 1942), PRO PIN 8/116.
201. *Current Trend of Population in Great Britain*, Cmd 6358 (May 1942), p. 11.
202. Memoranda by: Professor E. Mellanby (2 October 1943); Sir H. D. Henderson (26 October 1943); and Sir A. M. Carr-Saunders (n.d., prob. October 1943), PRO MH 58/407. Carr-Saunders, for example, listed twenty-six important questions relating to population change that he thought the Royal Commission should answer, but the pro-natalist effect of family allowances was not one.
203. Memorandum, 'Paymaster General. The form of the population

inquiry' (n.d., *c.* early 1943), ibid.
204. Memorandum by Vivian (n.d., prob. June 1943), PRO RG 26/11.
205. Contained in PRO RG 24/9—11.
206. *Report of the Royal Commission on Population,* Cmd 7695 (June 1949), pp. 166, 169—70.
207. E. Slater and M. Woodside, *Patterns of Marriage* (1951), pp. 189—90.
208. Mass-Observation, *Britain and Her Birth-Rate* (1945), pp. 103, 129—30.
209. N. McKeran (Harrow Trades Council) to TUC (30 June 1946), TUC Records, File 118.

Conclusion

The 1945 Family Allowances Act was seen by Eleanor Rathbone as 'the triumph of a great principle', and she intended to continue campaigning for similar measures.[1] But in January 1946 she died, and thus the great driving force behind the Family Endowment Society was removed: the campaign for family allowances was seen by contemporaries as largely her creation,[2] and without her it inevitably lost its momentum. The Society continued campaigning on minor issues for a short time,[3] Eva Hubback even wanting it to turn its attention to the USA.[4] But her death in July 1949 killed the Society. The extent to which it had been dependent on these two leaders was demonstrated by the fact that without them nobody was quite sure how many members the Society had, or who belonged to its committee.[5] From then until the formation of the Child Poverty Action Group in 1965 no family allowances pressure group existed.

From 1945 onwards, family allowances were allowed to slip behind rises in the cost of living and become a notoriously neglected area of social policy. In 1952 they were raised to 8s 0d, but this was to compensate for the removal of food subsidies and represented no real increase. In 1956 the allowance for the third and subsequent children was raised to 10s 0d and the age limit raised from 16 to 18 years. Between 1956 and 1968 the purchasing power of the second-child allowance fell by 39 per cent, and that of other allowances by 31 per cent. In 1967 increases were introduced by stages so that in 1969 allowances amounted to 18s 0d for the second child and £1 each for subsequent children. This brought them up to their original real levels, relative to other benefits: in 1948 the real value of family allowances paid to three children as a percentage of the standard rate of national insurance benefit for a married couple was 24 per cent; by 1967 this figure was down to 12 per cent; but by 1969 it was back at 24 per cent again. However, in order to have remained at the Beveridge-recommended levels this figure would have had to be maintained at 40 per cent.[6]

Why were family allowances so neglected in the 1950s and for most of the 1960s? Various reasons have been put forward, such as the disappearance of the demographic argument thanks to the rise in the birth-rate (from 13·9 per 1000 population in 1941 to 18·0 in 1962), but the most important factors were probably low unemployment and rising real wages.

Family allowances were, of course, taken into account in both the new unemployment insurance and assistance schemes. The 1946 National Insurance Act provided benefits of 26s 0d per week for an adult man, 16s 0d per week for an adult dependant, and 7s 6d for the first child — with subsequent children receiving only the family allowance: a man, wife and three children thus received a total of 59s 6d. Under the 1948 National Assistance Act family allowances were taken into account as 'resources' when calculating family needs: a man, wife and three children aged 14, 9 and 4 years thus received 67s 0d (exclusive of rent allowance). When both schemes were launched, *The Times* expressed concern over the gap between assistance and low wage levels, giving as an example a man with a wife and three children aged over 10 years normally earning 100s 0d per week who, after deduction of insurance contributions and addition of family allowances, had a net income of 105s 0d; if he became unemployed and had a rent of 18s 6d per week, he would receive 59s 6d per week in unemployment benefit plus family allowances, to which the National Assistance Board could add a supplement of 30s 6d, resulting in a total of 90s 0d. This, warned *The Times*, was dangerously near such a man's normal wages, given that the means test 'has been liberalized and no longer has much deterrent force'; somewhat remarkably, it suggested that the obvious solution was to double family allowances in amount.[7]

However, such cases were becoming increasingly rare. Social security benefits have always maintained a fairly constant relationship to average wage levels — in 1938, for example, a married couple on unemployment assistance received 25 per cent of average manual earnings and in 1970 the equivalent figure was 29 per cent[8] — and thus by the late 1940s rising real wages were pulling assistance and, to a lesser extent, benefit rates above Rowntree-type minimum subsistence levels. This can be illustrated in the case of a married couple with three children aged 14, 9 and 4 years old. Such a family would have received 28s 0d per week (exclusive of rent) unemployment assistance in 1936. This was equivalent to about 47s 0d in 1948, taking into account a rise in the cost of living of about 70 per cent. Yet under the 1948 National Assistance Act such a family received 67s 0d (exclusive of rent) — equivalent to a money rise of about 140 per cent over the 1936 figure. Interestingly, this is almost exactly the percentage by which average weekly earnings of adult male manual workers rose in money terms over the period 1936—48.[9] On the Beveridge Report's calculation of necessary minimum subsistence, such a family would have required about 43s 0d for its minimum needs (exclusive of rent) in 1936; it was thus receiving about 35 per cent less than it required.[10] By 1948, however, such a family was receiving from the National Assistance Board only about 8 per cent below the equivalent Beveridge subsistence figure — 67s 0d as against 73s 0d (exclusive of rent). Thus the arrival of subsistence benefits owed everything to rising real wages and very little to the Beveridge Report; in fact, it is probably true to say that Beveridge's much-proclaimed 'subsistence principle' appeared almost exactly at the point at which, thanks to rising real wages, social security benefits would have reached subsistence levels anyway. Not surprisingly, therefore, social scientists in the 1950s believed that 1930s-style subsistence poverty in large families had all but disappeared, and there was little pressure for increased family allowances.[11] (It was only when social scientists began to re-define poverty in relative terms that the cause of family allowances was revived: for example, Abel-Smith and Townsend found 18 per cent of households in Britain, containing 14·2 per cent of the population, to be living below the 140 per cent National Assistance level in 1960, of which nearly 30 per cent were children — equivalent to 17 per cent of the child population.)[12] With an unemployment rate of barely 2 per cent in the 1950s, all that was needed to force the low-paid, large-family unemployed man back into work was a wage-stop, a four-week rule, and a deliberate policy of stigma, which continued to be subtly woven into the social security system. In this connection, it is interesting to note that the rise in unemployment since the 1960s has been accompanied by a revival of interest in family allowances.

This study has tried to examine the process of social policy development by asking the question: *on what grounds* were family allowances acceptable to policy-makers? In asking this question, it has been necessary to draw a rather artificial distinction between those outside government (the campaigners) and those inside (ministers and civil servants). Such a distinction obviously implies an over-simplistic definition of 'the State', equating it with the formal structure of government: it is quite evident that the prominent members of the Family Endowment Society (such as Beveridge) came from exactly the same social elite that produced senior civil servants, and shared many of the latter's attitudes. Again, this study has perhaps adopted a rather crude method of measuring the impact of ideas on policy-making: the Public Record Office may reveal to the historian no explicit evidence that eugenic fears influenced civil servants, but in some more subtle (and immeasurable) way demographic concerns widely held among the political intelligentsia in the late 1930s and early 1940s may have made policy-makers less inclined to dismiss family allowances outright.

However, despite these and other drawbacks inherent in such an approach, this study *has* clearly demonstrated that family allowances did not come about through a rational response by those in government to evidence presented by campaigners. In the final analysis, it can be seen that despite all the arguments relating to working class family poverty and the need to raise the birth-rate, family allowances were acceptable to policy-makers only for reasons of economic control: in the short term, they came into favour at the start of the Second World War as part of an anti-inflation wage control policy; in the long term, they were seen as a means of enforcing work-incentives, assisting labour mobility and concealing the problem of low pay. Although they undoubtedly gave some financial relief to large working class families, primarily they were introduced as a means of preserving the economic *status quo*.

In the final analysis, the role of the main pressure group, the Family Endowment Society, seems not to have been of crucial importance. It certainly provided the most coherent forum for debates which would have taken place anyway. But ministers and civil servants generally remained impervious to its campaigning, except on very minor issues such as Kingsley Wood's promise to publish the 1942 White Paper. Of course, the importance of any pressure group is dramatically thrown into proper perspective when reference is made to other countries, for then one is reminded that welfare development is essentially the product of long-term economic forces at work in all industrialised societies, or societies with similar social structures. Although there was some variation in the nature and timing of family allowance developments in other countries, the general trend of the arguments was much the same as in Britain — from the controversy over wages in the 1920s, to the demographic concerns of the 1930s, to the anti-inflation wage-control arguments of the 1940s. To give but one example, the 1941 Child Endowment Act in Australia (which provided 5s 0d per week to each child after the first up to the age of 16 years, as did the 1945 Family Allowances Act in Britain) was introduced as an anti-inflationary alternative to all-round increases in the basic wage[13] — exactly the grounds upon which family allowances were considered by the Treasury in 1939–40.

By contrast, those within government appear to have played a very influential part. Power seems to have remained firmly in the hands of civil servants, with ministers playing rather a secondary role. Admittedly, arguments for family allowances were often confused, for a long time trade union hostility appeared an insuperable obstacle, and there seems not to have been strong pressure from any of the main political parties. But at no time were civil servants willing to take seriously the arguments of the campaigners: by and large, they were able to manipulate situations with consummate ease, to 'set the agenda' and decide on what terms family allowances would be acceptable. Only on rare occasions (such as the public response to the Beveridge Report) did they give way. The political influence of civil servants, and their accountability, has frequently been discussed in policy studies literature in relation to the general question of 'representative bureaucracy' – in particular, whether senior civil servants (through background, and methods of selection and promotion) display class loyalties that cause them to act in a highly partial manner.[14] Given the British civil service's traditions of secrecy, and the impossibility of measuring, in any quantitative sense, the power of civil servants in policy making, such discussions have tended to produce little more than general speculation. All that can be said is that in contrast to pluralist accounts of welfare development, which tend to see civil servants as neutral arbiters, the picture that emerges from this study is one in which a predominantly upper-middle class, public school/Oxbridge-educated elite of senior civil servants possessed great power and exerted it in a very biased way.

To say this is not, of course, to uphold some sort of naive 'conspiracy theory' interpretation. History is undoubtedly full of little conspiracies: this study has shown the succession of minor deceptions that were perpetrated, such as the discrepancy between the public and private reasons for paying family allowances originally to the father, or the conduct of Ministry of Health officials in the malnutrition controversy of the 1930s (where defending the low-wage sector in industry was considered more important than carrying our proper investigations into public health). But to posit some sort of grand conspiracy, in which a ruling class clearly perceives its long-term 'real interests', is ridiculous: as many ideological battles are fought within the corridors of power as outside them, and the historian who expects unpublished sources to reveal dramatic secrets will usually be disappointed. Such a view would imply that welfare development can be explained by a new crude functionalism: that is, all social policies are introduced because they are 'necessary' for capitalism's continuance.

In fact, welfare simultaneously performs both 'control' and 'ameliorative' functions, which merge into each other and inter-relate with great subtlety. One is always analysing a process that is dynamic, not static: while a particular social policy may be introduced primarily to appease political discontent, perpetuate inequalities, engineer consent and impose new forms of control, it may also improve living standards and raise expectations, thus giving rise to popular demands for further social policies to effect a genuine redistribution of wealth — and so the process continues. 'Concessionist' arguments for welfare, relating to its control functions, are always counterbalanced by fears of what might happen if popular demands are too readily met. This is the answer to the obvious question that presents itself: if family allowances were so necessary if the new social security system was to assist economic growth, then why was there not general agreement within government that they should be introduced? Clearly, civil servants felt very unsure about whether family allowances really *were* necessary: on the one hand, they recognized the validity of the work-incentive arguments and, in the light of them, were prepared to defer slightly to public pressure; but on the other hand this was more than balanced by a realization that to introduce family allowances could be to encourage demands for further measures to redistribute wealth to working class mothers and children — which they were determined to resist. Not surprisingly, therefore, the 1945 Family Allowances Act was very different to what feminists and socialists had been demanding twenty-five years earlier.

Notes and References

1. Speech for Family Allowances Reception (to celebrate the passage of the Act) (13 November 1945), Eleanor Rathbone Papers, XIV. 3.82.
2. See, for example, James Griffiths, *Pages From Memory* (1969), p. 81. Griffiths was Minister of National Insurance when the first family allowances were paid.
3. For example, in February 1946 it tried to persuade the government to raise the proposed benefit of 7s 6d under the National Insurance Bill for the first child of widows, the unemployed and the sick. Eva Hubback to Beveridge (26 February 1946), Beveridge Papers, IIb. 45 (pt 2).

4. Hubback to Beveridge (10 March 1946), ibid., IXa. 102 (pt 1).
5. Mary Stocks to Gilbert Murray (16 February 1950), Gilbert Murray Papers.
6. Peter Kaim-Caudle, *Comparative Social Policy and Social Security* (1973), pp. 264—5. Space does not permit an account of the child benefit scheme of the 1970s.
7. *The Times* (4 June 1946). I owe this reference to Dr Alan Deacon.
8. J. C. Kincaid, *Poverty and Equality in Britain* (1973), p. 15. Figures exclusive of rent allowance.
9. These calculations are based on information in: *Report of the National Assistance Board for 1948*, Cmd 7767, (1948) pp. 11—12; B. R. Mitchell and H. G. Jones, *Second Abstract of British Historical Statistics* (1971), p. 148; A. H. Halsey (ed.), *Trends in British Society Since 1900* (1972), p. 122; D. Butler and J. Freeman, *British Political Facts, 1900—1968* (1969), p. 223.
10. *Social Insurance and Allied Services*, Cmd 6404 (1942), pp. 87—9. This is in fact the 1938 subsistence level.
11. Thus Francois Lafitte could declare in 1962 that 'the causes of poverty *are* shrivelling up'. F. Lafitte, *Social Policy in a Free Society* (1962), p. 12.
12. B. Abel-Smith and P. Townsend, *The Poor and the Poorest* (1965), pp. 39—41.
13. T. H. Kewley, *Social Security in Australia, 1900—1972* (1973), pp. 190—5.
14. Two interesting discussions of this, taking contemporary and historical viewpoints respectively, are Michael Hill, *The Sociology of Public Administration* (1972), esp. chs. 1, 2 and 9; and Max Beloff, 'The Whitehall factor: the role of the higher civil service, 1919—39', in Gillian Peele and Chris Cook (eds.), *The Politics of Re-appraisal, 1918—39* (1975), pp. 209—31.

Bibliography

(Place of publication is given only when it is outside Great Britain.)

Unpublished Sources

1. Private Papers

Beveridge Papers (British Library of Political and Economic Science).
Dalton Diaries (British Library of Political and Economic Science).
Marjorie Green Papers (in the possession of Mr W. Soper).
Lloyd George Papers (House of Lords Record Office).
Violet Markham Papers (British Library of Political and Economic Science).
Gilbert Murray Papers (Bodleian Library, Oxford).
Sir George Newman Diaries (Department of Health and Social Security Library, Alexander Fleming House, Elephant and Castle).
Sir George Newman Papers (Library of the Wellcome Institute of the History of Medicine).
Eleanor Rathbone Papers, Fawcett Collection (City of London Polytechnic Library).
Eleanor Rathbone Papers (University of Liverpool Library).
Sir Arthur Steel-Maitland Papers (Scottish Record Office).
Graham White Papers (House of Lords Record Office).

2. Public Record Office Material

Assistance Board: AST 7, 11.
Board of Education: ED 24.
Cabinet Papers: CAB 23, 24, 27, 65, 66, 87, 89.
Health and Local Government Board: HLG 30.
Ministry of Agriculture and Fisheries: MAF 38.
Ministry of Health: MH 55, 56, 58, 61, 79.
Ministry of Labour: LAB 27.
Ministry of Pensions and National Insurance: PIN 1, 3, 7, 8, 17, 18, 19.
Prime Ministerial Files: PREM 1, 4.
Registrar-General: RG 24, 26.
Treasury: T 160, 161, 162.

3. Miscellaneous Collections

Allen & Unwin E. Rathbone File.
Bev. Coll. Misc. 9: Beveridge and the Family Endowment Society (British Library of Political and Economic Science).
Bev. Coll. T. vol. X: Coal Commission, 1925-6. Family Allowances (British Library of Political and Economic Science).

National Union of Societies for Equal Citizenship Archives (Fawcett Collection, City of London Polytechnic Library).

Political and Economic Planning: unpublished memoranda. 'Population Policies Committee: Scope of Investigation' (25 May 1938), and 'Population Policies Committee: Family Allowances as a Population Policy' (17 October 1938) (British Library of Political and Economic Science).

Scottish Record Office File: C B 7/5/28.

Trades Union Congress General Council Minutes and Economic Committee Minutes (Congress House).

Trades Union Congress Records, Files 117 and 118 (Joint Committee on the Living Wage, and Family Allowances) (Congress House).

Sidney Webb, 'Eugenics and the Poor Law' (1909) (London School of Economics Coll. Misc. 181, British Library of Political and Economic Science).

4. Unpublished Theses

Bentley Gilbert, 'The British Government and the Nation's Health, 1890–1952' (University of Wisconsin PhD thesis, 1954).

Hartmut Kopsch, 'The Approach of the Conservative Party to Social Policy During World War II' (University of London (LSE) PhD thesis, 1970).

John Macnicol, 'The Movement for Family Allowances in Great Britain, 1918–45' (University of Edinburgh PhD thesis, 1978)

Sylvia Mann, 'Trade Unionism, the Labour Party and the Issue of Family Allowances 1925–30' (University of Warwick MA thesis, 1978).

Published Sources

1. Government Publications

(a) Command Papers

Reports of the Commissioners of Inland Revenue, 1918–45.

Report of the War Cabinet Committee on Women in Industry, Cmd 135 (1919).

Report of the War Cabinet Committee on Women in Industry: Appendices, Summaries of Evidence, etc., Cmd 167 (1919).

Final Report of the Committee of Inquiry into the Scheme of Out-of-Work Donation, Cmd 305 (1919).

Minutes of Evidence Taken Before the Committee of Inquiry into the Scheme of Out-of-Work Donation, Cmd 407 (1919).

Report upon the Physical Examination of Men of Military Age by National Service Medical Boards, 1917–18, Cmd 504 (1920).

Unemployed Workers' Dependants (Temporary Provisions) Bill. Report by the Government Actuary on the Financial Provisions of the Bill, Cmd 1529 (1921).

Interdepartmental Committee on Health and Unemployment Insurance: First and Second Interim Reports, Cmd 1644 (1922), and *Third Interim Report*, Cmd 1821 (1923).

Report on the Possibility of Developing Unemployment Insurance by Industries, Cmd 1613 (1923).

Report of the Royal Commission on the Coal Industry, 1925, Cmd 2600 (1926).

Report on Investigation in the Coalfield of South Wales and Monmouth, Cmd 3272 (1929).

Report by the Court of Inquiry, Concerning the Matters in the Dispute Regarding Wages in the Northern Counties Wool Textile Industry, Cmd 3505 (1930).

Royal Commission on Unemployment Insurance, Final Report, Cmd 4185 (1932).

Report of the Departmental Committee on Sterilisation, Cmd 4485, (1934).

Annual Reports of the Unemployment Assistance Board, 1935–9.

Report of an Inquiry into the Effects of Existing Economic Circumstances on the

Health of the Community in the County Borough of Sunderland and Certain Districts of County Durham, Cmd 4886 (1935).
Ministry of Health: Report of an Investigation into Maternal Mortality, Cmd 5422 (1937).
Ministry of Health: Report on Maternal Mortality in Wales, Cmd 5423 (1937).
Current Trend of Population in Great Britain, Cmd 6358 (1942).
Family Allowances: Memorandum by the Chancellor of the Exchequer, Cmd 6354 (1942).
Social Insurance and Allied Services, Cmd 6404 (1942).
Social Insurance, Part 1, Cmd 6550 (1944).
Report of the National Assistance Board for 1948, Cmd 7767 (1948).
Report of the Royal Commission on Population, Cmd 7695 (1949).

(b) Other Government Publications
Parliamentary Debates (Hansard): House of Commons (5th series) and House of Lords.
The Poor Law Report of 1834 (Penguin edition, ed. S. and E. Checkland, 1974).
War Office pamphlet, *Recoverable Advances, Supplementary Separation Allowances and Temporary and Special Grants Authorised under Part II of the Regulations* (1916).
War Office pamphlet, *Regulations for the Issue of Army Separation Allowances, Allotments of Pay and Family Allowances During the Present War* (1916).
Ministry of Labour, *Report on National Unemployment Insurance to July 1923* (1923).
Report of the Unemployment Insurance Committee, 1927 (1927).
Ministry of Health, *Reports on Public Health and Medical Subjects, No. 68: High Maternal Mortality in Certain Areas* (1932).
Ministry of Health, *Final Report of Departmental Committee on Maternal Mortality and Morbidity* (1932).
Ministry of Health Advisory Committee on Nutrition, *The Criticism and Improvement of Diets* (1932).
Ministry of Health, *Nutrition: Report of a Conference between Representatives of the Advisory Committee on Nutrition and Representatives of a Committee Appointed by the British Medical Association* (1934).
Ministry of Health Advisory Committee on Nutrition, *First Report* (1937).
War Office pamphlet, *Regulations for the Allowances of the Army* (1938).
War Office pamphlet, *Special Army Order, 25 April 1938. Family Allowances for Soldiers* (1938).
Annual Reports of the Unemployment Insurance Statutory Committee on the Financial Condition of the Fund (1934–9).
Annual Reports of the Chief Medical Officer at the Board of Education: the Health of the School Child.

2. Reference Works
D. Butler and J. Freeman, *British Political Facts, 1900–1968* (1969).
D. Butler and A. Sloman, *British Political Facts, 1900–1975* (1975).
C. P. Cook, *Sources in British Political History, 1900–1951*, Vols. 1 and 2 (1975), Vols. 3 and 4 (1977).
Dictionary of National Biography.
A. H. Halsey (ed.), *Trends in British Society Since 1900* (1972).
B. R. Mitchell and H. G. Jones, *Second Abstract of British Historical Statistics* (1971).
United Kingdom Statistical Office, *Annual Abstract of Statistics, No. 84, 1935–46* (1948).
Who's Who and *Who Was Who*.

3. Journals and Newspapers
British Medical Journal.

Bulletin of the Committee Against Malnutrition.
Economic Journal.
Economica.
Eugenics Review.
Journal of Hygiene.
The Labour Woman.
The Lancet.
Liberal Magazine.
Liberal Woman's News.
The Medical Officer.
New Leader.
New Statesman.
Proceedings of the Royal Society of Medicine.
Public Health.
Sociological Review.
The Times.

4. Publications by Leaders of the Family Endowment Society
(a) By Eleanor Rathbone

Report of an Inquiry into the Conditions of Dock Labour at the Liverpool Docks (1904).
How the Casual Labourer Lives (1909).
with E. Mahler, *Payment of Seamen* (1911).
Disagreeable Truths About the Conciliation Bill (1911).
Report on the Conditions of Widows Under the Poor Law in Liverpool (1913).
The Muddle of Separation Allowances (1915).
'The remuneration of women's services', *Economic Journal*, 27 (March 1917), pp. 55—68.
'The New South Wales scheme for the grading of wages according to family needs'. *Economic Journal*, 30 (December 1920), pp. 550—3.
The Disinherited Family (1924), republished as *Family Allowances* (1949) with additional chapters by Lord Beveridge and Eva Hubback.
Family Endowment in its Bearing on the Question of Population (Family Endowment Society pamphlet, 1924).
with Mary Stocks, *Why Women's Societies Should Work for Family Endowment* (1925).
Memorandum on Widows', Orphans' and Old Age Contributory Pensions Bill (1925).
Wages Plus Family Allowances (Family Endowment Society pamphlet, 1925).
Memorandum of Evidence by Eleanor Rathbone to the 1925 Royal Commission on the Coal Industry (Family Endowment Society pamphlet, 1925).
Memorandum on the Application of the Family Allowance System to the Mining Industry (Family Endowment Society pamphlet, 1925).
The Ethics and Economics of Family Endowment (Beckley Social Service Lecture), (1927).
The Goal of Our Housing Policy (c. 1928).
Milestones: Presidential Addresses at the Annual Council Meetings of the National Union of Societies for Equal Citizenship (1929).
The Use and Abuse of Housing Subsidies (1931).
Memorandum on the Scale of Needs Suitable for Adoption by the Unemployment Assistance Board in Assessing Assistance to Applicants Under Part II of the Unemployment Act, 1934 (Children's Minimum Council pamphlet, July 1934).
Child Marriage, the Indian Minotaur (1934).
The Case for Direct Provision for Dependent Families through Family Allowances (Family Endowment Society pamphlet, 1936).

'Changes in public life', in Ray Strachey (ed.), *Our Freedom and its Results* (1936), pp. 15–76.
The Case for Family Allowances (1940).
The Case for the Immediate Introduction of a System of Family Allowances (Family Endowment Society pamphlet, 1940).
Rescue the Perishing (1943).
Falsehoods and Facts About the Jews (1945).
(The Fawcett Collection, City of London Polytechnic Library, contains some more pamphlets by Eleanor Rathbone of minor importance.)

(b) By Other Family Endowment Society Leaders
W. H. Beveridge (ed.), *Six Aspects of Family Allowances* (1927).
K. D. Courtney, *et al., Equal Pay and the Family* (1918).
Mrs E. M. L. Douglas, *Some Objections to the System of Family Allowances Answered* (Family Endowment Society pamphlet, 1927).
Marjorie Green, *The Theory and Practice of Family Allowances* (Rome, 1933).
Marjorie Green, *Rent Rebates* (Family Endowment Society pamphlet, November 1935).
Marjorie Green, *Family Allowances* (Family Endowment Society pamphlet, 1938).
Marjorie Green, 'Family allowances', *Labour Management* (November 1938), pp. 206–7.
Marjorie Green, 'The case for family allowances', *Social Service Review*, 20 (February 1939), pp. 45–51.
Eva Hubback and Marjorie Green, 'Family endowment: a proposal for constructive eugenics in England', *Eugenics Review*, 25 (April 1933), pp. 33–6.
Eva Hubback, 'Family allowances in relation to population problems', *Sociological Review*, 29 (July 1937), pp. 272–88.
Eva Hubback, *Family Allowances To-day* (Family Endowment Society pamphlet, 1941).
Eva Hubback, *A New Plea for Family Allowances* (Family Endowment Society pamphlet, 1943).
Mary Stocks, *The Meaning of Family Endowment* (1921).
Mary Stocks, *The Case for Family Endowment* (1927).
Mary Stocks, *The Floor of Wages and the Ceiling of Relief* (Family Endowment Society pamphlet, 1937).
Olga Vlasto, *Foreign and Colonial Experiments in Family Allowances* (Family Endowment Society pamphlet, 1925).
Olga Vlasto, 'Family allowances and the skilled worker', *Economic Journal*, 36 (December 1926), pp. 577–85.
Paul Western, *Family Allowances – a Policy for Liberals* (Family Endowment Society pamphlet, 1929).

(c) Other Family Endowment Society Publications
Annual Reports, 1925–30.
Monthly Notes, 1924–30.
Family Endowment Chronicle, 1931–7.
Anonymous Family Endowment Society pamphlets:
The Endowment of the Family (1924).
The Living Wage and Family Allowances (c. 1925).
Will Family Allowances Mean Lower Wages? (c. 1925).
Trade Union and Labour Opinion Favourable to Family Allowances (1928).
Memorandum on Family Allowances Presented to the Royal Commission on the Civil Service (1930).
The Family Endowment Society (1930).
Family Allowances Abroad and in the British Dominions (1932).

Memorandum on Family Allowances in the Teaching Profession (1932).
The Case for Family Allowances Among the Clergy (c. 1933).
Family Allowances and the Labour Movement (July 1941).
Family Allowances — the Case for a National Scheme (1941).

5. Publications by Political Parties and Pressure Groups
(a) Conservative Party
Conservative Party Annual Conference Reports.
Conservative Party pamphlet, *What the Conservative Government Has Done for Women and Children, 1925—1928* (1928).

(b) Labour Party
Labour Party Annual Conference Reports.
National Conference of Labour Women Reports.
Labour Party, *Report on Motherhood and Child Endowment* (1922).
Labour Party Executive, *Labour and the Nation* (1927).

(c) Liberal Party
W. H. Beveridge, *Insurance for All and Everything* (1924).
Liberal Party pamphlet, *Give the Children a Chance* (1927).
Women's National Liberal Federation Annual Reports.
Reports of the Council Meetings of the Women's National Liberal Federation.
Interim Report of the Family Endowment Enquiry Committee set up by the Women's National Liberal Federation (1926).
Women's National Liberal Federation, *Final Report of the Family Endowment Enquiry Committee: Children's Allowances* (1927).
Women's National Liberal Federation pamphlet, *Liberal Policy for Women* (1929).
Britain's Industrial Future, being the Report of the Liberal Industrial Inquiry (1928).
Liberal Policy: A Speech Delivered to the Council of the Liberal Party Organisation on the 15th March 1939 by Sir Archibald Sinclair.
Liberal Policy: Resolutions Adopted by Meeting of the Assembly of the Liberal Party Organisation (May 1939).
Family Allowances: Report of the Special Committee on the Liberal Party Organisation (June 1941).

(d) Trade Union Movement
Trades Union Congress Annual Reports.
Trades Union Congress and Labour Party, *Unemployment Insurance* (c. 1921).
Trades Union Congress and Labour Party, *Resolutions to be Discussed at the Special Conference of the Trades Union Congress and the Labour Party, 27th January* (c. 1921).
Notice of First Annual Women's Trade Union Conference for 1926.
Trades Union Congress General Council and Labour Party Executive: Joint Committee on the Living Wage, *Interim Report on Family Allowances and Child Welfare* (Parts I—III) (1928), and *Final Report* (1930).
Manchester and Salford Trades Council pamphlet, *The Demand for 'Family Allowances'* (1930).

(e) Independent Labour Party
Independent Labour Party Annual Conference Reports.
Independent Labour Party pamphlet, *Labour's Road to Power* (c. 1926).
Independent Labour Party pamphlet, *The Living Income* (c. 1929).
H. N. Brailsford, 'Equal pay and the family wage', in *A Share in Your Motherland* (1918), pp. 9—17.

H. N. Brailsford, *Families and Incomes: the Case for Children's Allowances* (1926).
H. N. Brailsford *et al.*, *The Living Wage* (1926).
H. N. Brailsford, *Socialism for Today* (1928).
Ernest E. Hunter, *Wages and Families* (1928).
Dorothy Jewson, *Socialists and the Family* (1926).
A. Creech Jones, 'Family income — a trade union view', *Socialist Review* (August 1926), pp. 27–31.
Minnie Pallister, 'The justice of family allowances', *Socialist Review* (June 1926), pp. 38–43.

(f) Children's Minimum Council
Marjorie Green, *Evidence on Malnutrition, Supplementary to Memorandum on Scale of Needs Previously Submitted to the Unemployment Assistance Board* (Children's Minimum Council pamphlet, September 1934).
Marjorie Green, *Malnutrition Among School Children* (Children's Minimum Council pamphlet, June 1938).
Marjorie Green, *Nutrition and Local Government — What Your Local Authority Can Do* (Children's Minimum Council pamphlet, November 1938).
Marjorie Green, *School Feeding in England and Wales* (Children's Minimum Council pamphlet, 1938).
Children's Minimum Council pamphlet, *Observations on the Draft Unemployment Assistance Regulations* (1936).
Children's Minimum Council pamphlet, *Special Areas Bill: Memorandum on Proposed Provision for Additional Food, etc., for Mothers and Children in Distressed Areas* (February 1937).
Children's Minimum Council pamphlet, *Memorandum on Milk for Mothers and Children Under Five* (1937).

(g) Other Organizations
British Medical Association, *Report of a Committee on Nutrition* (1933).
British Medical Association, *Nutrition and the Public Health* (1939).
Eugenics Society Annual Reports.
Eugenics Society Library File A 11/1 (contains miscellaneous pamphlets).
Family Allowances Labour Group pamphlet, *Family Allowances and the Labour Movement* (July 1941).
Family Allowances Labour Group pamphlet, *The War Time Case for Family Allowances* (July 1941).
Family Endowment Society, *Observations Explanatory of the Principles and Practical Results of the System of Assurances Proposed by the Family Endowment Society* (1836).
International Association for Social Progress, *Report on Family Endowment* (1927).
International Association for Social Progress, *Report on Family Provision through Social Insurance and Other Services* (1928).
Invitation to Labour Family Allowances Committee Conference, 23 May 1929.
National Industrial Alliance, *The Case For and Against Family Allowances* (1939).
National Union of Societies for Equal Citizenship, *National Family Endowment* (1920).
Political and Economic Planning, *Report on the British Health Services* (1937).
Political and Economic Planning, *Report on the British Social Services* (1937).
Save the Children Fund, *Unemployment and the Child* (1933).
Socialist Party of Great Britain, *Beveridge Re-organises Poverty* (c. 1943).
Socialist Party of Great Britain, *Family Allowances, a Socialist Analysis* (c. 1943).
State Bonus League: E. Mabel Milner and Dennis Milner, *Scheme for a State Bonus* (1918).

State Bonus League: E. Mabel Milner and Dennis Milner, *Labour and a Minimum Income for All* (1920).
State Bonus League: Bertram Pickard, *A Reasonable Revolution* (1919).
Women's Co-operative Guild Annual Reports.
Women's Co-operative Guild, *Notes for the Study of Family Allowances* (*c*. 1925).

6. General Contemporary Works (Published to 1945)

(a) Books

E. W. Bakke, *The Unemployed Man* (1933).
E. W. Bakke, *Insurance or Dole?* (New Haven, 1935).
Margaret Balfour and Joan Drury, *Motherhood in the Special Areas of Durham and Tyneside* (1935).
H. L. Beales and R. S. Lambert, *Memoirs of the Unemployed* (1934).
W. H. Beveridge, *Unemployment, a Problem of Industry* (1910 edn).
W. H. Beveridge, *The Unemployment Insurance Statutory Committee* (1937).
W. H. Beveridge, *The Pillars of Security* (1943).
C. P. Blacker (ed.), *A Social Problem Group?* (1937).
C. P. Blacker and D. V. Glass, *Population and Fertility* (1939).
A. L. Bowley, *The Division of the Product of Industry* (1919).
A. L. Bowley (ed.), *Studies in the National Income* (1942).
A. L. Bowley and M. Hogg, *Has Poverty Diminished?* (1925).
Eveline M. Burns, *British Unemployment Programs, 1920—38* (Washington, 1941).
L. J. Cadbury, *A Population Policy and Family Allowances* (1939).
A. M. Carr-Saunders, *World Population* (1936).
R. B. Cattell, *The Fight for Our National Intelligence* (1937).
Enid Charles, *The Twilight of Parenthood* (1934).
F. le Gros Clark (ed.), *National Fitness* (1938).
Joan S. Clarke, *The Assistance Board* (1941).
J. L. Cohen, *Social Insurance Unified* (1924).
J. L. Cohen, *Family Income Insurance* (1926).
Percy Cohen, *The British System of Social Insurance* (1931).
Percy Cohen, *Unemployment Insurance and Assistance in Great Britain* (1938).
G. D. H. Cole, *et al., What Is Ahead of Us?* (1937).
Leonard Darwin, *Eugenics and National Economy* (1913).
Leonard Darwin, *An Address on Practical Eugenics* (1914).
Ronald C. Davison, *The Unemployed: Old Policies and New* (1929).
Ronald C. Davison, *British Unemployment Policy, The Modern Phase Since 1930* (1938).
Paul Douglas, *Wages and the Family* (Chicago, 1925).
M. D. Eder, *The Endowment of Motherhood* (1908).
R. A. Fisher, *The Overproduction of Food* (1929).
R. A. Fisher, *The Genetical Theory of Natural Selection* (1930).
R. A. Fisher, *The Social Selection of Human Fertility* (Herbert Spencer Lecture) (1932).
P. Ford, *Work and Wealth in a Modern Port* (1934).
P. Ford, *Incomes, Means Tests and Personal Responsibility* (1939).
G. A. Gaskell, *Social Control of the Birth-Rate and Endowment of Mothers* (1890).
Mary Barnett Gilson, *Unemployment Insurance in Great Britain* (1931).
D. V. Glass, *The Struggle for Population* (1936).
D. V. Glass, *Population Policies and Movements in Europe* (1940).
Alexander Gray, *Family Endowment, a Critical Analysis* (1927).
J. B. S. Haldane, *Heredity and Politics* (1939).
Wal Hannington, *The Problem of the Depressed Areas* (1937).
Wal Hannington, *Ten Lean Years* (1940).

E. M. Hampson, *The Treatment of Poverty in Cambridgeshire, 1597—1834* (1934).
Henry Harben, *The Endowment of Motherhood* (Fabian Tract no. 149, 1910).
R. F. Harrod, *Britain's Future Population* (Oxford Pamphlets on Home Affairs, 1943).
Mrs R. J. Hawkes, *What Is Eugenics?* (1910).
Lancelot Hogben, *Dangerous Thoughts* (1939).
International Labour Office: Studies and Reports, Series D. No. 13, *Family Allowances — The Remuneration of Labour According to Need* (Geneva, 1924).
D. Caradog Jones, *The Social Survey of Merseyside* (3 vols.) (1934).
J. M. Keynes, *How to Pay for the War* (1940).
Juergen Kuczynski, *Hunger and Work* (1938).
The Lancet pamphlet, *Family Allowances* (1940).
E. J. Lidbetter, *Heredity and the Social Problem Group*, Vol. I (1933).
G. F. McCleary, *Population: Today's Question* (1938).
G. F. McCleary, *Race Suicide?* (1945).
William McDougall, *National Welfare and National Decay* (1921).
G. C. M. McGonigle, *Nutrition: the Position in England To-day* (1936).
G. C. M. McGonigle and J. Kirby, *Poverty and Public Health* (1936).
Harold Macmillan, *The Middle Way* (1938).
C. E. McNally, *Public Ill-Health* (1935).
H. Corry Mann, *Diets for Boys During the School Age* (1926).
Sir James Marchant (ed.), *Rebuilding Family Life in the Post-War World* (1945).
T. H. Marshall (ed.), *The Population Problem* (1938).
Mass-Observation, *Britain and Her Birth-Rate* (1945).
John D. Millett, *The Unemployment Assistance Board* (1940).
Sir George Newman, *The Building of a Nation's Health* (1939).
Sir Arthur Newsholme, *Fifty Years in Public Health* (1935).
Sir George Nicholls, *A History of the English Poor Law* (1898 edn).
J. W. Nisbet, *The Beveridge Plan* (1943).
John Boyd Orr, *Food, Health and Income* (1937 edn).
Sir John Boyd Orr, *Not Enough Food for Fitness* (1939).
Karl Pearson, *The Groundwork of Eugenics* (1909).
Pilgrim Trust, *Men Without Work* (1938).
Piotr Prengowski, *Workers' Family Allowances* (1931).
W. B. Reddaway, *The Economics of a Declining Population* (1939).
J. H. Richardson, *A Study on the Minimum Wage* (1927).
W. Robson (ed.), *Social Security* (1943).
B. Seebohm Rowntree, *Poverty a Study of Town Life* (1902 edn).
B. Seebohm Rowntree, *The Human Needs of Labour* (1918 and 1937 edns).
B. Seebohm Rowntree, *Poverty and Progress* (1941).
B. Seebohm Rowntree and F. D. Stuart, *The Responsibility of Women Workers for Dependants* (1921).
John A. Ryan, *A Living Wage* (New York, 1912 edn).
Clive Saxton, *Beveridge Report Criticised* (1943).
H. Llewellyn Smith, *et al.*, *The New Survey of London Life and Labour*, Vol 3 (1932).
Sir Josiah Stamp, *Wealth and Taxable Capacity* (1921).
R. M. Titmuss, *Poverty and Population* (1938).
R. M. Titmuss, *Birth, Poverty and Wealth* (1943).
R. M. and K. Titmuss, *Parents Revolt* (1942).
H. Tout, *The Standard of Living in Bristol* (1938).
Hugh Vibart, *Family Allowances in Practice* (1926).
Sidney Webb, *The Decline in the Birth Rate* (Fabian Tract no. 131, 1907).
S. and B. Webb, *Industrial Democracy* (1919).
S. and B. Webb, *English Local Government: English Poor Law History: Part I, The Old Poor Law* (1927).

H. G. Wells, *Socialism and the Family* (1906).
H. G. Wells, *The New Machiavelli* (1911).
W. C. D. and C. Whetham, *The Family and the Nation* (1909).
George Whitehead, *Socialism and Eugenics* (1911).
Gertrude Williams, *The State and the Standard of Living* (1936).
G. Udny Yule, *The Fall in the Birth Rate* (1920).

(b) Articles and Essays

Sir Percy Alden, 'The nutrition problem', *Contemporary Review*, 151 (January 1937), pp. 46—52.
Leo Amery, 'Family allowances in industry', *Co-Partnership* (June 1938), pp. 3—6.
W. H. Beveridge, 'Population and unemployment', *Economic Journal*, 33 (December 1923), pp. 447—75.
W. H. Beveridge, 'Mr Keynes's evidence for over population', *Economica*, 4 (February 1924), pp. 1—20.
W. H. Beveridge, 'The fall of fertility among European races', *Economica*, 5 (March 1925), pp. 10—27.
C. P. Blacker, 'The sterilisation proposals', *Eugenics Review*, 22 (January 1931), pp. 239—47.
J. S. Blackmore and F. C. Mellonie, 'Family endowment and the birth rate in the early nineteenth century', *Economic Journal*, 37 (May 1927), pp. 205—13.
H. S. Booker, 'Parenthood and poverty', *Economica* (new series), 4 (November 1937), pp. 448—54.
John Brownlee, 'The present tendencies of population in Great Britain with respect to quantity and quality', *Eugenics Review*, 17 (July 1925), pp. 73—6.
Eveline Burns, 'The economics of family endowment', *Economica*, 5 (June 1925), pp. 155—64.
A. M. Carr-Saunders, 'The Unemployment Assistance Board', *Political Quarterly*, 7 (1936), pp. 538—50.
E. P. Cathcart, 'Nutrition and public health', *Public Health*, 48 (May 1935), pp. 286—91.
Enid Charles, 'The effect of present trends in fertility and mortality upon the future population of Great Britain and upon its age composition', *London and Cambridge Economic Service, Special Memorandum No. 40* (August 1935).
Leonard Darwin, 'Some birth rate problems', *Eugenics Review*, 11 (October 1920), pp. 147—57; and ibid., 12 (January 1921), pp. 277—90.
Leonard Darwin, 'Population and civilisation', *Economic Journal*, 31 (June 1921), pp. 187—95.
Paul Douglas, 'Some objections to the family wage system considered', *Journal of Political Economy* (Chicago), 36 (October 1924), pp. 690—706.
Paul Douglas, 'The British discussion of family endowment', *Journal of Social Forces* (North Carolina), 3 (November 1924), pp. 118—24.
A. F. Dufton, 'Food for thought', *The Lancet* (26 December 1936).
J. C. Dunlop, 'The fertility of marriage in Scotland: a census study', *Journal of the Royal Statistical Society*, 77 (February 1914), pp. 259—88.
'Endowment of motherhood' by E. I. C., *Eugenics Review*, 14 (July 1922), p. 134.
Mrs H. A. L. Fisher, 'Family allowances', *Quarterly Review*, 480 (July 1924), pp. 73—87.
R. A. Fisher, 'Income-tax rebates', *Eugenics Review*, 20 (July 1928), pp. 79—81.
R. A. Fisher, 'Family allowances', *Eugenics Review*, 24 (July 1932), pp. 87—95.
Victor Freeman, 'Weights, heights and physical defects in school children', *The Medical Officer* (18 August 1934).
D. V. Glass, 'The population problem and the future', *Eugenics Review*, 29 (April 1937), pp. 39—47.

T. E. Gregory, 'The endowment of motherhood', *The Common Cause* (18 October 1918).

'Hungry England report', *Week-End Review* (1 April 1933).

R. Huws Jones, 'Physical indices and clinical assessments of the nutrition of schoolchildren', *Journal of the Royal Statistical Society*, 100 (1938), pp. 1–52.

F. C. Kelly, 'Fifty years of progress in nutritional science', *The Medical Officer* (16 February 1935).

Ruth Kenyon and Maurice Reckitt, 'The policy of family endowment, for and against', *The Commonwealth*, 18 (June 1927), pp. 169–74.

J. M. Keynes, 'A reply to Sir William Beveridge', *Economic Journal*, 33 (December 1923), pp. 476–86.

J. M. Keynes, 'Some economic consequences of a declining population', *Eugenics Review*, 29 (April 1937), pp. 13–17.

F. Lafitte, 'The work of the Population Policies Committee', *Eugenics Review*, 31 (April 1939), pp. 47–56.

Robert McCarrison, 'Problems of nutrition in India', *Nutrition Abstracts and Reviews*, 2 (July 1932), pp. 1–8.

William McDougall, 'A practicable eugenic suggestion', *Sociological Papers, 1906* (1907), pp. 55–80.

William McDougall, 'Family allowances as a eugenic measure', *Character and Personality* (Durham, North Carolina), 2 (December 1933), pp. 96–116.

D. H. Macgregor, 'Family allowances', *Economic Journal*, 36 (March 1926), pp. 1–10.

J. F. Maurice ('Miles'), 'Where to get men', *Contemporary Review*, 81 (January 1902), pp. 78–86.

J. F. Maurice, 'National health, a soldier's study', *Contemporary Review*, 83 (January 1903), pp. 41–56.

V. H. Mottram, 'The physiological basis of the minimum wage', *The Lancet* (22 October 1927).

A. C. Pigou, 'Eugenics and some wage problems', in *Essays in Applied Economics* (1923), pp. 80–93.

'Population Investigation Committee: first annual report', *Eugenics Review*, 29 (January 1938), pp. 240–3.

J. H. Richardson, 'The family allowance system', *Economic Journal*, 34 (September 1924), pp. 373–86.

D. H. Robertson, 'Family endowment', in *Economic Fragments* (1931), pp. 145–54.

B. Seebohm Rowntree, 'Family allowances', *Contemporary Review*, 154 (September 1938), pp. 287–94.

A. H. Seymour and J. E. Whitaker, 'An experiment in nutrition', *Occupational Psychology*, 12 (Summer 1938), pp. 215–23.

T. H. C. Stevenson, 'The fertility of various social classes in England and Wales from the middle of the nineteenth century to 1911', *Journal of the Royal Statistical Society*, 83 (May 1920), pp. 401–32.

H. Tout, 'A statistical note on family allowances', *Economic Journal*, 50 (March 1940), pp. 51–9.

R. M. Titmuss and F. Lafitte, 'Eugenics and poverty', *Eugenics Review*, 33 (January 1942), pp. 106–12.

A. F. Tredgold, 'The feeble-minded', *Contemporary Review*, 97 (June 1910), pp. 717–27.

'Wages and allowances for workers' dependants', *International Labour Review* (Geneva), 10 (September 1924), pp. 470–85.

Mary T. Waggaman, ' "Family wage" systems in Germany and certain other European countries', *United States Department of Labor: Monthly Labor Review* (Washington, 18 (January 1924), pp. 20–9.

7. Biographies and Autobiographies

Leo Amery, *My Political Life, Vol.* III. *The Unforgiving Years, 1920—1940* (1955).

Janet Beveridge, *Beveridge and His Plan* (1954).

Lord Beveridge, *Power and Influence* (1953).

Asa Briggs, *Social Thought and Social Action: a Study of the Work of Seebohm Rowntree* (1961).

Pamela Brooks, *Women at Westminster* (1967).

Alan Bullock, *The Life and Times of Ernest Bevin*, Vol. I (1960) and Vol. II (1967).

Max Cohen, *I Was One of the Unemployed* (1945).

Bernard Donoughue and G. W. Jones, *Herbert Morrison, Portrait of a Politician* (1973).

S. E. Finer, *The Life and Times of Sir Edwin Chadwick* (1952).

Margaret Gowing, 'Richard Morris Titmuss', *Proceedings of the British Academy*, 61 (1975), pp. 401—28.

James Griffiths, *Pages From Memory* (1969).

Jose Harris, *William Beveridge, a Biography* (1977).

Roy Harrod, *The Life of John Maynard Keynes* (1951).

Diana Hopkinson, *Family Inheritance: A Life of Eva Hubback* (1954).

Milo Keynes (ed.), *Essays on John Maynard Keynes* (1975).

Harold Macmillan, *Winds of Change, 1914—39* (1966).

Violet Markham, *Return Passage* (1953).

Sheila Marriner, *Rathbones of Liverpool, 1845—73* (1961).

D. E. Moggridge (ed.), *Keynes: Aspects of the Man and His Work* (1974).

Lord Morrison, *Herbert Morrison, an Autobiography* (1960).

Harold Nicolson, *Diaries and Letters, 1939—45* (1970).

Lord Boyd Orr, *As I Recall* (1966).

Eleanor Rathbone, *William Rathbone, a Memoir* (1905).

Eleanor Rathbone Memorial Lectures (by various authors, on various topics, some containing personal reminiscences of Eleanor Rathbone).

Peter Rowland, *Lloyd George* (1975).

Lord Salter, *Memoirs of a Public Servant* (1961).

Anthony Sampson, *Macmillan* (1967).

T. S. and M. B. Simey, *Charles Booth, Social Scientist* (1960).

Mary Stocks, *Eleanor Rathbone* (1949).

Mary Stocks, *My Commonplace Book* (1970).

8. General Secondary Works (Published Since 1945)

(a) Books

Brian Abel-Smith and Peter Townsend, *The Poor and the Poorest* (1965).

Mark Abrams, *The Condition of the British People, 1911—45* (1946).

Paul Addison, *The Road to 1945* (1975).

S. Andrzejewski (Andreski), *Military Organisation and Society* (1954).

Adela S. Baer (ed.), *Heredity and Society* (New York, 1973).

J. A. Banks, *Prosperity and Parenthood* (1954).

Theo Barker (ed.), *The Long March of Everyman* (1975).

H. L. Beales, *The Making of Social Policy* (Hobhouse Memorial Lecture) (1946).

Lord Beveridge, *The London School of Economics and its Problems, 1919—37* (1960).

C. P. Blacker, *Eugenics, Galton and After* (1952).

N. Branson and M. Heinemann, *Britain in the Nineteen Thirties* (1973 edn).

Vera Brittain, *Lady Into Woman* (1953).

Maurice Bruce, *The Coming of the Welfare State* (1966 edn).

David Bull (ed.), *Family Poverty* (1971).

John Burnett, *Plenty and Want* (1966).

Eveline M. Burns (ed.), *Children's Allowances and the Economic Welfare of Children* (New York, 1968).
Angus Calder, *The People's War* (1971 edn).
D. N. Chester (ed.), *Lessons of the British War Economy* (1951).
F. le Gros Clark, *A Social History of the School Meals Service* (1964 edn).
G. D. H. Cole, *A History of the Labour Party from 1914* (1948).
Robert E. Dowse, *Left in the Centre* (1966).
Derek Fraser, *The Evolution of the British Welfare State* (1973).
Victor George, *Social Security, Beveridge and After* (1968).
Victor George, *Social Security and Society* (1973).
Victor George and Paul Wilding, *Ideology and Social Welfare* (1976).
Bentley B. Gilbert, *The Evolution of National Insurance in Great Britain* (1966).
Bentley B. Gilbert, *British Social Policy, 1914—1939* (1970).
D. V. Glass, *Numbering the People* (1973).
P. Hall, R. Parker, H. Land and A. Webb, *Change, Choice and Conflict in Social Policy* (1975).
Mark Haller, *Eugenics* (New Brunswick, 1963).
W. K. Hancock and M. M. Gowing, *British War Economy* (1949).
J. R. Hay, *The Origins of the Liberal Welfare Reforms, 1906—1914* (1975).
Michael Hill, *The Sociology of Public Administration* (1972).
Peter Kaim-Caudle, *Comparative Social Policy and Social Security* (1973).
T. H. Kewley, *Social Security in Australia, 1900—1972* (1973).
J. C. Kincaid, *Poverty and Equality in Britain* (1973).
F. Lafitte, *Social Policy in a Free Society* (1962).
S. Leff, *The Health of the People* (1950).
S. and V. Leff, *The School Health Service* (1959).
Robert Lekachman, *The Age of Keynes* (1967).
J. M. Mackintosh, *Trends of Opinion about the Public Health, 1901—51* (1953).
J. D. Marshall, *The Old Poor Law, 1795—1834* (1968).
T. H. Marshall, *Social Policy* (1975 edn).
E. W. Martin (ed.), *Comparative Development in Social Welfare* (1972).
Ralph Miliband, *Parliamentary Socialism* (1973).
Ramesh Mishra, *Society and Social Policy: Theoretical Perspectives on Welfare* (1977).
C. L. Mowat, *The Charity Organisation Society, 1869—1913* (1961).
C. L. Mowat, *Britain Between the Wars* (1966 edn).
David Owen, *English Philanthropy* (1965).
Nicholas Pastore, *The Nature—Nurture Controversy* (New York, 1949).
Gillian Peele and Chris Cook (eds.), *The Politics of Re-appraisal, 1918—39* (1975).
Henry Pelling, *Britain and the Second World War* (1970).
Robert Pinker, *Social Theory and Social Policy* (1971).
J. R. Poynter, *Society and Pauperism* (1969).
J. H. Richardson, *Economic and Financial Aspects of Social Security* (1960).
R. S. Sayers, *Financial Policy, 1939—45* (1956).
Karl de Schweinitz, *England's Road to Social Security* (Philadelphia, 1947 edn).
Henry C. Sherman, *The Nutritional Improvement of Life* (New York, 1950).
Margaret Simey, *Charitable Effort in Liverpool in the Nineteenth Century* (1951).
Eliot Slater and Moya Woodside, *Patterns of Marriage* (1951).
R. M. Titmuss, *Problems of Social Policy* (1950).
R. M. Titmuss, *Essays on 'The Welfare State'* (1976 edn).
Neil Tranter, *Population Since the Industrial Revolution* (1973).
James C. Vadakin, *Family Allowances, an Analysis of their Development and Implications* (Miami, 1958).
James C. Vadakin, *Children, Poverty and Family Allowances* (New York, 1968).
Sir John Walley, *Social Security: Another British Failure?* (1972).
Margaret Wynn, *Family Policy* (1970).

A. F. Young and E. T. Ashton, *British Social Work in the Nineteenth Century* (1956).

(b) Articles and Essays

P. Abrams, 'The failure of social reform, 1918—20', *Past and Present*, 24 (April 1963), pp. 43—64.

P. Abrams and S. Andreski, 'The military participation ratio', *Past and Present* 26 (November 1963), pp. 113—14.

Judith Blake, 'Are babies consumer durables?', *Population Studies*, 12 (March 1968), pp. 5—25.

Mark Blaug, 'The myth of the old Poor Law and the making of the new', *Journal of Economic History*, 23 (June 1963), pp. 151—84.

Mark Blaug, 'The Poor Law report re-examined', *Journal of Economic History*, 24 (June 1964), pp. 229—45.

H. S. Booker, 'Income tax and family allowances in Britain', *Population Studies*, 3 (December 1949), pp. 241—7.

Eric Briggs and Alan Deacon, 'The creation of the Unemployment Assistance Board', *Policy and Politics*, vol. 2, no. 1 (1973), pp. 43—62.

Allan M. Cartter, 'Income-tax allowances and the family in Great Britain', *Population Studies*, 6 (March 1953), pp. 218—32.

Victor George and Paul Wilding, 'Social values, social class and social policy', *Social and Economic Administration*, 6 (September 1972), pp. 236—48.

John Goldthorpe, 'The development of social policy in England, 1800—1914', *Transactions of the Fifth World Congress of Sociology, 1962* (Louvain, 1964), pp. 41—56.

Roy Hay, 'Employers and social policy in Britain: the evolution of welfare legislation, 1905—14', *Social History*, 4 (January 1977), pp. 435—55.

D. Heer and J. Bryden, 'Family allowances and fertility in the Soviet Union', *Soviet Studies* 18 (October 1966), pp. 153—63.

J. P. Huzel, 'Malthus, the Poor Law and population in early nineteenth century England', *Economic History Review*, 22 (December 1969), pp. 430—52.

Hilary Land, 'The introduction of family allowances', in P. Hall, R. Parker, H. Land and A. Webb, *Change, Choice and Conflict in Social Policy* (1975), pp. 157—230.

Bernice Madison, 'Canadian family allowances and their major social implications', *Journal of Marriage and the Family* (Wisconsin), 26 (May 1964), pp. 134—41.

T. H. Marshall, 'Citizenship and social class', in *Sociology at the Crossroads* (1963), pp. 67—127.

T. H. Marshall, 'Value problems of welfare—capitalism', *Journal of Social Policy*, 1 (January 1972), pp. 15—32.

Arthur Marwick, 'Middle opinion in the thirties: planning, progress and political "agreement"', *English Historical Review*, 79 (April 1964), pp. 285—98.

Arthur Marwick, 'The Labour Party and the welfare state in Britain, 1900—1948', *American Historical Review* (Richmond, Virginia), 73 (December 1967), pp. 380—403.

M. E. Rose, 'The allowance system under the new Poor Law', *Economic History Review*, 19 (December 1966), pp. 607—20.

John Saville, 'The welfare state: an historical approach', *New Reasoner*, 3 (Winter 1957—8), pp. 5—25.

Neville Vandyke, 'Family allowances', *British Journal of Sociology*, 7 (March 1956), pp. 34—45.

Joseph Willard, 'Some aspects of family allowances and income redistribution in Canada', *Public Policy* (Cambridge, Mass.), 4 (1954), pp. 190—232.

Index